MAKING WAVES

DEDICATION

For Simon, Anna, Gracie and Henry

Take a chance. Life is not a dress rehearsal.

DISCLAIMER

This book about exploration, risk and perseverance is based on a true story. Events are described with the help of detailed personal journals, my recollections and a few educated guesses, because many of these experiences happened some time ago. Recalled conversations may not be the exact words spoken, and most people's names, numerous identifying details and some locations have been changed to ensure privacy. With the obvious exception of my business partners, boat captain and family, no one should think he or she is the basis for any character.

MAKING WAVES

LIBBY BROWN

CROSSROADS PRESS

Editors: Jeanette Felton McKittrick and Marilyn Shaw

The following photos courtesy of Gregg Gandy: 1.14, 2.4, 2.6, 2.7, 2.8, 2.9, 2.10, 2.11, 2.12, 2.13, 2.14, 2.15, 3.5, 3.11, 3.23

Photo 1.2 courtesy *Richmond Times-Dispatch*

Cover Photo by David Hunter Hale

Printed by Worth Higgins and Associates, Richmond, Virginia

Typeset in Sabon and Eason Inline fonts

Book design by Carol Roper

First printing November, 2006

ACKNOWLEDGEMENTS

These words are mine. The recollections in this book are based upon my personal experience of them, and not intended to speak for my husband, our children, our business partners or our boat captain. Like the rest of us, I am the sum of my life's adventures. Although I have been a willing partner to the gambles we shared, I have not been the sole author of them. For that, much of the credit is due my husband Stewart, a risk-taker of a higher order. Without his vision, there would be no story.

To my fellow wave-makers Steve Robertson and Randall Ward, who always believed in the value of my motor-mouth. Thanks for the party.

To my stalwart boat captain Gregg Gandy who meant it when he said his most important responsibility was my safety. Thanks for the loyalty.

To my son Stew and his wife Johannah for doing a job in which most young families wouldn't last a day, let alone years, and for helping make sure my tale about the difficulties of managing a resort on an out-island didn't wander out of bounds when my emotions did. Thanks for freeing up my time so I could write.

To my daughter Ellie who persuades customers to send money to a P.O. box in Virginia so they can land on a tiny airstrip to visit an unheard-of island resort in the middle of the sea. Thanks for inspiring me with your generosity of spirit, depth of strength in time of crisis and unwavering faith that anyone who doesn't think I'm great is wrong. And to Matt for your tolerance of and affection for Fowl Cay when it gobbles up so much of your wife's time.

To past colleagues I was privileged to work with who helped me accurately remember dates and facts. To a couple of stateside buddies who watched this story flutter inside me like a wild bird in a cage and encouraged me to let it fly. To fellow boaters who invited us aboard and refreshed my memory of the good and the scary. To my circle of island property owners who reminded me during the hard times we *do* live in Mother Nature's paradise. Good friends all, my appreciation.

To the Bahamians of the Family Islands who taught me to understand the good side of "what is, is." Thank you beyond measure.

To teachers who set me, in big and little ways, on the right path for this endeavor: Jenna Johnson, David Knuth, Phyllis Theroux and Mary Lou Weisman.

To readers and their wise counsel who never made me feel like the novice I am: Carol K. Billingsley, Marilyn and Cully Culwell, J.R. Hipple, Gary Johnson, Lee Knapp, Eleanor Minus, Bill Robertson and June Rosen.

To rainmakers of such generosity it takes my breath away: Barney Michael, Bob Schmetterer and Dave Wilson.

To my mother Tatum Robertson for bequeathing me the courage and endorsement to be an intrepid traveler of life.

And to my patient and good-natured husband Stewart. Your steadfastness in the face of my volatility is a gift greater than the biggest diamond you ever gave me in the years when I used to wear jewelry. Thank you for opening your private soul so that I might tell the story of how you helped me find my way because you never lost yours.

I am indebted to you one and all.

PROLOGUE

It seems as if one night, I went to bed as a member of the Personnel Department at a stodgy old bank—"Libby, hire me somebody who can type more than 40 words a minute, will you?" Before I knew it, I woke up in a first-class seat headed from my home in Virginia to my private island in the Bahamas. The solicitous man seated next to me asked, "So where do you live?" The answer was easy, but it didn't seem quite honest.

I could tell him where my two homes were, that wasn't the quandary. But those answers avoided the truth that where I really lived, where I was most at home, was on the precipice of risk.

Although sometimes risk chooses us, usually, taking chances is our choice. Since from childhood most of us are taught to be risk-averse, our voluntary leaps stay small, avoiding inconvenience and anxiety. There is, however, a category of devotee that doesn't just tolerate risk but seeks it— as well as its discomforting edge of exposure.

Challenge comes in degrees. Sometimes these are small—enrolling in a college course at sixty years of age. Sometimes they're not so small— retiring early to scale the world's most formidable mountains. The big lifestyle-altering ones that I savor are out in the margins and have the capacity to bring you to your knees, but also the promise to fulfill your sweetest dreams.

At least once in your life, if you're lucky, you encounter the temptation to step out, a beguiling chance that is yours for the taking, or for the leaving. You've had one I'll bet—one wink, one whisper. Did you pass on it because it wasn't a good time, because you were scared it might shake up your familiar routine or keep you awake at night? Or because you had too many responsibilities, or you were too young or too old? Wimp.

Easy for me to say. I've spent thirty years on the edge with one eye cast toward the heavens and the other on the yawning chasm below.

The polite inquirer had no way to know of my three plunges into the deep end. Why would he think a sedate-looking woman like me would have risked her mortgage on a venture concocted by two hung-over bachelors with a shipping crate? He couldn't have guessed I gave up driving carpools and left my teenagers to sail off into a life of pirates and pleasure-seekers. He didn't suspect I had hopscotched from babysitting a desk job to developing a resort.

So, where do I live? What a great question.

I live where risk lives, seeking out the edge of dearly-acquired pleasures where many of my days are hard, and the exhaustion of disappointment and age occasionally overtakes the prize. I live in a place so rare for my gender and generation that my singularity has brought me hurt, anger and intense joy.

I live where I can play chicken with my own destiny, Mr. Seat 2A, because unless I take that head-on ride, I haven't really lived.

PART ONE

THIS END UP

Mos' any po' ole fish can float
And drif' along and dream.
But it takes a reg'lar live one
To swim against the stream.

—Anonymous

CHAPTER 1: This Way Out (1)

*S*tewart, who hadn't worn a suit, let alone tie-up shoes, except to weddings during his near decade-long life on the lam from business-as-usual, threw on an old gray one that smelled of the cedar closet. A too-wide, too-loud paisley tie from his collection of similar choices added insult to the injury his frayed shirt sustained. Once in the taxi, he crossed an ankle over his knee, revealing a dusty shoe with a hole worn through two layers of sole.

"I'll get them polished when we get to the airport," he said in a familiar non sequitur. On Stewart's list of what made a man worthy, clothes were a footnote.

In contrast to my husband, I had dressed with keen attention to detail on this remarkable morning. With nerves slipping out like unruly lingerie, I took cover under a black suit and heels, the big city costume of professional women, even though I was a small town girl, and donned my pearls over a blouse of periwinkle blue, my best color. If only the ruckus in my guts could be smoothed into submission by a sleek outer veneer.

Soon after their initial visit several months earlier to the offices of our small company in Richmond, Virginia, the Melville Corporation sent us encouraging feedback and a request for more sales figures. Three days after we produced that information, a phone call. "The officers want to get to know you and Libby better," the president of this giant retail conglomerate said to Stewart. "Can you come to New York for a meeting and lunch next week?"

Thunderstruck, but cautious, we agreed.

Of the companies that had shown curiosity about our nine-year-old furniture business with the oddball name, this one was our favorite. That there was any firm that wanted to buy us seemed an otherworldly prospect, let alone one of Melville's sphere.

This End Up had belonged to our two partners, Stewart and me since we sat in a smelly old building together to draw up a floor plan for a shop in Richmond. It seemed a short leap from September 1975 to November 1984. Today, Stewart and I would sit across the desk from

Melville's chief executive officer to discuss the buyout of a business that had drawn its first breath at a drunken brawl.

The flight to New York was easy. Melville sent a car for the hour and a quarter drive to their corporate offices, and the 10 a.m. appointment seemed like perfect timing. Then, a wardrobe gaffe, perhaps the most memorable in a long string.

"Where's your belt, Stewart?" I asked, hoping against experience there would be an answer other than the one I was pretty sure I knew.

As he folded down his USA Today, Stewart sloshed a little coffee on the knee of his trousers, not that it made any difference, and pulled back his coat. "Hmmm. Guess I forgot it." His imperturbable attitude yawned its first "oh well" of the day. "Maybe we better try to find a men's store along the way."

Find a men's store? He had to be kidding. We had exactly 35 minutes to be in the Melville Corporation's headquarters for the mother of all interviews. We needed to be good, real good. And we needed to be on time. Our grab at the gold couldn't chance a misstep.

Finally, with only 15 minutes before our meeting, even nonchalant Stewart was showing a little fret over our inability to find a leather store that would let him in before the normal 10:00 start of the retail day. Our driver spotted a person sweeping the sidewalk outside a ritzy men's clothing store. Stewart jumped out. In 60 seconds he had the young man chuckling, as I knew he would. Back in the speeding car with an expensive black braided belt, the likes of which his wardrobe had never seen, he threaded the new purchase around his waist. I told him he had missed a loop. He was still making the adjustment when we screeched to a stop at the front door of Melville's headquarters.

A major-league audience was on our docket. We knew that going in, and the pressure to be at our best weighed hard upon me. The result could change the lives of our employees, our partners and us, but I never dreamed of the magnitude of change that morning's encounter would have.

As we moved into his private offices, the charming chief executive officer put Stewart and me at ease around a table laden with coffee and pastries. My goal for the day was to see if our personalities meshed, and his easy smile, twinkling eyes and effortless manner of inclusion earned this man a gold star from me. Things were off to a good start, and I had stopped trembling inside when Stewart moved on to talk with Melville's financial team, leaving me to interview with the CEO.

I met Stewart in the hall as he returned from his meeting with the chief financial officer. "No b.s.," he whispered, an accolade worth three gold stars, had he kept a tally. As we gathered our coats for lunch, the CEO asked if we would like to stay with the company should a merger come to pass. My heart slammed at the portent of his question. Were we on the verge of converting a mere nine years of work into a sizeable return? Stewart felt the weight of the question too, and even though he was composed, I could see excitement flush his skin. A cool-headed answer from him took the focus off me, as I stood like a deer in the headlights, wide-eyed and mute.

"We would both be interested in staying," said Stewart, "but we couldn't sign an employment contract. If continuing to work together caused problems between us, we would need to be able to leave for the sake of our marriage."

A barely detectable smile between the two Melville honchos made me suspect that a gold star had just landed in our column.

The atmosphere at lunch was easy and business was discussed only in a peripheral and humorous manner. Introduced as "the rose between seven thorns" to the all-male cast already seated at the restaurant, I mentally removed half a gold star for the sexist comment. As I was just beginning to breathe normally when the waitress came for orders, reading the menu required more attention than I could settle into, so I chose a salad without even looking. Stewart, who sat across the table from me, ordered a Reuben sandwich with extra sauerkraut. Few things weigh on him enough to modify his eating or sleeping patterns.

Sitting between the Melville CEO and the founder of CVS drugstores, I relaxed under their kind questions about my life outside This End Up, small though it was in those years, and minded my manners by asking the same of them. When my salad was served, the ripe cocktail tomatoes looked like a good place to start. Poke. Into a plump one went my fork. I'm not sure how something that little could have so many insides, but one tine sent a jet of juicy red guts onto the monogrammed cuff of my partner to the left, and another tine shot a runny glob of tiny seeds dribbling down my periwinkle bosom.

As we walked to the car that was to return us to the airport for our trip back to Richmond, I was confounded and a little jealous of how, once again, the tables turned in Stewart's favor under his offhand bearing of benign neglect. Sometimes I couldn't find the payoff for the *planning and precision I first cultivated as a high school teacher. Here I was, lipstick-less, not having wanted to perform such a girlie task at a table full of men. A wide run slithered down the front of one stocking, and the polish of my pearls screamed "charlatan" as they lay atop the grubby pink smear on my chest. Although I didn't want to be a rose among the thorns, it would have been nice to look more like the flower than the compost.*

On the other hand, Stewart was obliviously dapper in spite of himself with his pinstripe suit jacket slung over a shoulder, braided belt placed neatly through all seven trouser loops around a trim waist, and richly polished shoes that hadn't betrayed their shabby secret. Stewart's aquamarine eyes, fed by tiny lines of experience, and his casual mop of thick, wavy hair topped off the picture of a man in full control.

When the limo pulled away from the gathering, I glanced through the rear window to make sure the smiling bigwigs weren't a mirage and blinked fast, as you might do trying to awaken from a vivid dream. Could we be looking at enough financial security to guarantee fun and contentment from now on? I snuggled into the soft leather seat while my mind reeled, intoxicated by the chance of untold riches.

CHAPTER 2: The Good Life

The first ring of the phone caught me on my pantyhosed knees, where I was holding off the dog with my elbow while cleaning up the lunchtime shambles of fruit and toast that my two toddlers had launched from matching high chairs. The phone's curly cord was strangling a naked doll. To unwrap it with bananas slimed on my hands would further aggravate my frisky temper.

A bout of diarrhea had kept me changing children all morning. I'd had to change my own dress when the dog barfed on the matching shoes, and feeling the pressure of being late to my weekly volunteer job for the Junior League, I had slung my pearls around my neck only to have them spill on the floor one by one. No way I'd make it to the country club to drop off the check for the dues that were already a week late. Where the hell was the babysitter? *(Photo 1.1)*

The phone continued its harangue while I wished the intruder would give it up. At the fourth annoying jangle I snatched up the receiver, loaded for bear.

"Hey, Libbo. Sounds like a party." My brainy kid brother was there, unwittingly in the crosshairs of a barely missed verbal onslaught.

Our mother had mentioned recently that Steve and a college buddy were making furniture in their Raleigh apartment. Details were in short supply, as they often were in relation to my independent, rolling stone of a brother. I decided to loft a throwaway inquiry about this hobby since I figured it was an embarrassing stopgap on the road to real employment, but before I could, Steve intervened. "Did Mom tell you about what Randy and I are doing? How about opening a store up there in Richmond to sell our crate furniture?"

Not in a lifetime of guesses would I have recognized that as the landmark question of my life.

Holding the receiver between my chin and shoulder, tethered by the grimy spiraled cord just out of reach of my two- and three-year-olds, I tossed out a couple of crackers.

"The business has kind of exploded. We only take orders on weekends, but we're pretty much swamped," said my normally understated brother. "We really like to make it, but it's not our thing to talk to customers. You'd love that part. You do the selling. Randy and I'll make the orders and drive up to Richmond to deliver them."

I remembered vaguely that Mom had told me the story one afternoon over the din of Ellie's playgroup. Something about a wild party and a weekend booth at the flea market where they peddled their homemade furniture. She said they were having a hard time keeping up with it, but I attributed that to too much bachelor fun.

"No way, Steve! After two babies back-to-back, I can't wait to get back to my job at the bank next month. I got a great promotion in the Personnel Department. Anyway," I challenged from the eminence of big sisterhood, "who would ever buy furniture made from crates?"

"This could really work, Libbo. Stewart could keep the books and you could do the selling. Hell, you've always been able to shoot the shit with a lamppost."

Considering the source, I decided to count that as a compliment. A piercing scream sounded from highchair No. 2, out of all proportion to the tiny body issuing it.

"Let me think about it a few days and I'll get back to you."

* * *

Steve was our mother's favorite. Small and sickly as a baby, he absorbed every free moment she had, while my older brother and I had to settle for the attention of sitters. Looking to solve that problem, Bill and I put baby Steve in a turkey roaster, flipped on the oven and shoved him in. Fortunately for all, Mom turned off the vacuum just then and heard the muffled shrieking of "Rat," as we called Steve when we were tormenting him.

After that inauspicious start, Steve found his niche at the tiller of sailboats, where at age 10 he started raking in racing trophies. Quiet and inquisitive, his report card was always the best in the house, and a summer job with an architect during high school presaged his talent for design. When it was time for college, the product design program at North Carolina State University was a natural choice. After graduation, Steve placed an ad in *Yachting*—"Experienced crew available for hire anywhere in the world"—and sailed off to faraway places for several years with only an occasional postcard to tell Mom he was alive.

By the time he returned to the United States, I had an agenda of husband, babies and tennis lessons. Each of us was forging opposite types of adult lives, but his individualism intrigued me. Never did I suspect his wandering path and my straight one would merge into the ride of my life.

Preparing dinner, I was unable to dismiss Steve's phone call. But still, why opt for change, for a leap from the security and convenience of the pleasant status quo? Nothing felt so safe as habit. As I reflected on my life, reasons for shaking it up seemed slippery, and reasons for staying put, sure-footed. Why rock the boat?

My husband and I come from traditional backgrounds. Our childhood values read like a 1950s "How to Succeed" guidebook: 1.) Work hard, play fair and strive to be the best. 2.) Don't lie, steal, cheat or hurt other people. 3.) Be loyal to family, friends and those in your charge. 4.) Leave something of merit behind. These tenets were so deeply ingrained in us by both sets of parents that I thought nothing on earth could threaten them. We swallowed them whole and were told that we would get what we gave.

And we did, for many years.

When we moved to Richmond in 1968, Stewart and I were comfortable from the start. Newly married and newly careered, we were befriended by likeable people who were hatching children, so we did too. Our background and agenda fit perfectly into the quiet enclave of the handsome old southern city's West End district.

Through Stewart's University of Virginia ties, we had an entrée into the Capital of the Confederacy surpassed only by one's birthright. We purchased a white brick, two-story Georgian in an established section, much like the one I lived in as a teenager in Wilmington, North Carolina, once my family stopped moving around the world.

Comfortable friends with like backgrounds took us in right away. Our country club was similar to the one of Stewart's childhood, where we felt right at home dining in the Grill Room after a game of paddle tennis with our group. On fall weekends, the maid kept the children while we traveled to Charlottesville for U.Va. football games. Those road trips were a social highlight, and we joined up afterward with fraternity brothers whom we still called by their college nicknames. Tradition was a lively art in the hands of our adopted state.

Stewart worked downtown, selling stocks and bonds in a genera-tions-old brokerage house. He loved the firm he worked for. Cigarette smoke hung thick from the ceiling in this town made wealthy by tobacco. The ticker tape clattered its good news/bad news messages, and bawdy jokes and gossip shot through the financial community like spindrift.

As young wives, many of the women debated the merits of different garden clubs and which decorators they might use when they had the money to re-do. Everyone wanted jewelry to add to her collection at Christmas, and we speculated for a whole year about where the family would go for spring break. We snapped up privilege and place without a second thought.

Volunteerism was the sole outside-the-home career for most women of our circle in the early 1970s. Some seemed born to be community leaders. That role was tended with the single-minded dedication of a *Fortune 500* CEO. An invitation to join an elite board or garden club was cause for green-eyed jealousy from those who wished they could be in that coterie, and the social-climbing that ensued in pursuit of the prize was an Olympian sport in Richmond.

More serious were the conversations about our children. The topics ranged from pediatricians, carpools and playgroups, to cotillion, manners and the right kind of clothes. I'm sure it was similar in many southern towns, and in the beginning I joined the discussions as vigor-ously as any new mother. The provenance of neighborhood and educa-tion gave me a voice.

Perhaps the most important marker of ratification for young parents was their children's acceptance to certain private schools. Most people we knew would have hocked everything to pay for a spot at the right academic address for their pre-schoolers—*if* they could get in. With many more applicants than spaces, competition began at conception. On the day the letters of decision were delivered, mailmen found parents pacing at the end of the driveway. Acceptance was orgasmic, wait list a bitter letdown and rejection a staggering blow to the gut. Two years in a row I spent a stomach-churning afternoon on the front steps of our house, feeling that I might die if our mailman didn't deliver a thick envelope instead of a thin one.

On weekends we grilled hamburgers in the backyard while we watched the children in the blow-up swimming pool. We talked about plans to add on to the house, which friends were having another baby and what repairs the car needed. Stewart practiced his putting and I worked on my handmade Christmas ornaments. We needed nothing, and almost anything we wanted could be obtained with just a little time and effort. Our lives were comfortable, filled with the soothing white noise of busy-ness. Things were good in the most traditional sense of the word, but life as I knew it was about to take an untraditional turn.

CHAPTER 3: Boxed In

I shiver to think how close I came to passing on an offer that diverted my run from a lifetime of sheltered straight-aways to a ride of hairpin turns with no guardrails. I was almost too lazy, too afraid of change and too worried about what others would think to take a peek at a different path, a path that could be charted with nothing but my own free will.

I was growing bored with the status quo—the bank, the club, a few square miles of lovely homes and time-honored tradition. I loved my family, enjoyed my friends, and with two toddlers and a full-time career, I had more than enough to do. But boredom caused a discontent that percolated just under my skin. I held that uneasiness inside, though, because it was too confusing to understand. Why would I be unhappy with a life of such comfort? What kind of person would consider risking it for who knows what?

My recently under-stretched mind returned over and over to the earlier phone conversation as I wound down the day's duties, tending a tub full of children with Jell-O hair. Steve's words, "This could really work," had rung with confidence—no, rather, with conviction.

Looking back, I realize now that my uneasiness was directly proportionate to my life of ease. While others may be risk-averse, I was (and am) in need of the charge achievable only by taking a chance. Everyone has his comfort zone, and mine, paradoxically, is at the glinting edge of risk.

I thought with increasing curiosity about individuality, about superlatives, about deep-down satisfaction. I didn't want to be different just for the sake of it. More than anything, I wanted to do something different, to move beyond what I knew, but I was troubled that non-conformist behavior would exile me from the hermitage of West End acceptance.

The evening after the phone call, I broached the idea of opening a furniture store with Stewart. I told him of the conversation with my brother and expected that Mr. Stockbroker would think it was outrageous to jeopardize perfectly happy surroundings with such a harebrained retail venture. His reaction was not what I anticipated, and we talked late into the night.

"I'll call Steve tomorrow and get more information. Then I can run some numbers." With a mighty yawn, the family budget director was out for the night.

I don't know what made us focus so fast and hard on opening a store to sell furniture made from crates. Stewart and I both admitted we had a burgeoning restlessness we had never discussed. It seemed disrespectful, almost irreverent, and certainly ungrateful to voice unhappiness in the midst of all this happiness. Our children, our health and our bank account were in sound condition. We belonged to clubs, we took vacations, we owned toys of privilege. Friends we loved rounded out the fullness of our daily lives. How could we not be bursting with contentment? On the face of things, Steve's suggestion seemed as illogical as betting our house in a craps game. For me, though, the idea was a crossroads, a choice between two fated lives. The narrowness of my life wasn't painful; it just wasn't exciting. And I wanted to be tingling with anticipation when I pulled back the covers every morning.

So I embraced my first big chance, and indulged what would become a lifelong taste for taking a risk.

That first step wasn't such an earth-shattering event. Curiosity and enervation prodded me onto the launch pad. The courage to ignite came from a husband who had kept us financially sound since we married, a brother who was loaded with smarts and abilities and the fluke that brought us all together—luck. That combination was good enough for me.

Stewart and I decided to open a store selling the unheard-of crate furniture with me at the helm. I would forgo a salary and benefits along with a promotion at the bank. As I mentally checked what I was giving up against an illusory future, I wondered whether I would be diminished or enhanced by the decision.

Unbeknownst to us, Steve's phone call had created a fork in the road of our lives. Choosing the off-road trail rather than a well-marked path gave us the wherewithal for freedom that I never knew existed. Our decision to open a tiny store jump-started the first of three wild rides, unimaginable to me in 1975.

CHAPTER 4: Crate Expectations

Our first furniture store opened on Strawberry Street in Richmond's historic Fan District in September 1975. The small spot was located in a rat-infested, run-down building that we spruced up with $500, the sum of my egg money. On weekends, Stewart stapled rolls of bamboo fencing on the walls so it would hide the holes in the rotting barnwood siding. The two of us put down a used carpet from the Goodwill store over the torn linoleum. How Stewart didn't electrocute himself as he hung the track lights I'll never know, because as long as that store was open, the fluky wiring had a hissing mind of its own. *(Photo 1.2)*

Steve and his college buddy, Randy, brought the furniture from Raleigh—a couch and chair covered in orange and brown acetate and nylon, a fabric they named "Bigfoot Brown," with matching end tables, a coffee table and some magazines to set them off. They said they had chosen the dimensions of the pieces because they were exactly what would fit in Randy's VW bus. That idea was the first piece of research for the two men, and the furniture stayed those sizes long after we no longer delivered it in a Volkswagen bus. I placed a handwritten sign on the display: $395 for the five-piece set.

A neighborhood wino ambled by to welcome us to the block as we locked the doors for the night.

"Hey, man. My name's Reverend," he shouted from the curb with a fling of his Willie Nelson pigtail. "It's just spiritually uplifting to see you guys going in here. I bunk in the park across the street so I'll be a regular customer."

Reverend was such a fragrant old soul that his breath signaled his upcoming arrival, and as much as I wanted regular customers, I hoped he would not be one of them.

"I was wondering if you'd be serving, uh, anything at the opening tomorrow, because I got some good friends and we could swell up the crowd for sure," he said as he winked.

Reverend had a bottle in a crinkled paper bag wedged between a worn leather belt and his jeans. The blessing of a spare bounced in his jacket as he moved down the street, shouting, "God bless you, God bless you," to everyone and no one. The four new proprietors moved on to do some celebratory drinking of our own.

At a local café, we took a table next to the salad bar, which was offered up in a footed bathtub. A rowdy group sat next to us toasting one comrade's short story publication. We raised our beers to acknowledge the author's success.

"So, Steve, you and Randy explain how this project started," I said. "Mom was so vague that I never really understood it."

"Well, it started with a party and a shipping crate. And it went from there."

* * *

The evening of revelry happened in the best tradition of recently graduated fraternity men everywhere. This wingding occurred in Raleigh, not far from the campus of North Carolina State University, Steve and Randy's alma mater. Having visited all the world they cared to see with no money, the two chums drifted back to the town of their raucous college careers.

After years of crewing on sailboats in the South Pacific, Steve surfaced, hauling his life's possessions in a heavy-duty wooden shipping crate. Several cold winters in his Volkswagen bus caused Randy to turn temporarily to the cozy comfort of his parents' home, but soon he had his bachelor pad.

To celebrate the friends' reunion, festivities ensued at Randy's place. As the night wore on and the empty bottles piled up, his thrift store furniture became missiles, launched from the second-story apartment, shattering to toothpicks on the ground below. The next morning, the only things left in the bachelor pad were some hung-over people sleeping on the ragged pillows of the destroyed furniture pieces. And in a corner, standing unfazed in the morning-after fog, was Steve's perfect crate.

Even though Randy had recently started a construction company, his bank balance hovered at the poverty line. Facing monastic accoutrements, the two friends turned to the empty shipping crate for inspiration. By the end of the day, the sturdy container was dismantled and reconfigured into a boxy couch frame. Liquor-soaked foam cushions salvaged from the debris were thrown onto the new creation.

For the first time since Steve and Randy's graduation, their product design and textile degrees had taken a successful run at reality. With that effort, one of the most remarkable entrepreneurial stories of the 1970s and '80s would unfold.

Within a few days of the birth of the first couch, the unsuspecting businessmen had a trickle of requests from equally-strapped friends. Then the mailman wanted one. And the building superintendent. Soon a phone call came in from a stranger who had been referred. Steve and Randy were shocked. Where should they go from there?

The next weekend they hauled three pieces of the crate furniture to the flea market at the North Carolina State Fairgrounds. A wildly successful patchwork of small booths, the bazaar showcased bits of people's lives in a folksy panorama of commerce. Steve and Randy's spot was in the back pasture with the rest of the newcomers. As the entrepreneurs paid the $10 for their two-day booth, they received a warning from the manager. "You fellas cain't open up tomorrow mornin' without no sign on your space."

On the ride home, Randy and Steve mulled over what to name their furniture. When they opened the front door to their apartment, there stood the original crate couch. On its side was stamped the instruction from the manufacturer: a large black arrow pointed at the ceiling with the words, "THIS END UP," in the traditional stencil style. A national brand logo took its first breath.

* * *

It had to have been the best and the worst store opening ever. We painted a leftover crate panel to use as a sign. "THIS END UP." Stewart hung it above the doorway on a rusty old bracket. Anyone it fell on would have been knocked unconscious, but we were innocent then of liability concerns.

We were also innocents on the subject of marketing. Without realizing it, our opening day coincided with the Strawberry Street Craft Fair. The celebration was an annual neighborhood event that drew people from all over Richmond's Fan District. In 1975, "the Fan," anchored by then-sleepy Virginia Commonwealth University, sat squarely between the ultra-conservative West End and the downtown Capitol. It was home to a mix of Bohemian humanity: starving artists, musicians, center-city lovers, renovators of old houses, the gay contingent and the homeless. Lazy with sunshine, a light autumn breeze and leaves turning yellow and red, the day was custom-made to suit the Saturday fair underway in the park across the street. Children laughed, balloons bobbed and adults wandered the friendly crowds.

The store was mobbed from the start with a heterogeneous crowd of happy contrarians. They wore hiking boots and L.L. Bean shirts, their square, uncool Volvos waiting at the curb. These young customers, who would later be regarded as the economically powerful baby boomers, prided themselves on owning earthy things counter to their parents' culture. Our rugged, original-design furniture suited them perfectly.

Within an hour I had taken the first order. By that afternoon I had written three. One man used his last check for a purchase, and he made it out to "Up Your End." I was so excited I took it anyway.

While I helped a woman interested in furnishing her mountain house, my mind scrambled furiously to calculate how many VW bus trips it would take to deliver such an order.

"How soon could I get all this? I'm in a bit of a rush," said my customer, thumbing her wallet.

Oh my. How much better could this be?

Just then I heard people chuckling. Putting aside our book of 12 fabric choices, I turned to see the reason. Unable to find mom in the crowd, my two-and-a-half-year-old, almost-potty-trained son was doing what he thought was right. With flawless aim, he had set sights on the side of the This End Up chair and was, well, keeping his training pants dry. I could have kissed the kindly woman sitting in it for her graciousness as she rose from the ersatz toilet.

Years later in response to a This End Up customer satisfaction questionnaire, that woman wrote in the comments section, "I was sitting in the chair when the owner's little boy went to the bathroom on it during the opening day of your Strawberry Street store. Please tell her that I bought my furniture several months later because of that accidental demonstration. Every piece is still like new after eight years. Thank you for a wonderful product."

After settling my son on my hip, I slid the abused chair over the wet spot on the rug and returned to the mountain-house order in time to witness a granddaddy rat scurry beside the customer's foot and smush its fat body under the couch. Baby Stew, who was learning animal names, screamed "WAT" at the top of his lungs. The woman screamed, "OH MY GOD," at the top of hers. I barely got out of her way as she fled the store, tinkling toddler and super-rodent.

We couldn't bear to shut the door as long as there was interest. By 9:30 that night, I had waited on so many people and answered so many questions I could hardly remember where I had placed the day's receipts. Hiring help was immediately put at the top of my to-do list. At the top of his, Stewart listed to remind me to charge sales tax. I had forgotten it all day.

As we locked the door, headed for home exhausted and hungry while hugging two sleepy children to our shoulders, guilt about balancing work and family rumbled. The challenge I had been seeking crowned that day, like a newborn. What would this infant entity demand of me? How could I nurture it without turning my back on my own needs? I wondered why I felt so exhilarated. Three orders, a rat, tax evasion, and bodily fluids would not be a cause of euphoria for most people. But I was elated, and in my naiveté I believed that it would be fun to join my joyful new independence with my familiar, comfortable life.

By the end of the first week, we had at least two paying customers a day, sent in by friends who had visited the store during its opening. I puffed up with pride when they said they were told, "Ask for Libby." After a couple of deliveries put the product in customers' houses, referrals took on a geometric progression, all with no advertising.

Unrecognized by us, ambassador-customers evangelized about This End Up, extolling value and customer service. The product created a market for itself, speaking to a vast blue-jeaned generation bent on self-expression, set to extend their casual style into the home. These customers turned the unheard-of into the must-have by framing our company as the answer to their desire for authentic, functional furniture. Growing word of mouth and an irreverent name helped brand crate furniture with lightning speed.

The feeling of accomplishment for me in those early days came from being the solution to a problem of that scope. Not a quickie problem like taking a forgotten lacrosse stick to school, or finding the perfect dress for a party, or locating a fourth for tennis. Rather it came from standing in a store we built, selling goods we invented to a public that clamored for simple, solid furniture, sold at a fair price. Fulfillment came from the gratitude and respect I received from those strangers. Their admiration was my first acquaintance with the power of personal impact on people I didn't know. My part in the success of that hole-in-the-wall store began to clarify what kind of person I wanted to be. For the first time, I felt pride of identity in a sphere broader than the five square miles of red clay and carefully groomed lawns of my own neighborhood.

CHAPTER 5: This Way Out (2)

When Stewart and I returned home from our interview in New York, exhausted and bedraggled from our long day at Melville, we called Randy and Steve about the stunning events of the trip. We told them what we'd learned about some of the "big box" retailer's mega-chain stores: Marshalls, CVS, Wilsons Leather, Thom McAn, Linens-N-Things, Kay-Bee Toys. Their interest in a company the size of This End Up seemed like an elephant sniffing at a peanut, yet it appeared genuine.

Visions of fiscal sugarplums danced in our dreams that night. We vacillated between dismissing the buyout as fool's gold and accepting the possibility as a lead-pipe cinch. It would be hard not to tell anyone about these almost surreal events, but the four partners swore on a piece of yellow pine not to do it.

"How are things at work going?" asked my mother the morning after our return from Melville.

"Oh, you know. Same old, same old. A few more stores, a few more problems." I bit my lower lip as I stumbled over such an understatement. It didn't come easy to lay a big whopper on the mom who had taught me never to lie.

"Anything new at This End Up?" inquired my sister-in-law over the weekend. Everyone seemed to have a premonition.

Sitting at supper two nights after we'd returned to Richmond, Stewart and I looked at each other with a shake of our heads. There seemed to be a disconnect between now and 48 hours ago. Here we were, a regular couple eating pot roast with our preteen children at the kitchen table in our suburban brick house. Stewart folded his hands behind his head, exposing a big hole in the right elbow of his sweater, while Ellie and Stew cleared the table in preparation for chocolate pudding. Had we dreamed the Melville thing?

CHAPTER 6: Mavericks

Steve, Randy, Stewart and I had a fortunate blend of abilities that created the new furniture trend. In only a few months, we had given shipping crates a second chance at life. But, really, what did a sailor, a builder, a stockbroker and a personnel interviewer know about running a furniture business? Not much. That may have been a good thing since what we didn't know was that we were swimming against the tide of the industry.

Our Strawberry Street store sometimes seemed like a teenage boy: unruly, demanding and growing into his size-12 feet. As the orders rolled in, we realized we were no longer road-testing this venture. Randy and Steve, now referred to as The Boys, hired a strong deliveryman named Gunther. Every few weeks he filled a bigger rental truck with orders and drove 160 miles north to deliver to Richmond.

Until the neighbors complained, Gunther parked the truck in front of our house—to save money. Ellie and Stew came to expect him on Friday nights, when he would crash on the couch in our den—to save money. I would go downstairs the next morning to wake him for deliveries, with the kids watching cartoons and sucking their thumbs as they sat on the end of the slumbering giant's bed. Those moments of quiet at dawn on Saturdays were his last rest for 15 hours: 12 hours of lugging solid wood and three hours of driving back to Raleigh. Gunther had to return the truck before midnight—to save money.

We worked hard to cut costs. Stewart and I had little excess cash to devote to This End Up, but it never occurred to us to take a bank loan. The customer deposit of half an order's price was enough to pay for the raw materials to build the furniture. In this early stage, the time elapsed between the outlay of those funds and the incoming second-half payment, due upon delivery, was only two weeks. Even with our lack of business knowledge, the partners knew it was important not to get in debt. If the store were going to make it, it would have to make it fast. Otherwise, we'd just close it up—no great loss.

One Saturday, it got too late for Gunther to deliver the last order on the truck. The waiting customer was not happy, but I negotiated an alternate plan with her. A different deliveryman would bring her five-piece set on Monday evening after he got off his day job.

Mrs. Dunn lived on the outside edge of our delivery area. I rushed home from the store right at five o'clock to help Stewart jam the furniture into our first company-owned vehicle, a used sky-blue Suburban. When we stuffed the beige corduroy cushions in the front seat, they made a wall that plastered Stewart against his door. Other than the windshield and driver's side window, every view was obscured as he drove away, looking like a blue phone booth stuffed with college kids in tan car coats.

Having helped load the heavy furniture and send my husband off, I turned to find two dirty little faces beside me, searching for attention. As I gathered Ellie and Baby Stew for another hasty dinner before bath and stories, Mr. Crotchet from down the block walked up.

"Somebody told me you and Stewart were running a little business on the side."

"We sure are," I answered, wondering where he was going with this.

Growing bolder, he grilled me, finally questioning Stewart's departure "right at dinnertime."

"He's delivering furniture to a customer in Doswell," I explained, hoping to get back to my children.

"Well, that'll never work."

One of the many naysayers to come, Crotchet hurt me with his mean-spirited remark. I kept it from Stewart, though, when he stumbled in the front door several hours later.

"We need to give Gunther a raise," he said.

The next day, the phone rang as soon as I opened for business. Mrs. Dunn was calling with a story and a suggestion.

"Last night, your nice delivery boy came out here without a helper and hauled all that heavy furniture in by himself. He was as cheerful as could be even though he said he'd worked all day at his regular job. But he was awfully slim for a moving man. When I offered him a sandwich, he said he had a wife and two babies waiting supper for him at home. And then when I offered him a tip, he refused to take it!"

I wasn't at all sure where this conversation was going since it was my first-ever customer callback.

"Now I dislike getting anybody in trouble," said Mrs. Dunn, "and I don't want to take a job away from a person who obviously needs it, but I think your company should hire bigger delivery boys before some-body gets hurt."

My reaction started at stunned and ended at tickled. I called Stewart "delivery boy" for months after that. And I felt set free to have a job that provided such entertainment.

On the manufacturing side of things, though, entertainment was short. Producing a fast-increasing amount of furniture put a crimp in the leisure-time activities of the bachelors. At the ages of 27 and 30, Steve and Randy needed to free themselves for the important things in life. The only solution was to hire help.

The partners turned to sources of personnel not normally sought by manufacturers: college graduates unready for button-down shirts, hippies looking for freedom from regimentation in the workplace, women breaking away from the pink-collar ghetto, and Vietnam veter-ans newly returned from the war. With money tight, Steve and Randy cast about for people they could afford, for people who would like working alongside the freewheeling young owners.

The first in a long line of mavericks signed on. In 1975, we were a great match, those first iconoclastic carpenters and This End Up. The scrappy bunch sought different things from their workplace and we needed a different breed of employee. Some wanted money for untitled dreams of their own, a few wanted to smoke weed on their lunch break, a couple were working through a bit of depression and one longed to bring her newborn every day and nurse him in the shade of a tree. Seemingly an aberrant group, they turned out to be harbingers of This End Up's ideal craftspeople. And they helped us keep our heads above water as business surged.

CHAPTER 7: No End to the Day

We now had a team that handled the design and manufacture of our product as well as the selling of that product. Although Stewart did as much as he could at night and on weekends, we needed more of his time to manage the setup of the retail side and its finances. Since it was just my brother, his friend and me in charge of the operation, the three of us were handling the steady flow of money in a relaxed style. That began to worry my financially-trained husband.

At night, after Stewart got home from selling bonds and I had closed another round of furniture sales, the two of us sat down at our dining room table. While I arranged the day's take in orderly stacks of bills and checks, he whipped out the calculator, wrote a deposit slip, and into the pocket of his suit jacket would go the receipts, held together with a fat rubber band. The money would be put in the bank the next day, except for the time Stewart forgot and dropped his suit off to be dry-cleaned. That discovery caused a mad dash back to the cleaner's.

The accounting task completed, we turned to the tally of furniture that needed to be produced. After listing each piece sold that day under the appropriate category, I added up the number of cushions required in each fabric for the seating frames. Then Stewart and I turned to the most dreaded job—marking the location of every order on four taped-together maps of the city and surrounding counties for Gunther's use on the next delivery.

Finally, the social, family and household chores surfaced. After those were finished, we stumbled toward bed, rarely falling to sleep before midnight, just in time to be awakened by our three-year-old's perpetual nightmares.

At the end of those days, there was no end of the day. Stewart and I were so tired, pushing against a wall of fatigue night after night, that even minor tasks such as closing our downstairs draperies were abandoned. Years after this period of dogged endurance, our next-door neighbor told us he used to see us do the reckoning exercise with its humble stacks of scrip, admiring its growing dimension. Christian said he knew the business was going somewhere big. I'm glad someone thought so; we were just scrambling to keep the bases covered.

With sales on a monthly upswing six months after our first store opening, Stewart decided to leave eight years in the brokerage business, assuming the leading role in This End Up's retail expansion. With house, car, club, insurance and school payments on our docket, this move far surpassed my earlier personal leap of risk. The two of us were now gambling with our financial security; we would not have one penny of income unless we sold enough crates to pay the company bills. If money was left over, most of it would go to This End Up's growth, and the crumbs would feed our family. I was still too sheltered to know that I should have been scared to death.

The disparate strengths of the four partners, which were bound together by our common goal of building a one-product company, allowed for harmonious decision-making. Day to day, The Boys focused on manufacturing, Stewart on growing the business and I on training our expanding staff in sales and management techniques. *(Photo 1.3)*

Our first important decision as a team was to open another store, to be located in Alexandria, Virginia. We lucked into a plum corner in historic Old Town, and I asked Barbara, our capable employee from Richmond, to move there and open it. She accepted, and seven months into our venture we had the second of what would ultimately become a chain of 253 furniture stores.

The reception of Steve and Randy's crate design was favorable again, but the Alexandria store had a much larger customer base. Barbara said she had appeals for more fabric choices from the sophisticated Washington, D.C., crowd, so we increased our selection from 12 to 18. Some additional furniture pieces were added, including bunk beds, which would turn out to be the best-selling items in This End Up's history.

Soon we had a staff of four in the new location, and the search was on to find a local man to help Gunther with the D.C. delivery territory. To keep complaints down as we fell behind getting orders into people's homes, the all-female store staff delivered pieces from the small stock of extra items we kept in the basements of their apartments. After retail hours, they loaded whatever furniture would fit in the back of their small cars and took the pieces to the customer who had been waiting longest, sometimes a trip of 20 miles each way. The guts and get-it-done spirit of that first batch of sales associates, most of them just graduated from southern women's colleges, defied their stereotype. Much like the original carpenters, these yearling managers set the model for our future store personnel.

Three months after the second location opened, we were swamped. Struggling to keep appearances calm and professional, our skeleton store staff remained undertrained, overworked and underpaid for what we were asking of them. With no retail, delivery or manufacturing background, with double-time hours and slave wages, so were we.

At this early point in our enterprise, we sought store managers who had backgrounds similar to ours. Familiarity made it easy to work together. As friends, we didn't need sophisticated management skills, skills that Stewart and I were short on from our former jobs as paper salesman and stockbroker, teacher and human resources assistant. The company grew, and we cut our executive teeth on these first employees.

The young women who started This End Up alongside us had something in common other than their education and upbringing. Many of the candidates we hired were willing to work on commission in order to get a job with some autonomy. We supplied what bright women moving into the workplace wanted in 1976: trust, confidence and principled leadership. They supplied what an entrepreneurial business wanted: work ethic, independence and a will to succeed. It turned out to be a winning formula.

Stewart's pay-for-productivity philosophy scared a few of our saleswomen at first, but that arrangement was the only way we could afford them. In addition, Stewart and I felt strongly that This End Up would be a sounder company in the long run if it lived by that compensation plan. As we grew, the idea turned out to be one of the linchpins of employee loyalty. Most of these young women learned quickly that their smarts and hard work paid off under such an arrangement, but some struggled at the start and kind parents helped out occasionally.

A few years later, however, fatherly fiscal concern took a passing shot at us in the middle of dinner.

"Is this Mr. Brown? Mr. Stewart Brown who owns This End Up?" asked the peeved man on the phone.

"It is," I heard Stewart say.

"My name is Julian Franks and my daughter Hazel works for you in your Cobble Creek store. I just have to tell you that you don't pay her enough for all the things she does. She even delivered a table to a *trailer* yesterday," bellowed Mr. Franks. "I didn't send her to college to do that. She's going to have to find another job if you can't raise her salary."

I agitated over how Mr. Franks had the nerve to call us at home to demand anything on behalf of 24-year-old Hazel's employment, and I feared for her adult independence. But Stewart handled the scene with his normal aplomb, explaining the company's compensation philosophy and the trust we had in Hazel's abilities. I fumed in the background at the effrontery of the caller.

When our own children became young adults, I found more empathy for parental protectiveness. But the Hazel incident inspired Stewart and me to teach our daughter how to handle her own differences with people before she left our custody.

CHAPTER 8: This Way Out (3)

I had decided not to get myself in a twit by asking Stewart every day whether he had heard from the men who could change our lives. He was happy to oblige my silence. Our different styles of communication often put the two of us at loggerheads. Stewart measured all his words. I was happiest spilling out whatever came to mind. But two weeks had passed since our hopeful interview with the Melville Corporation, and I couldn't stand it any longer.

"Stewart, haven't they called back yet? How long can it take to decide if they want to go forward? The CEO sounded so encouraging when we were up there, didn't you think? What could be the holdup?"

Stewart disclosed a few snippets of information about daily requests coming in from Melville for an avalanche of information. And then, as was his habit, he dropped a bombshell.

"There's a second company interested in us. They'd like to come for a meeting in the next week or so."

Suddenly, there were two big-time, renowned businesses taking the measure of This End Up. Two days later, Randy and Steve arrived in Richmond to discuss our improbable popularity. The conversation started with Stewart recalling for us the original inquiry from the Melville Corporation in 1982.

This End Up was only seven years old when Melville contacted Stewart the first time. The partners had been too excited about its exploding growth to give that exploratory call serious consideration. All four of us were steamrolling its expansion, and each day was more successful than the one before. Stewart had said thanks but no thanks to Melville, and we moved through the next 24 months without further thought of parting with our creation.

Now we had Melville back at the table, and suitor No. 2—The Wolverine Company—was sniffing around. And Steve and Randy wanted an exit plan from their side of the company. Stewart believed he could run both the retail and manufacturing parts of This End Up. The economic environment was perfect for mergers and acquisitions. We had already *experienced one lesson in the meaning of right time, right place. This opportunity had all the same markings.*

Stewart would coordinate the potential sale. His financial background made him the natural choice. Since he would head This End Up in its entirety once Steve and Randy left, potential buyers would want to negotiate with him. But the responsibility became more complicated with the surprise entry of a second company, and we knew we needed professional help. The game had ratcheted up.

From the days of his former career, Stewart had connections with a reputable regional brokerage firm out of Charlotte that had a strong mergers and acquisitions department. Steve, Randy, Stewart and I felt encouraged after our interview with that company's new whiz kid, Peter Thomas. Peter had an Einstein brain, a lawyer's attention to detail and the courtly manner of a southern gentleman. We signed with his firm to be This End Up's representative in any negotiations with the two companies.

CHAPTER 9: Nailing It

R andy and Steve had moved This End Up's manufacturing facility from the basement of their apartment building to an abandoned flower shop after a couple of months in business so they could store more than one day's worth of raw materials. The hobby part of this furniture gig was over, and they needed to purchase some serious tools. The Boys maxed out their credit cards on a radial arm saw for starting the workday and a mini refrigerator for winding it down.

The time had come to stop buying the inferior wood stock carried by building supply companies, but Randy and Steve weren't sure where to get the wholesale goods they needed. They chose the name of a nearby lumber company from a reference book at the N.C. State library. On their first inquiry, the sales manager hung up on them. After wangling a personal appointment, the guys combed their ponytails, gave their best pitch and were turned out of the office in less than five minutes.

Sitting on the empty flatbed truck they had rented in the hopes of bringing back their first load of serious wood, The Boys were a dejected-looking sight at the nearby gas station. When the same sales manager pulled in for fuel on his way home for the day, he appeared at first not to recognize Randy and Steve. Making a U-turn in his path, he walked over to the two mavericks, and without preamble, he got in their faces and growled.

"Pay your bill. If you don't, it's over. I must be nuts but I'll give you one try."

With that, Account #66441-8 was opened, and stayed open for most of the life of This End Up Furniture Company.

The consequences of sharply increased sales were sparking up like flashpoints in the delivery, manufacturing and design parts of the business. We were fast becoming one of Ryder's premier mid-size truck accounts, and The Boys were already looking for another location in which to build the expanding line of furniture.

Around the beginning of our second year, the old HeavenRest Mattress Factory came available for rent in downtown Raleigh, and

Steve and Randy signed a lease for the tall, skinny building. The cut-up space of the first floor could only be used for housing raw materials, so the manufacturing process, which needed a large unobstructed place, had to be upstairs. The Boys hoped the two-floor layout wouldn't be quite the stumbling block it appeared.

It was worse.

The ancient freight elevator groaned and screeched, protesting its load of solid wood furniture. On days it broke down, our complement of second-floor carpenters played darts and checkers while a backup of raw materials gathered in the humid heat of the first floor. The soupy air of eastern North Carolina caused some of the boards to curl in distress. And the ones that had their grain on straight required quick transformation into meaningful purpose before their knots started to pop.

At the same time, the drivers and delivery trucks stood around the ground floor with nothing to do. On those days of manufacturing, employee and truck stoppages, The Boys usually brought out the beer while they waited on Buddy, the elevator repairman.

On the retail side, our first few locations belonged to young landlords. When This End Up could pay the rent on time, they celebrated along with us, enjoying the work-together-party-together approach. Both sides scrambled and prodded and scratched each other's backs in whatever way we could to get the job done and have some laughs at it.

Occasionally, we traded furniture for rent with our struggling proprietors. In a bar one Kentucky Derby day, Stewart and one of our landlords bet on the horses and Stewart's choice won. As the payoff, This End Up got a budding real estate mogul as a delivery helper on its next truck. When one owner couldn't afford to re-glaze the leaky picture window in the store we rented, he gave us stacks of old towels to sop up the water. We understood. The rat running between our customer's feet at the Strawberry Street store didn't cause us to ask the landlord to hire an exterminator. We bought our own giant traps and a big hunk of cheddar at the market down the block.

After the fourth or fifth store, all of them quickly profitable, Steve, Randy, Stewart and I decided to go full tilt toward making this furniture company as big as we could—say, 20 or 25 stores. Stewart and I had placed those first few stores in the tight geographic triangle between the beaches of Virginia, its capital city and the teeming bedroom communities of Washington, D.C., and we soaked up graduates of nearby colleges to run them.

Connected to the young crowd that wielded influence around the original locations, a close-knit team of friends manned each store within those cities. Every manager, whether at work or play, was a strong ambassador for This End Up's products. Being women somewhat outside their traditional roles, they were determined to be successful in a non-traditional job, and they weren't shy about passing the word wherever they went. These salespeople and I spent hours together, selling and critiquing each other's skills. Because of their affability, intelligence and confidence, I had the perfect platform on which to develop This End Up's sales training program which became one of the secrets to its overall success.

Many of the young women we interviewed for sales positions admitted they needed to deal in something more glamorous than crate furniture to be happy on the job: jewelry, clothes or perfume, for instance. The ones we hired, however, were more interested in learning the craft of the job. The cultivation of first-rate selling and management techniques was at the core of their ambitions, and we did all that we could to support these young professionals, many of whom have gone on to distinguish themselves as leading players in retail America.

At that time, the nation was coming out of a widespread recession, and the Woodstock generation was beginning to set up house. Young people in the '70s rejected the cheap, assembly-line furniture they could afford, and they embraced Randy and Steve's refreshingly simple and solid designs. The value inherent in these pieces was clear to see, and after hard times, the modest price tag was a balm for tight budgets. The combination of quality, affordability and casual style was utterly unique in the marketplace. No one sold a product where you paid a moderate price and got excellent durability—not until This End Up.

CHAPTER 10: Searching for Me

The profitable Richmond and Alexandria locations were working smoothly. Three other Virginia stores, a couple of stores in North Carolina and one Maryland store were bursting with business, and strong personnel had set them on a path to profit. As their managers became more independent and were able to keep the inevitably rough ride of fast growth in hand, Stewart began to search for new store sites and look for ancillary ways to spur sales.

On sporadic weekends, he and I set up a small portable showroom at craft shows in the Central Virginia area, trying to increase our exposure to the public without spending money to advertise. While Stewart wandered around with our toddlers, I manned the booth, wedged between hummingbird feeders and ceramic mugs and across from sun catchers and wooden whistles. Our first commercial customer discovered This End Up at one of those shows. A sizeable success ensued and I made periodic trips to help furnish the ski resort at Snow Mountain.

I no longer worked standing up in the back of the Strawberry Street store. My six-month stint as a This End Up store manager came to a close once we opened a tiny office in downtown Richmond, where I got to sit at a desk and try my hand at long-distance management.

What a challenge. What a learning curve. I loved every minute of it, but as the pace and stress of the enterprise pressed into my time at home, I began to realize some of the consequences of my gamble. Our children needed more attention; the time had come to find someone to help us raise Stew and Ellie, who were now four and five years old.

At first, the only after-nursery school requirements of our youngsters were lunch, Sesame Street Band-Aids and stuffed animals, until I got home and relieved the maid to honcho baths and supper. Before long, though, they began to have the usual earaches and tummy bugs, hurt feelings and art projects just at a time when I needed to be away for longer days and overnights. Susan joined our family and completely exceeded our expectations for a house manager/nanny. I couldn't have dreamt of anyone so competent, calm and caring. Luck continued to love us.

* * *

The roles of wife, mother, daughter and friend held the same amount of importance to me as ever, and I wanted those blessings to have every shred of care they deserved. That created a delicate balancing act, as I had pledged to be in service to This End Up's success, and I recognized that I would need to put forth extraordinary effort to keep up with all my commitments. It seemed there was less and less time in the day and sometimes my life seemed not quite what I had intended.

I felt inspired, motivated and fulfilled with my job, but when it came to those I loved, my antagonist—doubt—paced inside me. Was I being inattentive and inconsiderate? I would try not to think about business during normal conversations with friends, to quit mentally slighting their everyday interests and to rediscover the value in our easy familiarity. Soon, I promised myself, Ellie and Stew would clap their hands upon arriving home from school to find me baking chocolate chip cookies. My mother would be pleased at how often I called her instead of being patiently accepting of how seldom she heard from me. And Stewart would discover a smiling wife instead of one so preoccupied with work she forgot to say hello.

They were promises I failed to keep.

* * *

The first time I ever lost sleep over an employee began with a frightening event involving a store manager. We were inexperienced at handling serious personnel matters when a phone call into the Richmond office broadsided us.

"Mr. Stewart Brown? Officer Mike Donohue with the Bethesda, Maryland, Police Department. We have a major problem here with your employee, a Miss Daley Harrington. She's threatening suicide by hanging on the outside of the third-story railing above the children's daycare area that's just below your store."

We were stunned. Daley had cut her clothes to ribbons and was waving big scissors at anyone who approached her. I could visualize those scissors, the ones we packed in every new store box so the salespeople could cut fabric swatches for customers.

We arranged for Daley's transfer to the psychiatric floor of a nearby hospital, and afterward, Stewart jumped into our car to drive the

50 miles to Fredericksburg so he might tell her parents in person what had happened. It was raining when he left the office for a rush-hour drive to Daley's home. At 8:45 Stewart dragged in wet and quiet. As he sat down to a leftover dinner, I asked what Mr. and Mrs. Harrington's reaction had been.

"Nothing."

"NOTHING? What do you mean nothing?" I said. "Weren't they home? Weren't they shocked?"

In a somber tone, Stewart told a tale of resigned parents who wanted no details other than the name of the hospital where their daughter had been admitted.

"Then they closed the door in my face," he said.

Finding it hard to believe that was the whole story, I prompted my less than loquacious husband with a question about their thanks.

"There weren't any."

The halcyon days of our start-up were over. Our initiation had begun into the most overwhelmingly difficult but often rewarding aspect of our responsibilities—people.

Tossing and turning later, I fumed over Daley's ingrate parents as the clock's hands circled around. In the morning hours, though, the anger faded to sadness and I hurt for them, because they seemed all too acquainted with Stewart's distressing tale. I prayed that my own children would never be aggrieved with whatever demon possessed our beautiful Daley.

CHAPTER 11: The Golden Rule

In 1977, while Stewart and I were managing the human side of the business, the design-build team was working on the supply side. Randy and Steve needed to expand both manufacturing and distribution to keep up with the 20- to 25-store plan, so they bought land in Raleigh on which to build a bona fide factory. Once again, their design and construction experience, along with their confidence in breaking conventional rules, gave This End Up an edge over competition. Rapid production called for creative plant layout to build the volume of furniture that plans demanded. The goods had to be easy to produce, because we knew by this time they could be sold as fast as we could open stores.

Success came through like a storm. Such an atmosphere was a heady place for the 29- and 32-year-young men as they watched their investment take shape. The Boys had been granted several design patents for the crate furniture and the copyright for the This End Up trademark. That would later prove to be a bothersome deterrent to several would-be copycats. Legitimate now, with a real factory, the entrepreneurs had suppliers coming to them instead of the other way around. And people wanting jobs lined up at the door of the clever company that melded high-speed production with the warmth of family.

Steve and Randy's exterior design for the new plant resembled a country store more than a 40,000-square-foot factory. Ruffled curtains in the windows and wooden rocking chairs on the covered porch welcomed visitors. They might have expected to find cats stretching in the sun and the aroma of vegetable soup coming from a wood-burning stove, rather than carpenters operating radial arm saws, filling the air with the sharp, fresh odor of sawdust. *(Photo 1.4)*

Behind the rustic façade, over a hundred pieces of furniture could be built in a 24-hour day. For years, vendors who made their first call on This End Up would turn around at the entrance to the driveway and telephone from a nearby phone booth, saying they were lost. When directed back the same way, salesmen all had a similar response.

"But that can't be your factory."

In a business world filled with slick-talking proclaimers, our plant's unassuming exterior delighted every supplier, customer and reporter who toured the sophisticated facility within. Even when we had 253 stores in the United States and Canada, most people never realized the scope of This End Up. The quiet manner in which we developed the company was a well-thought-out plan that matched three of the partners' four personalities. And I, the most talkative, animated partner, was in my proper niche—sales—where it was productive for me to be able to "shoot the shit with a lamppost."

Frequently, a diverse group of people might be seen relaxing in the rockers on the factory's front porch: a carpenter waiting to start work, a driver picking up a load of furniture destined for the Northeast, a store manager from Louisiana taking a factory tour. Because all our employees were paid on incentive, we never had to ask why they were on that porch at two o'clock in the afternoon. And they never had to scurry around when one of us came out the door.

In the factory, quotas were met without delay so the carpenter could move into the lucrative area of overage pay. This End Up's builders knew the goals and managed their own way to achieve them. Our pay concept was based on common sense; it screened out slackers and royally rewarded hard workers.

Allowing people the freedom to pilot their own lives at work, though, sometimes masked unacceptable behavior that went undiscovered for too long. A gentle carpenter named Freddy came to work when the new factory opened. His breadth almost matched his height, and he was always nearby when we needed a strong body. Freddy's corrugated brow formed cliffs over deep-set eyes whenever he put his massive back to the problem at hand. And afterward, a little-boy smile as if to say, "Happy to help."

When Freddy finished his time on the factory floor, he said goodbye and lumbered out the back door, presumably for home. One day, the cleaning crew turned in a bag with some XL clothes and a toothbrush they found stashed behind the candy machine. Freddy's checkbook was at the bottom of the bag. When confronted with the evidence, he said he saw no reason to pay rent on an apartment. He could be more readily available to work if he lived in the break room. And for six months, Freddy had done just that while The Boys were engrossed with the new plant.

Randy and Steve's noses had been pressed hard to the grindstone over the past two years, as manufacturing outgrew each successive location—from a basement apartment to a former flower shop to an old mattress factory. There were no creaking elevators now; it was quiet inside the new plant's soundproofed offices. But to open the door from the office to the factory was a startling experience. There, in a din painful to unprotected ears, carpenters worked at 14 individual stations, building without interruption one piece of furniture at a time, tended by runners who anticipated their every need.

Boxes of nails balanced in crooked stacks, ready to be loaded into pneumatic guns that made the factory sound like a firing range. Belt sanders screamed in a duet with routers. Tools whined and jackhammered above the constant whoosh of suction equipment vacuuming wood dust from the air. When the factory was at its peak, your chest would vibrate like you were at a stoplight next to a four-wheel subwoofer with bass and volume knobs wide open.

Lumber was stacked 10 feet high in a 4,000-square-foot space that opened onto a huge receiving dock. Fifty-five gallon drums of stain and furniture glue, containers of braces and bolts, belts of sandpaper and carts of spare tools were scattered among intent carpenters. Working in the factory was a job where negligence carried serious physical consequences.

In the bid to employ capable people to work in the factory, one of This End Up's drawing cards was the partners' conviction that work could, and should, be fun. We wanted our employees to learn how to meet goals with a balance of reliability and self-direction. Since our workforce was young, they brought with them an innate passion for change, and they were perfectly cast to work in a start-up company with its flexible hours, dress and compensation.

Start to finish, each carpenter built his weekly quota alone. That setup was unheard of in a furniture company that produced a cookie-cutter design of only 30 pieces. Conventional wisdom held that This End Up was perfectly suited for an assembly-line layout, but our one-person, one-piece approach gave us excellent quality control. Each carpenter signed his initials to the underside of his completed goods. That mark was a guarantee to the customer that he accepted sole responsibility for quality. Upon delivery, if customers rejected a piece, the faulty item was returned to the signatory for rebuilding and deducted from his pay.

Quotas for every This End Up factory employee were set with the individual's input. To issue ultimatums seemed a great indignity, an indignity to us as well as to them. We offered little direction so long as the results were timely. A number of years into our development, we formalized a management philosophy that gave some structure to our ways. It worked wonderfully but no better than our seat-of-the-pants instincts did when we were small enough to look in the face of every person who worked for us.

People still ask: How did you become so successful in so short a time? We're not sure. Possibly it worked because we were in the right place at just the right time. Or perhaps it worked because of the unique harmony among our four personalities, our employees and our product. It probably didn't hurt that we wanted people to enjoy their jobs. But maybe it worked because, when we were setting down our company roots, we simply lived by the Golden Rule. I know also that we strived to hire as many people as we could with strong values and a sense of fair play. Skills we could teach. Integrity they had to bring with them. *(Photo 1.5)*

One example of a perfect match between a good-hearted employee and This End Up's entrepreneurial style was Billie. Having spent six years in the grinding, regimented work of North Carolina's textile mills, Billie was able to save enough money to enter college at age 24. She came to us in desperation after her son was born two years later.

With wire-rim glasses and a strawberry blonde braid, she was a small woman whose face was sharpened by the burden of single parent-hood. Her widowed sister brought Billie's year-old son to the factory for lunch almost every day. That way Billie could spend time with her child even though she worked long hours to support the three of them.

Billie became an efficient producer of coffee tables. I always stopped at her workstation on my factory tours because I was attracted by her soft-spoken, guileless manner and determination. Once I asked her how she judged the quality of her tables before she sent them out to be delivered.

"Well, Libby, I just look at every piece I build, and I say out loud to myself, 'Billie, would you want that in your own home?' If I can't answer yes, then I tear it down and build it again, no matter how long it takes."

Some things were so simple and so sweet at the outset and meshed so perfectly with our belief that we really could create a different kind of company—one based on fairness and trust and honesty. Most of the time, doing unto others as we would have them do unto us solved just about any problems that came our way.

CHAPTER 12: Men and Boys

Our factory was open around the clock, and often carpenters worked without any formalized schedule; if it suited you to work at 3:00 a.m., you could. Camaraderie was thick and loyalty of the familial sort. Picnic tables, play areas, basketball nets and vending machines were available for your family if they wanted to hang out and wait for you to finish your work.

We asked for excellence from every individual. Hardworking employees became easy to come by when we handed out paychecks more than double the furniture industry's average; in return, our typical carpenter produced almost four times the industry's average. The energy of our young employees, in the factory as well as the stores, created the dynamism that was a large part of what built This End Up so rapidly.

Unlike the predominantly male manufacturing part of the business, the retail side had mostly female employees. With the women, we sometimes acquired additional human resources—their brash and controlling men. These buckoes might come out swinging if they perceived a slight to their manhood through their women's careers. Often, embarrassed employees told Stewart and me they were mortified by their husbands, boyfriends or fathers butting in.

Several years into our history, our family was on vacation in North Carolina when we received another dinnertime phone call from another belligerent man. Her champion bristled with proprietary regard for his new wife. We let it pass that he had no regard for us.

High-and-mighty Barry Middleditch jumped through the phone in a white-hot rage. His wife, Emily, who was receiving anonymous, lecherous phone calls at work, was This End Up's highly regarded Kentucky/Tennessee district manager.

Stewart listened to the story of the scary events that had understandably put Emily on edge. But he was hearing about the incidents for the first time.

"How long has this been going on?" asked Stewart. Boiled shrimp and corn on the cob chilled in the air conditioning.

"For weeks. You'd better think up a plan quick, or I'll pull Emily out of that job so fast it'll make your head spin."

"Well, what would Emily like to see done?" I placed a cold beer in front of Stewart.

There was a pause. Perhaps the green-eyed monster on the phone was unnerved by Stewart's non-defensive approach. It seemed he had not thought to ask his wife her opinion on the subject. We had heard through the grapevine that the wealthy power broker thought it was demeaning to him for Emily to work, and I admired her for insisting on autonomy.

But Barry Middleditch was accustomed to picking confrontations, not walking away from them. Stewart listened to demands while he sipped his beer and watched the breeze play in the sea oats. "Fine," he said.

Emily's husband huffed and bullied and postured some more. And once again Stewart said, "Fine."

After another minute, he closed the conversation in his hallmark affable style. "Please give Emily a message for me, if you will. Tell her not to worry, that she's very important to us. If she'll call me in the morning, she and I can work out whatever will make her comfortable." I hoped Stewart's generous treatment of the raging bull had caused him to consider his behavior, but somehow I had my doubts. We sat back down at the table, and Stewart's face sparkled with mischief.

"If I were inclined to make sexy phone calls, I'd pick Emily too."

* * *

This End Up was awakening me to priceless lessons. My former wall of privilege had kept me segregated from a delicious variety of people. Compared with my new duties, my old routine seemed more boring than ever. Sometimes I would take a peek at my watch and wonder: What would I be doing if I were not at work? Arranging flowers? Shopping? Most of my friends seemed happy with domesticity and thrilled to be chasing down the latest designer trends. Why wasn't I?

New people and rigorous work was what slaked my desire for challenge. I went to bed most nights flagged with the fatigue of doing things that stretched me. And I rose most mornings eager for the demands of that workout.

CHAPTER 13: Diminishing Returns

When Stewart and I hung our lives on the line to start the crate furniture business, I was unaware of all the risks attendant to our gamble. The most difficult sacrifice for me was my personal relationships. The all-engrossing enterprise demanded almost everything I had to give, and what was left was guarded jealously for my children. Still, my friends were important, too, and I struggled to preserve familiar bonds, even as the path I had chosen diverged more and more from the familiar day-to-day life we once had in common. Our growing distance was sometimes painful.

A woman who had grown up in Richmond but moved away when she decided to marry "up North" returned for a visit after some years. I was asked by a mutual friend to join a group for the welcome-back luncheon for Franny. I had met the honoree only once, but I wouldn't have missed it because it was a chance to catch up with some friends.

On the day of the party, I left nine of our new store managers-in-training deep in an accounting lesson. Racing from our downtown offices with a stack of phone messages in my hand, I screeched into a service station. I would never make my 6:20 business flight the next morning if I had to stop for gas. Arriving at the private squash and tennis club a few minutes after the core crew had assembled, I found the guests revisiting old times.

"Franny, remember when you and Maryanne and I were all in Miss Granby's English class? Ninth grade, wasn't it?"

"And you and I used to have our birthday parties together," piped up another guest. "I remember to this day a yellow smocked dress you wore to one. It's impossible to find dresses like that anymore. I have to send off to a place in New Orleans to get the right kind for Elizabeth."

Relaxing in the warmth of a common memory, I flashed back to my own call to that same store for our two-year-old Ellie's Easter dress.

"You won't believe how much this club has changed since you lived here," complained the hostess. "Sometimes reserving a court takes forever, and then I might not even know who the people are playing next to me."

"Did you know my sister, Lila, lives in your aunt's house now? They just put on an addition that must have cost a fortune," added Lolly. "She's just had Fleming and Bates do the dining room walls."

Every old friend had some opinion or update to offer Franny. As a newcomer to her circle, I waited my turn.

"Sorry to hold everybody up," called a breathless new arrival.

"What a morning! I had to drive both carpools and that made me late for my tennis lesson. So when I got to the Pro Shop, Ted said he only had half an hour to work with me. Then after I broke my neck to make my pedicure, Yang Lin was out sick. Unreal!"

Franny empathized. "Bless your heart."

I thought of the calloused feet and plain nails inside my shoes. I really should try a pedicure from Yang Lin sometime.

"Anyway, I haven't seen you for eons, Franny. You look fantastic. Last time I saw you was in the Atlanta airport. You, Polecat and the kids were heading for a dude ranch in Montana."

I stepped into view as the smooth delivery of personal connections slowed for breath.

"Oh, Franny," said the hostess. "This is a new friend, Libby Brown. She moved here eight or nine years ago from North Carolina, and she, uh, she works."

With that, my credentials were complete. I faded to the perimeter to listen.

Their conversation made me feel sad, and whatever I had to offer to this mix was not of interest to them. Their happy reminiscing made me sorry that my early years had been spent in different places, that my memories of teachers and classmates and parties were unconnected to anyone here. In spite of my sorrow, I was reminded again of why I wanted to know life's margins.

Warning myself about being too touchy, I tried to put the stepsister feeling behind me. I asked questions during lunch and laughed at some of the funny stories about the childhood antics of the group. Was it their lack of interest in my life that caused me such a troubled reaction?

As we finished wine and lunch, separate checks were presented to each attendee. When the waiter waved the tab for the guest of honor in the air, one of her girlhood chums said, "Give it to Libby. She can afford it."

Not a pack from which someone would venture a stand on the side of a Johnny-come-lately, no one batted an eye. I was sure the comment was a joke, but I felt my face flush as I struggled with a tangle of conflicting emotions and the ringing endorsement of my place outside their comfortable circle.

* * *

As our business matured, so did the thickness of my skin. Remarks from other friends like, "I'm so proud of you and Stewart," helped me contain the vandals of my confidence, but questions of conviction seemed to be part of my genetic makeup. Sometimes my goals would waver in front of me in the face of soul-searching. But then my competitive streak, like a living entity, would grab me by the scruff of the neck and shriek in my face, "You chickenshit, weak-willed wimp!" After that nudge, I could usually circle back to the task.

CHAPTER 14: This Way Out (4)

I could tell Stewart was home because he stomped his feet on the doormat. From the sound of it, I knew the icy snow, the only type during Richmond winters, still had not melted from the driveway. Out the kitchen window, I saw the silhouette of his car stuck at the foot of the hill. The day was the kind where my neck stayed pulled into my shoulders and my scalp felt like plucked chicken skin. I wanted to sink up to my lower lip in a hot bath.

I was glad to be home after two days of driving in the shipyard and military base traffic of Tidewater, Virginia. Visits to each of the three This End Up locations in that area convinced me that the experienced district manager, with her streak of optimism, was behind the excellent sales of those stores. I was eager to tell Stewart how well they were doing since I now measured every success with an eye toward what Company No. 1 and Company No. 2 would think.

When I left Richmond on Wednesday, Stewart had said that he and Peter Thomas planned to spend a day pulling together "The Book." This important document would be given to the parties interested in buying This End Up. It consisted of a detailed history and mission, lists of stores and their sales, information on employees, factories, trucks and distribution centers, as well as financial disclosures about the company. The report opened with biographies and job descriptions of the four partners. There went privacy.

Stewart told me when I called to check in from the Virginia Beach store that Peter had contacted some other companies. Mild interest was expressed here and there but nothing noteworthy. He contacted Melville officials, who asked when they would receive The Book. He touched base with The Wolverine Company, whose spokesperson said top executives wanted to come to Richmond to see us, but the CEO had a busy travel schedule. I had the uneasy feeling Company No. 1 was cooling off and Company No. 2 was stalling.

The complexity of selling This End Up was coming into focus. I remembered my euphoric confidence of just a few weeks earlier during *our interview with Melville that surely we were only a formality away from a life of financial security. I hoped Stewart would bring in some hot news with the cold air.*

Without giving him a chance to take off his coat, I started popping questions like a string of firecrackers. "So, how have the last few days been? Did The Book go out? Have we heard from either company?"

"Not much."

That didn't answer any of my questions.

I served up beef stew as I waited for information I knew would trickle my way in time. Did Stewart do that on purpose? Was he that distracted? Did he want to keep me in the dark?

We talked about my trip and a lease problem with the Columbia, Maryland, store. The children spoke about school, friends and upcoming spring break. The phone rang regularly, the dog had to be put out and in and out again. Pans were scoured, mail read and homework done. I headed for a bubble bath. Stewart poked his head through the bathroom door.

"I forgot to tell you about U.S.B. Furniture."

"Who?" I asked in a sleepy voice.

"U.S.B. Furniture. Real big company. They say they want to sit down at the negotiating table with us. I'll tell you more about it when you get out."

But Stewart would be snoring by then.

CHAPTER 15: Mall Rats

Early on, Stewart made a decision that changed the face of This End Up forever. He decided that shopping malls were the right locale for our continued expansion. This was a radical departure from business-as-usual, and the idea was scorned by everyone from acquaintances to competitors to real estate developers.

Huge, stand-alone superstructures were the industry standard for furniture retailers. The courage to go forward was one of Stewart's greatest acts of grit and perhaps the most forward-thinking move that the stodgy furniture industry had seen in years.

We had begun to acquire a tough hide, developed from dealing with our hometown doubters, but they were amateur skeptics compared with mall leasing agents.

"Are you nuts?" they would ask, call after call, as Stewart's queries were cut short and shown the door. We lost track of the number of turndowns.

Finally, Fernwood Mall, a scruffy, midsize center in Virginia, gave us a grudging chance. A spot was available, vacated just before the October start of the holiday season. The cocksure mall manager waved the signed contract in our faces.

"Look. You've got three months to make it or break it. And if you can't make it at this time of year, then you'll never make it. You need to be open for business in 14 days, 10:00 sharp."

His face folded down on itself like he had sucked a lemon. He walked away muttering, off to spread his uncommon cheer to the other retailers.

Our first mall store had 650 square feet at a yearly rent of almost $10,000. We would have to sell the little-known crate furniture at a time of year when disposable income was slotted for jewelry and toys. The smart-aleck mall manager was unaware that not every product had its heyday during Christmas. But why would he know that? Furniture stores had never lived in malls before.

When Stewart signed our first mall lease in September 1978, my heart was happy and heavy at the same time. Finally, he held the winning card he sought tirelessly for two years, but now that he had cracked into the king-size retail world, we would have to play for keeps. From now on, I knew I would spend many of my days in the cities where our new malls would open. The push pins on the map in my office spread from Florida to Maine, and what was left of my regular life fell like a house of cards.

It took all 14 days and the whole night before the opening deadline to get the Fernwood store painted, carpeted, lighted and certified for occupancy. To save money, Stewart added tradesman and project manager to his job description, although he did hold the line at the much-needed plumbing duties. An exhausted band of the faithful helped Gunther carry in the heavy furniture pieces for the showroom. Just as they slid into place at 10:00, the front gate went up under the beady eye of the prune-faced mall curmudgeon.

After the opening of the initial mall store, we moved up the East Coast, scratching our way into imperfect mall locations in Maryland, Delaware, Pennsylvania, New Jersey and New York. Adding mattresses, lamps, wall art and throw pillows to our product line attracted flocks of browsers to This End Up stores. Sometimes Stewart would allow me a glimpse of a smile of vindication as the steady traffic of malls began to pay off. *(Photo 1.6)*

Requests for more pieces to go with our furniture came in, and people brought us sketches of products they wanted. Managers could count on a busy sales staff the day after deliveries, once customers' neighbors saw the furniture. The average buyer had a wealthier, more educated profile than we had originally envisioned, and they often bought pieces for dining and living rooms, not just for dens and play-rooms. We changed the look of the stores from rough-hewn to polished, and we hired an interior designer to update the stores and the fabric selection regularly.

Still the number of refusals almost equaled the number of calls Stewart made those first few years as he tried to obtain space in top-tier malls. But finally, as the second-rate mall locations began to generate first-rate sales, the big developers started to acknowledge us. What a triumphant day when one of them actually sought This End Up, a conquest that could not have been more gratifying. Developers were a long way from admitting us into their club, but at last, they let This End Up submit an application. I toasted Stewart's tenacity and redoubled my occasionally flagging resolve.

After having heard so often from others why This End Up was unacceptable in malls—"nobody sells furniture in malls," and "those wooden crates don't belong in our centers"—we worked on targeting the core issues that would win the big developers' approval. Stewart honed his sales pitch to those standards and started back at the beginning of our wish-list developers. We wanted just one chance at an excellent location in a Grade A mall to make a run at being a bona fide retail chain.

The leasing agents called Stewart obstinate, but at long last they called him. His unflagging courage and resolve got us booked into our first center court space, and that contract began the transformation of our business from homespun to spun gold.

Our mall store formula was tweaked to near-perfection. In an area of 600 to 700 square feet, we could show one of every piece of furniture we offered. Because we delivered the customer's request directly from our factory, we took orders from the showroom display. We rarely sold anything off the floor, which eliminated the need for inventory. And, more important to the consumer, this allowed for customized upholstery selection. The entire fabric display was housed in a flat, 5-foot-wide wall unit, which used the otherwise surplus vertical dimension of a store. Every costly inch of real estate was made productive.

The ultimate measure of success for any mall store was the dollars it could sell per square foot of space. This End Up soared off the chart from the beginning, achieving an unheard-of $2,180 per square foot at one notable location just before we sold the business. Our small stores, with 95 percent of the floor space devoted to product, brought in much higher average dollar transactions than neighboring purveyors of toys, toiletries and apparel. For developers, generating high-dollar sales from a small-scale space was like hitting a grand-slam home run. Stewart's relentless pursuit of mall locations hit pay dirt. When a couple of newspaper articles about This End Up were published, including a half-page lead article in *The Philadelphia Inquirer,* buzz in the retail world took off. We received a suggestion from an important developer that we come to the pinnacle of industry wheeling and dealing—The International Conference of Shopping Centers. Why not?

CHAPTER 16: Fish Out of Water

The International Conference of Shopping Centers met every year in Las Vegas. That venue was the most efficient place for This End Up to learn what was going on in the mall world, now that leasing agents had agreed to see us. When Stewart and I made our first trip there, our stores stretched along the East Coast, we were about to open our first one in the Midwest, and we had our sights set on Colorado, Canada and the West Coast. But this high-stakes conference and the sybaritic city where it was held were just about as foreign to two straight-talking, low-key people and our plain, rugged product as could possibly be.

Stewart and I heard three days of presentations about what was hot in retail space. The developers were the same bombastic characters who once had made a career of hanging up on Stewart. Now, impatiently watching every precious minute on gold Rolex watches, they occasionally allowed us the time of day. We usually were granted a late afternoon appointment with junior associates eager to put some martinis on their expense accounts before settling in at the blackjack table. The big boys were long gone to schmooze fatter cats than This End Up.

Stewart had a facility for negotiating leases with these giant companies, sophisticated organizations that hardly expected a "mom-and-pop" owner to work out his own deals. The men we called on had us up to their quarters, sumptuous suites of conference rooms, private bars, lounges and media rooms, all serviced by fleet-footed minions and swanked out in the ultimate high-roller accoutrements. Stewart showed up in a tattered blue blazer, no lawyer in tow, juggling a Diet Coke, a wrinkled, yellow legal pad with coffee stains on it and a dime-store calculator low on batteries. He usually had to borrow a pencil he would forget to return and manage to lose before the next appointment. After circling around the discussion like a dog settling in, he eased into the conversation, trading logic for cunning, in his patient, slow-talking way.

Observing Stewart's performance was exactly like watching him stalk a bonefish. He cast out a teaser once he spotted his prey. "So, how are things at Aspen Mall, Mort?"

Aspen was a mid-grade mall in downtown Denver that This End Up had no interest in. Mort was what Stewart was trying to trap, not Aspen.

"Couldn't be better. Square foot sales through the roof, and we're just finishing negotiations with Saks," boasted Mort. "It'll be the best mall in the area this time next year. A hell of a lot better than the Patella development going up on South Side."

Mort shifted in his seat and checked his costly timepiece.

Stewart threw out the next line with a near-perfect cast. "Great! Congratulations! But didn't I hear that Fantazium was leaving?"

We never gambled on deals without doing homework. My hours of mall crawling provided some of the grapevine bait that Stewart chummed with.

"How'd you know that?"

Mort's patronizing smile left his face blank. Stewart teased the line out a little further with his flair for changing conversational direction.

"Look at this color shot of our slick new store design. A perfect look for that Fantazium space at Aspen. When are they pulling out, by the way?"

After purposely exposing confidential information, Stewart had now provoked his quarry with a request to take over the soon-empty spot. I hoped that Mort wouldn't take the Aspen hook, though, since we didn't want a store with parking problems and a shopper profile above the age bracket of our customers. Trade-offs were valid currency in mall deals. If Mort turned down Stewart's set-up, we could use the rebuff to This End Up as tender in the future.

"You've got to be kidding. Nobody from that demographic wants *crate* furniture. You'd do better with that stuff being at Stonewall Landing."

A strike! "Great, I'll take 900 square feet, but not on the spoke leading down to the ice rink."

Stewart was pretending interest in a space much larger than he wanted, because our research on Stonewall showed only small places available, just the right size for a This End Up store. Once Mort's comeback for less than 900 feet surfaced, Stewart could act as if the step-down in size was a big sacrifice. Then he would have more bait for the rent negotiation.

Mort continued. "Five hundred eighty-five feet. That's it. But it's a package deal with 1,000 feet at Brookhaven in Cleveland. Take it or leave them both on the table."

The bonefish had just run for the mangroves.

The Brookhaven combo was a setback, a Grade B mall in a city where This End Up already had good coverage. A quick review of our Cleveland locations turned up one lease in a Grade C mall with an option out in December. Stewart went in for the catch.

"We'll sign a two-year agreement for no more than 800 feet at Brookhaven, to open in January. I guess we'll have to take the 585 at Stonewall, but it has to be within four stores of center court. And I don't like it one bit, I'll tell you, but I'll give up on Aspen this time."

Stewart released his catch; we never knew when we might need to hook Mort again. The two of us walked out with our primary goal accomplished for a relatively small compromise.

Our Stonewall Landing store was a good producer. We made a little money on Brookhaven but didn't renew its lease. And, unfortunately for its A-List tenants, Aspen Mall went slowly downhill.

A comment amused me once in a mall negotiation when Stewart introduced me simply as "Libby" and started the joking, easy kind of conversation that was his habit. After another victorious round, he walked out ahead of me while I gathered my things in the obscurity of a nobody. I heard the leasing impresario say to one of his underlings, "How the hell did you let him get away with *that*?"

I smiled that the quick rush to judgment about my partner had given him the advantage. Whatever these developers thought of us, Stewart had the right combination of skills to benefit our young enterprise. He started securing a few locations in premier malls at a rent competitive with better-known specialty stores. This acceptance by the mall kings was almost beyond our ken after so many frustrating months of being regarded as entrails in the slipstream of a royal barge.

Our Grade A malls were hard-earned and expensive. Needing to produce high revenues in a hurry to cover the eye-popping rents, we chose our brightest and most motivated people to run those stores. A mistake in hiring would be quick and certain disaster to our profit/loss line. *(Photo 1.7)*

A month before we opened our most expensive store ever, managers announced company-wide that This End Up would prosecute any employee caught stealing. We needed to stop a spate of internal petty theft. While we had issued the same statement before, Stewart and

I never had the stomach to go through with it. People who worked for us were like family. This time, though, we intended to keep our word.

Babs, a bright young mother of three children under the age of seven, was a perfect example of our extended family. An excellent store manager for several years, she had a stalwart husband named Bill whom Stewart and I had met briefly. We knew he had entered graduate school, and the couple was trying to make ends meet with her working full-time for us and him stocking shelves on the night shift at Kmart. When we were ready to open our Midwest flagship store right in Babs' backyard, we made the easy decision to promote her to Riverton Corner, by far our most sophisticated store and This End Up's costliest location.

Lee, our keen-eyed CFO, came to Stewart soon after our warning about employee theft. An audit had turned up serious irregularities in the high-volume store Babs would be leaving for Riverton Corner, which would be opening in just three weeks. The culprit had to be a member of her part-time staff. Babs, the Sunday school teacher and proud mom who had just been promoted to This End Up's top location, would be the last one we would suspect of larceny.

Isabel, Babs' district manager, and Lee, who had flown in from the main office, did the questioning. At first, Babs denied that she knew anything about the missing money, but her body language told a different story. Unfortunate experience had made us sadly skilled at pinpointing guilt. She was told to think about the matter overnight and to be at the store at seven the next morning.

At the appointed hour, Isabel and Lee encountered a tragic sight. The couple was weeping, grief-stricken. A vein, raised prominently down the center of Bill's blood-red forehead, throbbed with his broken heart. Babs was wracked with remorse.

She had confessed to her thunderstruck husband during the night. Babs had carried out the scheme alone through a complicated plan of rolling money, kiting checks and stealing from petty cash. The theft had been going on for a while, and it had netted her a substantial amount.

Babs was sentenced to a short term at a minimum-security prison for her crime. Though Stewart and I never saw her during this time, we mourned her loss. We hoped that by making the tough decision to prosecute, we saved other people from similar pitfalls, but when I tortured myself in a frenzy of second-guessing, I suffered headaches and heartaches over what happened to that family.

A few weeks after she was incarcerated, Stewart and I received a letter from Babs. It was a written confession, the first step to healing for this devastated young woman, and a brave and generous act on her part.

"If you think for one minute, no matter how badly you need the money, that it would be worth it to steal, just remember me. I have disgraced my parents to the point where they won't go out in their neighborhood. I have dishonored my husband of nine years who has had to drop out of school to pay our bills. God only knows if he will stick by me when I get out of jail. My kids will be saddled forever with a convict mother, and you know how cruel other children can be. We will have to move away and start over for them to have any chance of a normal life. They will always be guarding our family's dirty secret. And what will I tell them when they ask me why I did it? I have spit on the trust that a wonderful company has placed in me for the last three years. I can never ask them for a reference; I can only beg them for forgiveness. And what about me? I live every day with pain that never goes away. So remember this when you are tempted. If you give in, you may ruin your life forever.

Anonymous, for my children's sake."

CHAPTER 17: Pass the Nuts

While the courtship with mall developers advanced slowly, we gained regular notice from purchasing agents for colleges, resorts and government agencies. One of our favorite commercial customers was Madame Alexandra—Alex to her friends. She owned a "fine establishment for gentlemen," as she described it to us, which must have been a successful business since she frequently added to her This End Up collection. Alex said she loved its durability. She made tasteful fabric selections, paid upfront with cash and entertained us with her sense of humor. Although we were grateful for her loyalty, we did notice that Alex never sent us any referral business.

Our regular residential customers, on the other hand, told their families, friends, neighbors and co-workers. The repeat and referred orders exceeded 50 percent. Every person who sent a customer received a handwritten thank-you note from our store staff, leaving no doubt that we appreciated their effort. The success of asking people to pass the word about This End Up was easy to track. Whenever we opened a new store a large crowd showed up, much of it personal referrals, saying they heard about it at work, a party, or from a friend in another city.

In the early years, we had no advertising budget because we put all the money we could into costly mall leases. No one had ever heard of a furniture showroom of only 700 square feet or a furniture company that did no advertising. Our hope was that the constant stream of people walking by would more than offset the bursts of traffic driven into low-budget, out-of-the-way furniture locations from expensive newspaper and TV ads. But on the occasions when we opened our hometown newspaper and a six-page, four-color ad for a local furniture company fell out on the breakfast table, Stewart and I engaged in long bouts of Monday morning quarterbacking.

Our business was growing into a smash hit despite lack of press. Most customers loved the company, but not everyone thought our product was perfect.

Carol, our veteran district manager for North Carolina and Virginia, called to say she'd just had a remarkable encounter with a man who had bought his This End Up furniture three years earlier at the Hampton, Virginia, store.

"Now, lady, I've had this furniture in my living room for a long time and I really like it. But I need to trade in my end table for a different one," said the man, standing in a customer-filled store on a busy Saturday.

"What's wrong with it?"

"It's haunted."

"It's *haunted*?" echoed Carol, sure she was in for a joke.

He told a story of moving to a different place recently where his five pieces of This End Up furniture were arranged in the living room, same as in his other house. Within two days, demons that refused to be exorcized had entered the end table. The man said as far as he could see the only solution was for This End Up to retrieve that piece and bring him a new one. A spellbound crowd surrounded Carol and the customer.

"What does the table do that makes you think it's haunted?" asked our district manager, ever the defender of This End Up's reputation.

"It howls—and really loud too."

Although our replacement guarantee didn't specifically cover this circumstance, Carol made the exchange without further comment. The haunted table, which was in good condition, was sold at our Scratch and Dent sale, where the new owner never returned to complain about a blood-curdling wail.

Throughout This End Up's history, we tracked customer complaints with vigilance. It wasn't hard; sometimes months went by without a single one. Part of that good news was due to a product whose strength was immediately visible. What you got for what you paid was accepted as indisputably fair. A few customers didn't like the style or didn't like how heavy it was or couldn't find a fabric that suited them, but they always recognized the value. Our store personnel rarely heard, "This is too expensive." The pieces were made of yellow pine, not mahogany or walnut, where every blemish might be cause for comment. Our long suit was durability, not finish.

Infrequent damage during transit could usually be fixed in the back of the truck. The occasional piece rejected by one customer was gladly accepted by the next after a little touchup between stops. Seating cushions were all of uniform size, unattached to the frames and easy to replace. The pine, the price and the design held our furniture return rate to less than two percent, unheard of in our industry.

Unless the product was exceptionally abused in an organized campaign of mistreatment or was used in a way for which it wasn't designed, This End Up guaranteed to repair or replace it for free. Because of patent misuse of the furniture, we incurred one of our few lawsuits. I expect the college fellow who instigated that legal action never forgot which end was up.

A number of years into our history, a student in a fraternity at a large New England university was partying hard late into Homecoming weekend. Unable to stand on his feet any longer, but not wishing to miss out on the fun, Archer sat down nude on a deeply gouged This End Up coffee table which had become over the course of six years less of a table and more of a piece of yellow pine sculpture, rendered by fraternal graffiti artists. There, he continued dancing on his bare behind where a large splinter lodged in his exposed parts. The frat boy was taken to a nearby emergency room to have the injury tended to. He had no complications other than unmerciful ribbing, I suspect, but without letting us know of the episode, Archer had lawyers serve This End Up with a suit. Stewart and I thought we had heard it all after that incident. We were mistaken.

CHAPTER 18: A Good Man is Hard to Find

Our stores and customers spread throughout the South, Northeast and Midwest, and the distribution side of This End Up was literally being pulled in all directions. We discovered that poor delivery technique was the No. 1 reason for damage to the product and to customer happiness. The distribution business was an easy path to lost profits. Knowing that, we kept delivery in-house while other furniture companies farmed out this service to uncaring subcontractors.

Maintaining distribution service levels was always a struggle. Furniture distribution standards were so abominable, we had only to provide decent service to shine. Often, customer letters praised a pleasant delivery experience in contrast to a "fiasco" with XYZ Company.

Nobody could enhance This End Up's reputation with a customer better than a driver who spent an extra five minutes to take a discarded dresser down the stairs for a single mom. Nobody could sell more add-on pieces than our drivers by suggesting a TV cabinet for the living room, or a toy box for the playroom. Nobody could influence our profit margins quicker than a driver who would take the initiative to retouch and redistribute a truckload of furniture. And *nobody* had greater opportunity to wreak havoc than a driver. His potential impact was huge: organization of truck loading, repair of blemished pieces, management of his delivery helper, responsibility for the vehicle, collection of funds and overall customer service. And all on a tight schedule.

Hiring drivers was among our most challenging personnel tasks. We were after three attributes: brawn, brains and personality. If the driver lacked brawn, he got injured. If he was wanting in smarts, organization suffered. If he was low on personality, female customers called to inquire where that "other darling driver, Jamie" had gotten to. A good man was hard to find.

One of our first drivers *was* that darling Jamie. He was like a huge child who was so naughty we wanted to pull our, and his, hair out.

As he made his mischief, though, his engaging manner caused everyone to look the other way.

Jamie, who limped noticeably, had lost part of his left foot in a motorcycle accident in college. Despite that, he still went everywhere on a spit-polished Harley-Davidson, his only possession of note. We could always tell he was headed our way, thanks to the impudent habit of whistling loud and off-key, when he walked down the hall to our office. One thing we could never quite prepare ourselves for was his wardrobe of racy, XXL T-shirts. Even our feminist-leaning staff just "tsk-tsk'd" at the Big Johnson cartoon that expanded across Jamie's chest like a billboard. But with a face full of little boy freckles, a what-me-care? smile and long-lashed bedroom eyes, he more than delivered on our driver requirements, as long as you could keep him out of trouble.

After drinking his nights away in Richmond's singles bars, Jamie would sometimes crawl to the threshold of the company office and toss his cookies on our doormat where the first person arriving at work would find him face down. When questioned, he was contrite. He reasoned that he couldn't remember where he left his bike, so he wasn't able to go home. Therefore, he'd come to the only other home he had— This End Up. Nobody should have to clean up that "inexcusable mess" but him, so if he could just get into the supply closet, he'd take care of it immediately. That way he would still be able to start today's deliveries on time. But could he slip "quick as a wink" into the shower in the office and "borrow" yet another shirt so he'd be presentable to his "nice customers?" And off our driver would hustle in the mandatory This End Up T-shirt, after snatching somebody's Krispy Kreme doughnuts from the kitchen, leaving us treading the line between head-shaking amusement and panic attack.

Our long-suffering distribution manager Kevin went into Stewart's office one day and closed the door. Doors were rarely closed at This End Up.

"At the distribution meeting yesterday, Jamie had a pretty good suggestion about driver training." Kevin was a laid-back country boy, largely implacable. Today, he tapped his pencil on the arm of his chair.

"What was it?" asked Stewart, always looking for ideas to improve delivery.

"He wants to have a training session for the guys about how much money the company loses on some of the most common delivery mistakes. Then he wants to have bumper stickers printed for all the trucks that say, 'Do It Right the First Time.'"

Only Kevin's nervous pencil alerted Stewart to the coming reversal in conversational direction. He raised his eyebrows and waited.

"Right after his presentation, Jamie left the meeting for the Roanoke run. You remember how it rained all day?"

"Yeeeah? Did he have a wreck?" asked Stewart.

"Worse. He got a fully loaded truck of furniture soaking wet," Kevin said.

"How the hell can you do that?"

"Well, you can do that if the height of the overpass is lower than your truck. He peeled back the entire top like a sardine can and then drove 60 miles back to Richmond in the pouring rain. I swear to God, trying to control Jamie is about as successful as pissin' up a rope."

"So he ruined a truck *and* a full load of furniture?" Stewart tipped back in his chair. "That's something new. I guess he 'Did It Right the First Time.'"

Stewart's light-hearted manner and level head promoted This End Up's fortunes by disarming fear and spotlighting solutions. He seemed especially skilled at worrying only about things he had some control over, and the time had come to exert that control over Jamie. After his most recent performance, we decided we had misjudged Jamie in the smarts department.

At its peak, This End Up had 175 truck drivers and delivery helpers serving 253 stores in much of the U.S. and a small section of Canada. The clash between the stores' goal to keep customers happy and the distribution goal to finish every delivery day on time regularly created sore feelings between the two groups of employees. To promote better tolerance of their cross-purposes, we asked each of them to spend a day in the opposing job—salespeople on trucks and drivers in stores. Understanding the distribution procedure was important for me too, and because some Pittsburgh store personnel grumbled about the gruff style of many of their drivers, I decided to update my own experience by riding shotgun on a local delivery truck.

The driver was Ray, a heavily tattooed, wiry fellow in his late 20s who sported a Brillo Pad beard. Louie, his quiet, muscular helper, was a moonlighting family man, looking to augment his police officer's salary. Both men were shocked when they arrived at the store for directions and found the female owner of the company there to join them in a 12-hour delivery day. At seven o'clock on a midsummer morning, the three of us piled into the front seat, me squashed between my two disgruntled employees. Ray cranked up the country music to ear-splitting volume and shook his head silently at the coffee I offered. Louie crossed his arms over a buff chest and fell asleep.

By the third stop, I could tell from their relaxed posture they realized I hadn't joined them to search out fault but rather to refresh my understanding of the distribution process. As we bumped down the highway, the air conditioning failed to keep up with the heat. The thunder of the big truck's engine sounded as if it were about to blow all those things I didn't understand—pistons, fan belts and fuel pumps. Ray and Louie seemed unperturbed.

Poor mapping by the store personnel put us 15 minutes behind at our next drop-off, an apartment above a three-car garage. Louie handed me the order to look over. It involved six pieces of furniture. "Take off your dirty shoes," ordered the store manager's curt note. "The carpet is brand-new."

"OK, Brown. This one's yours. You been slacking off, sitting in this nice truck listening to good music while Louie and me been bustin' ass all morning. We're taking us a break now."

I knew from their joke the rest of the day would be instructive and fun. As the sweat dripped down my backbone, we shared funny customer stories, sang along with Jerry Jeff Walker and Lyle Lovett and talked about the cost of errors and the effect on their paychecks. I hit particularly hard on not leaving the distribution center without being prepared for the long trip, since I noticed neither of them had a watch, a thermos of water or any wood stain for repairs. I asked Ray how he felt about putting improved trip preparation on his goals; he said it was OK.

When we returned to the store early that evening, I asked Ray and Louie to join the store personnel and me for supper. The drivers and I probably smelled to the heavens but nobody seemed to care. The two men entertained the sales staff with three exaggerated repetitions of the "OK, Brown. It's your turn," story. I entertained them with a screeching rendition of Ray's toneless voice singing Lyle Lovett's lyrics, "Redneckness has got to be a disease. You catch it on your fingers and it just crawls right up your sleeves." Strained relations were like a hangover between the two factions, eased somewhat by sharing their headaches and a beer with each other and their boss.

"Please don't hesitate to call Stewart or me any time we can help," I said to the whole group as the evening broke up. It seemed the least

I could do for our employees who labored in malls and on roads so far removed from the home office.

At 2:15 in the morning several months later, the phone jarred me awake. I bolted upright, my heart and stomach on a collision course. Stewart and I had taken a middle-of-the-night call just two months earlier from a longtime employee who had been roughed up and held for several hours during an attempted robbery. I was extra jittery about calls after 10:00 p.m.

"Hello!" I shouted into the receiver.

"Yeah, uh, is this Libby?"

"Who is this?" I growled.

"This is Ray. Ray Stoddard? Your driver in Pittsburgh. I ran out of gas about 40 miles from home, and it's out in the sticks here. I don't have me no money, so could you call Melissa—she's the district manager—and ask her to come get me? I lost her number."

I asked Ray how he got my home phone.

"Well, when I met you out here in August you said to call you or your husband anytime if we needed help. There was only one Stewart Brown in Directory Assistance, so I just took a chance. Is it OK?"

This owning-our-own-business-stuff was interesting. Occasionally aggravating, but never boring. I lodged two things in my sleepy brain: check with Ray's manager on the goal of trip readiness and stop throwing out comments I didn't want taken literally.

CHAPTER 19: Truckin'

Delivering customer orders directly from the factory became untenable by 1979. Our motley crew was making too many trips at too many long distances, and we worried about accidents. With no centralized training for them, the quality of deliveries varied widely. More and more often, we were paying too much when we were forced to rent an oversized truck because the proper-sized ones we needed were unavailable. Growth had outpaced our initial delivery format. In response to all those concerns, Steve, Randy, Stewart and I decided to start a network of This End Up Distribution Centers and to switch management of home and commercial deliveries to the retail side of the business, an enormous additional responsibility for Stewart.

By this time, the company had an active commercial sales department that had sprung up from the humble beginnings of our craft-show days. Delivering one order from this burgeoning sector of our business could require a fleet of rental trucks. We had no idea that commercial sales would eventually have its own pieces, finishes, fabrics, salespeople and installation team, nor that resorts, schools and government agencies would buy nearly 20 percent of This End Up's total volume.

Stewart and I knew he would have to sign leases all over the country for the various distribution centers we needed. They had to be positioned near clusters of stores to be financially viable. Under this new arrangement, we could hire local delivery personnel in every city who would be trained by us and available to service our customers quickly. We were determined to keep our promise to the buyer—three to six weeks from order to delivery—but concerns about increasing obligations added to our emotional load.

To make the new distribution warehouses efficient, we needed our own fleet of midsized trucks. The time had come for us to stop being a rolling advertisement for Ryder. We wanted our own name on the highways of America. So Steve and Randy put in an order for a tractor-trailer to be used to drop-ship furniture at the new distribution centers from the factory. Stewart added several neighborhood-sized trucks to the order. The day they were all delivered in Raleigh, the whole factory team cheered wildly as the six-foot-tall—THIS END UP THIS END UP THIS END UP—rolled in, worn by three smaller vehicles, which soon looked like little guide carts leading the Concorde onto a runway.

As the tractor-trailer, lagging by several minutes, made the tight turn from the main road into the little driveway of our factory, the voice of the whole crowd died. It looked like the mother of all trucks bearing down on our dumbstruck party. It crunched over the gravel, sheared a few low limbs and swayed slightly before coming to rest at our feet in a shaft of sunlight. A low murmur built slowly to a deafening roar as we craned our necks to see the biggest THIS END UP logo ever. *(Photo 1.8)*

Beer came out, cameras clicked, toasts were made. And work for the rest of that bright afternoon came to a halt. When I stepped back later to snap a shot for the company album, I looked through the lens to see what we had become in only four years. The loading dock of our second 40,000-square-foot factory was jammed with furniture. Neatly stacked couch frames and colorful cushions waited to be loaded. The people who produced the product, dressed in jeans and T-shirts, talked animatedly with the people who sold it, dressed in tailored trousers and linen shirts. Stewart, Randy and Steve grinned like paid models for Colgate. I took the photo twice to make sure I didn't miss it.

As I joined my three partners over a beer, Randy raised his Budweiser and said softly, "Here's to us," and we all tapped our beer cans. I was happy beyond measure, and in my youthful exuberance, I couldn't imagine anything grander than that moment.

* * *

I am not a sentimental person, but every time I saw those towering trucks on the road, it made my heart race and my eyes mist over. I don't know why that particular experience affected me so. Maybe because I would be out driving on a freeway, absorbed in my day's agenda, and the giant THIS END UP looming ahead would catch me completely off-guard. It was a shock to see the sum of our efforts culminated in a national brand logo, plying the interstate highways. Maybe because, to most people, This End Up was the one or two small stores they saw in their hometown malls. But it was a stunning symbol of what we had achieved and the bracer that I needed. It helped subdue the squeeze of strain, the belittlement of doubt, and the fright of responsibility that caused my resolve to shy at times like a skittish pony.

* * *

This End Up's employee base exploded with the new distribution centers. We hired drivers, helpers, loaders, mappers and managers to reach our goals for faster response and happier customers. Sometimes the investment paid off. Sometimes it didn't.

Shortly after Christmas one year, I received a call from a customer in Nashua, New Hampshire. Mr. Flanagan told me a story about one of our drivers. He said when he got home on Christmas Eve his wife was in tears. The person who delivered their children's Santa present had failed to put it together. When Mom returned from errands, the bunk beds lay in pieces on the bedroom floor.

In the hopes that it would still be open, Mr. Flanagan called the This End Up store he and his wife visited during the decision-making process. The store manager had just pulled the gate down and was preparing to leave for Christmas Eve dinner with her family. She jotted down the Flanagans' address and said she would try to get one of our drivers to come set things right.

At nine o-clock, Allen, who worked at our distribution center 25 miles away, arrived in his family car with his two teenagers in tow.

"I'm sorry our driver who delivered your bunks today forgot to assemble them. It's not like us at all to do that," he said. "Show me where the beds are and I'll set them up."

Mr. Flanagan, trailed by Allen, stormed into the bedroom where the big surprise lay in pieces.

"Oh my goodness! Where did you get that bunk bed, Mr. Flanagan?"

"Well, I assume my wife got it from your Buckley Hills store. She was so upset that I never really asked her. Why? What's wrong?"

"This is a bunk bed that is made to look just like ours, but it is definitely not This End Up's. You can see the assembly instructions here with another company's name at the top."

The customer groaned. "What am I going to do? It's all my kids want for Christmas."

"Since I'm already here with my tools, I'll put them together for you," offered Allen.

As he walked out around ten o-clock, Allen was still smiling when he said, "Merry Christmas, Mr. Flanagan. I hope your children love their beds, even if they aren't This End Up."

I called Allen to congratulate him on superb service, made even more superb because Mr. Flanagan wasn't even our customer.

But there was occasionally a flip side. With so many trucks and drivers on the road, tracking the exact whereabouts of either became increasingly difficult. Myriad circumstances occasionally caused deliveries to take longer than expected: a drop-off in a center-city high-rise, a customer who forgot her delivery date, a mapping coordinator who mixed up 195 with I-95, a driver who had to clear the buyer's room of old furniture so there would be space to deliver the new, a blizzard, a traffic jam, a broken truck.

We trusted all our employees to do the right thing. It usually worked well and eliminated a degrading workplace atmosphere. But if someone were inclined to abuse our system, he could.

Hank was so inclined.

His delivery territory was the area between Raleigh and Wilmington, North Carolina. Our Mimosa Mall store in Wilmington was only 60 miles from South Carolina, a state where This End Up had one store and little name recognition. Our nearby South Carolina customers usually drove up to Mimosa Mall to pick up their furniture.

Hank packed his small truck straight out of the factory by himself. The plant managers got used to seeing him, and after a cursory glance, refocused on building furniture and loading the 18-wheelers. Once the affable driver became a regular part of the Raleigh scene, he was able to add, unnoticed, a few extra pieces of furniture to his truck every loading day. Quite some time went by before Hank was caught by a chance comment from a customer to our Wilmington store manager.

"You know, Tracy, I didn't know until I drove up here from Florence today that you guys sell your furniture from the back of This End Up trucks in South Carolina. I passed one in a parking lot on my way up here. That fellow was even busier than you."

Considering the number of far-flung people that we had handling money and goods, proportionately few incidents of internal stealing occurred. But because for so long we knew every employee personally, those incidents caused Stewart and me considerable sorrow. Perhaps our sheltered childhoods had protected us from the disappointing truth that sometimes you don't get back what you give. As we moved out of the realm of our beginnings, I battled to keep that evolving reality from making me bitter.

Later in life, I would need every ounce of that practice.

CHAPTER 20: This Way Out (5)

*A*t the quarterly regional manager's meeting in Richmond, our *key person in the powerhouse Northeast territory looked suspiciously at Stewart and me. "There sure have been a lot of men in business suits in my stores lately. What's up with that, do you know?"*

My grandmother, who had raised five children alone after my grandfather died young, used to say her "copers" were tired. So were ours. Acting as if it was business as usual was hard to cope with day after day. The tease of three possible purchasers for This End Up, all of whom seemed to want information ad infinitum, had caused me to revert to a childhood habit of biting my thumbnails. I wasn't sure how much longer I could keep the secret.

The hardest lies we told were to our management team. We were constantly on guard against a slip. Knowing us as well as they did, I couldn't fathom that they didn't spot a telltale twitch or a falter in my eye contact during the months of bargaining with our pursuers. In my suddenly adaptable conscience, I chalked up their innocence to trust. That only made the lies harder. True, they were lies of omission, and that made it easier. But only by a little.

The pursuers' courtship was taking longer than expected, even by our business broker's estimate. But we were not going to sell on price alone. Our hearts, souls and reputations were as deeply embedded in This End Up as if it were our child. The four of us were worried about the possibility of making the wrong match. There could be no mistake here. Our fine company, and the extended family that ran it, had to be perfectly paired with a suitor who would guard and grow its hard-won results with the same dedication of the original partners. The marriage arrangements were up to us. But we wondered if the groom was having second thoughts.

CHAPTER 21: Not a Real Job

In the early 1980s, Stewart and I bought an old building in the historic downtown section of Richmond to use as This End Up's retail headquarters. That came as a great relief to our 20-plus office employees who were stuffed into three nearby apartments where we kept our filing system in the bathtubs and where Stewart's office was the master bedroom. After restoring the old structure, we consecrated our center by returning the original couch to the new lobby. The Boys, who had sold that first piece at the Raleigh Flea Market for $95, bought it back from the customer for $2,000. Its red plastic plaque said, "The Original This End Up Couch, circa 1974." *(Photo 1.9)*

Stewart and I, Ellie and Stew moved into a new house we built in the midst of the chaotic store expansion of 1981. Overseeing the construction of one more project that tumultuous year hardly made the radar screen. The duality of my life, managed as tightly as Scrooge's money, juggled important mommy things for our 10- and 11-year-olds with time for friends and relatives and integrated nine-hour office days, except when I was on the road visiting stores and they lasted for 14. Our family traveled every holiday, foregoing the pleasure of building our own family traditions, to make time with parents and siblings. Managing this two-headed existence eroded my peace of mind, but the compromise kept the maximum amount of people moderately happy. My children were always the most important balls in the air, but the number, size and shape of the others required a lot of finesse. Focusing so hard on how much I could stuff into every day sometimes made me lose track of the end game—a future ordained by *my* script instead of other people's.

Many people who knew me had no idea of the schedule I kept. I often worked at home until one or two in the morning so there would be time to watch Stew wrestle or to take Ellie's birthday party roller skating. Because This End Up now had 70 stores and sales of $24 million, and I was one of the people who trained all those saleswomen, my travel load was heavy. Flight attendants began to recognize me as I flew from

Louisiana to Maine to Illinois to Colorado. I covered thousands of miles, frequently traveling just as the sun came up and long after it went down.

During this period, female business travelers were still uncommon. Especially on the early-morning flights into big cities, I would often be the only woman with a briefcase. I remember the discomfort of having 50 or more pairs of male eyeballs look up at me with curiosity from newspapers and reports as I passed by. When I opened my report on monthly and year-to-date sales figures, there were sidelong glances of curiosity. On the rare occasions when a seatmate asked me what I did, I grabbed the opportunity to tell the This End Up story to an invariably astonished listener.

For the most part, my friends and neighbors worked in their yards, went out for lunch, played their sports, had their dinner and nestled happily into bed around ten. Sometimes I felt my lot was better, sometimes I felt it was worse. As I sat in a driving snowstorm on a runway at Chicago's O'Hare Airport one night, waiting for the plane to be de-iced for the second time, feeling burned out and lonely, I felt envious of my friends with more conventional lives. In the dim light of the airplane cabin, I swore not to let my professional life sow divisions that would threaten valuable friendships.

* * *

At 40 years old, I struggled with self-doubt and looked fruitlessly to others for validation. I worked hard to do all my jobs and to build a sound company based on the ethics I was raised with, to provide a valuable product at a fair price, to create jobs where people could enjoy the dignity of self-direction and a fair reward for their work. Yet, for all my efforts, I felt unrecognized. For the courage it took to risk our future on our dreams, ignored. It seemed I was perceived as simply different.

I believed dreams, not memories, moved the world forward. But women seldom chose such a path in those days. I was so distressed about the differences between myself and many of my acquaintances that I began to overlook the value of my individuality and instead focused on its costs—the slap of disappointment, the pinch of hurt.

After we sold This End Up, the ensuing publicity brought accolades and some pockets of respect. By then, fortunately, I had discovered that self-esteem comes from inside. The conundrum of seeking acknowledgement for my risk-taking from people who never took a chance is still a puzzle to me.

* * *

In recent years, I was part of a conversation among several couples who had known each other a long time. They spoke about how much harder they felt it was for our daughters to raise their children than it had been for us, even though the girls had "married well."

"I don't know how they do it, as hard as it is to find good help. Kids, houses, friends—all the things we had to manage, plus Dorothy *works*," said one mama.

One of the husbands added, "None of you ever really worked. Well, volunteer work, but not a full-time job."

I should have known better, but I couldn't resist. "I worked a full-time job. And traveled."

"But not a real job," he replied.

In my younger days, I would have reacted. Clearly, while I was away, their old vision of my life had been kept warm for me. Idolizing people who had inherited money through happenstance without valuing those who had earned it through initiative continued to mystify me. I surprised myself by backsliding for a moment to the wailing wall of anger and hurt. I thought I had banished those sensitivities, although perhaps they will retain a tiny breath of life as long as I do. The knowledge of how remarkably fortunate I had been kept my mouth shut and my face serene. The effort to regain peace of mind took a baby step forward with my silence.

CHAPTER 22: Eating Chinese

Our staff of sales people was expanding to keep pace with store growth. The product was easy to make and easy to use, easy to find and easy to buy, but nothing sells itself. Sales training became my specialty. I was convinced that it would yield prodigious results. The showpiece of the Richmond headquarters was a life-sized mock store connected to a classroom. There, we honed the store managers' skills with my Five Steps of Selling program. They came from all over the country for four days of nonstop training. Some had never been out of their home state; many were nervous about the role-playing and taping of their selling techniques, an important part of the workshop.

The hours were jam-packed and run by our training department with the precision of a drill team and the humor of a comedy club. Attendees were oriented on a variety of subjects: our mission, accounting practices, hiring methods, customer service expectations. Then they were driven to Raleigh for a tour of the factories. Back in Richmond, the final day was devoted to coaching sales skills.

Shirley, a timid, 50-year-old widow from Bangor, Maine, was back in the workforce for the first time since raising children. She sat next to one of our few male store managers, Roger. He was a college-educated, bachelor clotheshorse from Paramus, New Jersey, who sported a flattop and a loud, honking twang. Shirley and Roger sat across from the pig-tailed Lily, a giggling, eyelash-batting, bleached blonde from New Orleans who was about as dumb as a fox. Lily sat next to Angela, a bilingual sexpot from San Diego with blood-red, three-inch fingernails.

The mix of backgrounds, personality types and geography was as much an education for many of our new managers as the workshop itself. And, for me, training sessions were a continuing lesson in not judging people by appearances. Shirley offered pearls of maternal wisdom about dealing with ill-tempered people, Roger pointed out an often-requested color which was missing from our fabric selection, Lily put her finger on why there was such difficulty with an aspect of store bookkeeping, and Angela inquired if we might be missing sales in our Miami store with no Spanish-speaking personnel.

The program was designed to operate in a wide-open forum and we regularly fielded questions about company politics, pay scales and personality conflicts. No subject was out of bounds, and sometimes the meekest participant launched the biggest bombshell in the last hour of the workshop. "What's going to happen when customers get tired of crate furniture? Should we be selling more than one style?"

Those sessions made a difference. Because the training was so all-inclusive, it anticipated any area of weakness. When new trainees returned to their jobs, they stood taller and spoke with more composure. Customers who happened into more than one of our stores could usually count on being treated in the same welcoming and informed manner every time. And I felt I had the benefit of getting to know our management staff, one-by-one, nationwide.

Eventually, we developed additional programs for district and regional sales managers, department heads and drivers, every one a salesperson no matter the job. It was expensive to fly, lodge and feed them for a week, but we had to have additional sales to support our new trucks, new distribution centers, factories three, four and five and all kinds of product demands.

During a management meeting where one of Stewart's favorite topics, cost-cutting, was on the table, the agenda turned to getting the training workshop budget in hand. Suggestions were hard to come by. Ideas from the normally creative management team ground to a chin-tapping halt. I was no help because every penny I could retain made my pet enterprise of employee education better. Stewart said he had a small idea.

"You all know Charlie Chao who owns the Golden Garden Restaurant around the corner?" Nods of assent. "He asked me awhile back if This End Up would be interested in a little exchange of trade— a few bunk beds for some Chinese food. At the time, I didn't think that would work, but now we might be able to save a little money."

No matter how far-fetched any of Stewart's suggestions were, they never got thrown out. He kept them in a little slot in his mind for review at a later date. They might pop out at an odd time, where they seemed unconnected to the issue being discussed. Sometimes they showed up on four or five occasions before they ever took root.

The meeting's participants were trying to follow Stewart's reasoning.

"Well, at least once a month we're paying for 12 or 15 people to have dinner in different restaurants when they're here for the workshop. Those nights have been averaging $400 a pop, times 10 months a year, times twice a month equals $8,000. We could put a little dent in it by exchanging dinners for bunk beds."

Sharon, our sales manager, dug deeper. "How many bunks do you think Charlie wants?"

"I'm not sure," said Stewart, "but whatever part of 8,000 retail dollars we can trade at our cost will be better than nothing."

"Great! Let's do it," said the group unanimously.

Some months later, our chief financial officer asked if we realized how much furniture Charlie Chao had ordered. Lee said Charlie must have furnished the entire Virginia Chinese community. Limiting his purchases to the $8,000 mark had never occurred to us. An immediate stop order was put on This End Up's all-time-best bunk bed customer.

Those of us who entertained the twice-monthly workshop groups at dinner thought we would turn into wonton soup. After almost a year of eating Chinese, we still had a long way to go to settle the furniture-for-food trade deficit. We never let Stewart get away with skipping any Chinese dinners.

By 1984, bunk bed production was high, helping This End Up snag a place in the bible of mall developers' "Top Dollar per Square Foot Stores." We also began to be noticed by other retailers, reporters and wannabes. Several copycat companies sprang up to nip at our heels, but they were never able to make a significant impact on our sales. Colleges started to contact us to speak to their classes on marketing and entrepreneurship, and we were asked if we would be willing to be a case study for MBA programs. The business writers for the Richmond and Raleigh newspapers checked in with us. A national magazine contacted us for an article about our business formula. There was particular interest in the part women played in our management structure.

The majority of the first group of women we had employed was still with us. Some of them had moved several times to open new stores or regions as This End Up marched across the country. Along the way, many had been promoted to managerial positions and had hired friends who referred friends. It amused Stewart when he introduced this young, all-female group to the heads of other furniture companies as "my management team." But management team was exactly what they were, and very good at it. In 1984, we had a retail enterprise of 500 part- and full-time people. More than 95 percent of them were women, an enigma in the predominantly male furniture world.

Because I traveled to all the different malls to help train our store staff, I saw why these women were perfect for the job. They related quickly to the primary decision-maker, a woman, who was interested in her home and budget. With their product knowledge and procedural training, these salespeople could also hold their own with the more technical and policy-oriented male customers.

Store personnel were highly trained in assertive selling skills and they were paid on incentive. They learned that, in the sales transaction, it was important to develop a relationship with the customer prior to discussing the product. That principle created a successful sales model: a win for the customer who was treated like the valuable asset she was, a win for the employee whose paycheck showed the results of education and effort, and a win for the company in its profits.

The founders never lost sight of the fact that if we couldn't sell and service the product, the rest of the business would wither away. Steve and Randy's manufacturing interest and Stewart's and my retail interest were mutually dependent; they never sold the product to any other company and we never marketed furniture from any other source. Admiration of each other's abilities stood firm on a foundation of staunch trust among the four of us, and that made it easy for This End Up to promise customers we would stick by them with great value and superb service.

And service the customer we did. When Nicole, one of our district managers in the Midwest, was about to walk down the aisle to be married, someone snapped a photo of her. There stood the bride, talking on a phone held to her ear by a bridesmaid. Another person had pulled Nicole's veil out of the way, and the little flower girl struggled to hold the big bouquet. The bride was jotting notes on a pad with the nub of a pencil held in her gloved hand. A familiar look of concentration overlaid her bridal glow.

The picture was sent to me with a caption, "Nicole handling an upset customer on her wedding day." Perhaps the customer would have been surprised to know about the dedication of this extraordinary employee, but I was not.

CHAPTER 23: This Way Out (6)

*S*ix and a half weeks after our interview and lunch with Melville, things were quiet in Rye, New York. Then suddenly, The Wolverine Company wanted a meeting. The "see and be seen" visit was scheduled for a Tuesday afternoon at our recently enlarged Richmond headquarters. Randy and Steve drove up to meet the muckety-mucks.

We had seen the CEO make guest appearances on financial segments of television news. I was eager to learn what kind of man he was, how compatible our management styles were and how this new suitor stacked up to Melville. So far, the purchase price discussions between Wolverine and Peter had not gone well. This face-to-face meeting could give a much-needed boost to negotiations if the important cultural issues were a fit.

The lieutenant to the bigwigs requested limousines for transportation to our office, which was on a crowded street in the historic district. To try to prevent questions among our staff regarding such an unusual event, Stewart asked his assistant to ask their assistant if we could pick them up in our Suburban at the airport. Wolverine snarled no.

The visitors gave off a slight air that This End Up was low on their hit parade as the afternoon proceeded with a sweep of complicated financial questions. Most of their astute comments were directed toward Stewart and Lee. A few gratuitous queries were aimed at the manufacturing partners. I was ignored and wouldn't have been surprised if they had asked me to go out for coffee.

Our dinner that night was at the Drewry Club, in a lovely old house on the grounds of one of Richmond's historic plantations. It had museum-quality paintings, random-width wood floors glowing with a century of paste wax, excellent food, and dignified, old-South service. The army of Wolverine's overconfident men entered that elegant atmosphere with a flourish and immediately requested a change of seating area. They settled in for a round of martinis and Manhattans before *dinner, while Stewart and The Boys had their usual Miller Lites and I, the house wine.*

They seemed to want to hold the floor, so we let them, out of hospitality but also a desire to see how they led this mating dance. The fast clip of conversation sprinted through a number of subjects and some polite cocktail party inquiries about the four of us. At the end of a superb dinner, we heard a few quick remarks about when they would be in touch again. Then, with a cursory thank you, those potentates of industry were whisked off in the black limousines with their black windows, hidden from people who never would have recognized them anyway.

Wolverine's style hit us like a sack of cement. They earned no gold stars from me. Because they had done most of the talking, we learned more about them than they did about us. The whole visit left me troubled. I knew that Stewart would want to keep the options open, but I questioned whether we really wanted to proceed with this smug group. On the other hand, I wondered whether we had blown the chance to make that choice. And I wondered if we would ever hear back from Melville.

CHAPTER 24: Barnyard Behavior

With continued fast growth in stores, sales and employees, more problems popped up in every corner of the business. Overnight, it seemed, there were worries about rising costs, personnel concerns and the lack of a cohesive management style in the widespread side of the business that Stewart and I oversaw. We needed to rein in some of the independence that had once worked so well, when we knew each employee personally. Ill-considered and, occasionally, shocking behavior emerged on the company and customer grapevine.

P.J., the manager of one of our Boston stores, was an excellent saleswoman. We had received many complimentary letters from customers about P.J. in her 18 months with This End Up. With huge brown eyes, double deep dimples and engaging people skills, she garnered consistently strong sales results. But, although she handled the sometimes-rancorous relationship with drivers better than most managers, she seemed unable to motivate her sales staff. This shortcoming held back P.J. from a promotion to district manager. It concerned us that we seemed more worried about it than she did.

This End Up's antiquated methodology for organizing deliveries was fraught with opportunity for mix-ups. Showrooms from all over the country sent orders they had taken from customers who lived near P.J.'s store to be included on her delivery trucks. Although this occurrence was common in the large malls, it complicated the store personnel's already difficult dealings with overworked local drivers. Deliverymen in large metropolitan areas knew that instructions from a store in Fuquay Varina, North Carolina, for a delivery in Boston could cause mayhem. The far-away staff person, inexperienced in the complexity of big-city bearings, and knowing the shit would not hit *her* fan, sometimes gave short shrift to delivery directions. And the out-of-town customer sometimes couldn't explain how to get there.

"Well, we're moving to a new subdivision outside Boston... let's see... 321 West. No, no, it's 231 West. Darn it, I mean 231 East. You go five or ten miles past Chuck E. Cheese, or is that Friday's? Anyway, whichever one comes first, there's a road on the left. Turn right there. Drive back in the woods and take the second right fork. There's no street sign yet, but there are some farms out there, so take a right at the one where the cows are in the field. You'll have to go over a real narrow, temporary bridge and we're the… um… fifth, sixth, seventh house on the left. I might have to run out to pick up the kids for a minute, so just hang in there till I get back."

Such demands were tough because the driver had to stick to the tight timeline necessary to reach numerous stops spread out over miles of terrain. They went berserk when the requests said something like, "The back door will be open, but grab the cat before she runs out and put her in the pantry. If the baby gate makes the doorway too narrow to get the loveseat through, just unscrew it from the doorframe. But put it back."

The delivery team might have 11 more stops, some with similar time-consuming demands, before the 7:00 p.m. deadline, after which the driver would lose his incentive pay for a punctual delivery. The store personnel might get huffy when they explained to the drivers, again, that the most important part of their job was keeping the customer happy. *They* were paid on incentive for that. Sometimes, the infighting was like the Hatfields and McCoys.

P.J. was a wizard at handling the frequent driver animosity triggered by this fossilized manner of routing trucks. Seemingly, she accomplished peace by scheduling herself in the store on delivery days when other managers often delegated the task to someone on their sales staffs. Compared with the turmoil of the average run, P.J.'s deliveries were a model of cooperation and planning.

Hoping to kick-start P.J.'s motivation for more responsibility, I asked her to teach a segment at a store manager workshop in Richmond. Titled "You and Your Driver—The Give and Take of a Smooth Relationship," I foresaw an impressive tag team presentation if I also included one of the many distribution fellows who sang her praises. There couldn't be a better teaching tool than a living demonstration of how great teamwork could solve recurring impediments to harmonious deliveries.

In double-checking P.J.'s credentials before I held her up as the guru on this subject, I discovered her key to driver satisfaction; an angry co-worker snitched on P.J. The reward for timely, accurate deliveries was a generous serving of adult entertainment in the store's backroom—immediate gratification for goal achievement.

When Stewart discussed with P.J. the impropriety of her incentive plan, she seemed slightly amused that anyone should care. We couldn't decide whether she was marvelously well-adjusted or dangerously screwed-up when she resigned without a backward glance.

Our retail and manufacturing divisions were managed as differently as their tasks required. The style Stewart and I preferred was straightforward, participative communication—a perfect match for so many young women laboring essentially alone with little work experience.

The Boys found a hands-off approach with their more seasoned staff worked well and that camaraderie and the occasional indulgence of high jinks created a productive workplace in the factory's tight space. Sometimes the high jinks came back at them.

At the complex of factory buildings in Raleigh, a new job was created for Bobby. He was one of the lovable, original carpenters who had started with This End Up in the HeavenRest Mattress plant. But Bobby smoked too much pot to continue on the new, fast-paced manufacturing line. So The Boys created a new position at This End Up, landscaper/handyman, a job at just the right speed for Bobby's attention span. The Boys could take advantage of his superb carpentry skills and also receive points from the brotherhood for keeping him on the payroll during his time of diminished willpower.

Once, when Steve was away on a sailing trip and Randy was clearing his desk for a vacation with a member of his harem, Bobby rushed in to ask permission to buy a little landscaping gear and build a small toolshed for it. Eager to leave, Randy said that would be fine as long as the shed was attractive and blended in with the surrounding landscape. Oftentimes, it took dedication to keep the mostly male work force connected to the finer points of aesthetics. But not Bobby. *(Photo 1.10)*

Upon their return, the company handyman escorted Randy and Steve to a newly landscaped plot, mulched with needles from the surrounding loblolly pines. A 14- by 18-foot concrete foundation with ramp supported the impressive new shed. Bobby's artful selection of exterior enamel, "Potting Shed Green," for the wood-sided structure caused it to nestle into the Carolina woods as if it had always been there, and the double-hung windows and brass hardware on the paneled doors glinted in the dappled sunshine.

The interior was designed for appearance and comfort, and Bobby apologized for having no rug on the floor, explaining that he was worried oil from the new lawnmower might stain it. He demonstrated how the fan, hanging from the center of the exposed beam ceiling, generated maximum air over a Pawley's Island hammock. Insulation throughout and architectural shingles would keep things comfortable most days in North Carolina's temperate winter climate. And, if The Boys would like, Bobby offered to add a furnace to the $20,000 "Tool Mansion," as it came to be called.

By this time in This End Up's history, Steve and Randy were finding it difficult to locate enough furniture-grade yellow pine to feed the voracious appetite of our customers. This type of wood was a staple in the exploding building industry in the Southeast. Much easier to mill for that purpose, few suppliers wanted to go to the extra expense of machining the pine properly for furniture. The Boys were scrambling to make sure we had this vital raw material at a cost that would keep us from having to boost our retail prices.

Steve and Randy were off to pay a call on a lumber supplier an hour up a back road from Raleigh, the second trip in as many weeks. They had bought wood from Ernest for years, but he was slowly squeezing them on quantity. The partners' minds churned for a new ploy to gain agreement from the weathered old veteran of Bainsboro Lumber Mill.

"STOP!" yelled Randy, and Steve swerved the truck to the side of the rural road only eight miles from Bainsboro. "Look at that goat."

A bent-over old man led a billy goat down the road by a worn rope. If they could buy him, Randy and Steve knew what they would do with the buck. Eighteen dollars later, with the goat tied in the back of Steve's truck, the three of them pulled into the lumber mill to pick up Ernest for lunch.

Ernest had put a note on the door. "Left a few minutes early. Meet me at Sam's Bar-B-Q."

Snickering in anticipation of their supplier's reaction, Randy and Steve sneaked the goat into his office and closed the door. Steve replaced Ernest's note with one of his own.

"Ernest, Here's a surprise from This End Up. You said this was one of your favorite things when we were here last week. We brought it up from Raleigh for you. Randy and Steve."

Not a word was said about the prank during lunch. On the way back to Ernest's office for the important meeting, The Boys could hardly contain themselves. After he read the note, Ernest opened the door to find the goat standing on the middle of his desk. The hungry beast had consumed every piece of paper on it, including all his customers' orders.

Ernest forgave the barnyard caper and did help us out with increased wood supply. He turned into one of our best vendors and always took the tricksters out to see Stud, who became the mascot of the mill. The last time Steve and Randy visited Bainsboro, the yard was flooded after heavy spring rains. Balanced with all four hooves on the top of a four-inch-square post was the goat, keeping his tootsies dry.

CHAPTER 25: Out of the Box

Stewart and I often thought back to the days when we managed the company like benevolent parents. For years, we considered our employees our family, rejoicing with them over life's triumphs and saddened by its reversals. We knew their families and their friends, attended their weddings, lent them money and visited them in the hospital. They babysat our children, gave us surprise parties and worked harder for us than we had any right to expect. Because we knew from their example our stores could remain staffed with people of reliability and conscience, we encouraged their personal referrals for This End Up jobs. But in the midst of this familiarity, it became obvious we were involved, ironically, in the re-creation of the homogeneous work environment Stewart and I had found stifling in our earlier jobs.

So we held tight to our belief in hiring people with strong values, but we began to look for them in different packages. In 1983 and '84, This End Up opened dozens of new stores. With such rapid expansion, we started recruiting through different methods: customers, waitresses, other shops and newspaper ads. The résumés of the applicants changed, and that added people outside our former milieu to the employee mix.

* * *

I stepped into a world of people whose looks, accents, lifestyles and personal yardsticks were often nothing like anything I knew. My views changed slowly. At first, I was blinded by their dissimilarities, just as others at home had been blinded by mine, but I began to see that I was the one who needed to change perspectives. As our stores continued to multiply in personalities as well as in number, I learned to appreciate and respect the very individuality in others I myself had sought acceptance for.

The geographic spread of our stores swept out the debris that remained of my sheltered old mindset. Discovering the diverse people of these new places was bracing, and I wanted to join in. Once I threw off the constricting comfort of my mental security blanket, I was free to take in the fresh air of an open mind.

* * *

After we opened stores in California, the lessons in diversity came quickly. No longer were all our stores staffed with the malleable young Southerners of our start-up days. And no longer was our customer wearing L.L. Bean plaid shirts and outfitting her cabin in the Blue Ridge. Who would take their places?

On the flight out to some of our new California locations, I wondered just what the differences would be between our Midwest and East Coast establishments. It would have been hard to imagine how the scene at Corannado Mall would unfold as the district sales manager Pam and I turned the corner of center court at 10:00 a.m.

Before us was a neat, gleaming This End Up store. The space was the perfect size and shape to display the most popular pieces of furniture. From outward appearances, prospects for sales looked bright. As I stood on the edge of the rug admiring it all, the door to the back room flew open and out sailed the store manager—on rollerblades.

Felicity was dressed in a drop-waist, black leather miniskirt that showed off carnelian beads on the gold hoop that pierced her belly button. Her low-cut, rhinestone-encrusted bustier pushed cleavage halfway to her neck. She sounded like wind chimes in a gale, one bare arm jangling with silver bracelets from wrist to elbow. Below her skirt, Felicity wore calf-length lace stockings; she had left her combat boots the night before by the fabric display shelf. Except for a long, linguini-thin, black rat-tail with glitter gel in it, her hennaed hair was short and spiky.

Any four-year-old would have sold her soul for Felicity's purple fingernail polish or the loops, drops and studs in each ear. The top of Felicity's This End Up desk served as a bulletin board for stickers touting her causes: Save the Whales, Redwoods, Air, Spotted Owl, Abortion Clinics and, in a stroke of circuitous thinking, Be a Proud Pioneer. Stop the Commercial Rape of California.

I heard Pam's sharp intake of breath and felt her sinews tense in anticipation of my reaction.

"Felicity, do you have a jacket?" she asked.

"Yeah, in the back. Why?"

"Put. It. On," commanded Pam.

When Felicity turned around to do as she was asked, a Celtic cross tattoo peeked out above her low-rise skirt.

Pam and I spent an hour checking paperwork. I tried unsuccessfully to wait on a family who spoke only Spanish. The Latino music that blared from the mall's sound system induced their children to dance wildly around the store. I was no help to the Velasquez group and neither was Pam. She said the extent of her Spanish vocabulary was limited to hello, goodbye, peso, taco and shit.

Since Pam and I were paying a drop-in visit to Felicity, she hadn't been notified to rearrange her workload to spend time with us, so she continued mapping her next morning's delivery. While I struggled to make headway with Mr. and Mrs. Velasquez, she sat by silently with her task.

On the way back to my hotel that night, Pam brought up the morning's Corannado visit. "You know, Felicity doesn't usually dress quite like that, Libby. I'll talk to her about it after you leave for St. Louis."

"Pam, I know that you know the closer in style your managers can be to their prototypical customer, the quicker a sale is made. People like to think that the salesperson is just like them in terms of taste and lifestyle."

This elementary hiring principle was taught to all our managers. I was concerned that Pam seemed to have missed it. Although I sometimes needed to address issues of appearance in the stores, it usually related to blue jeans, tank tops and tennis shoes, not mini skirts, belly rings and combat boots.

"Let's start by defining what the average customer is like at Corannado Mall," I said.

Pam's answer was slow in coming but sure in its content.

"Actually, they're very much like Felicity."

My vision of the typical This End Up customer and store manager was dawdling behind reality. It needed updating and enlarging. I had slipped back into being too long on comfort and too short on the hard work of change. What had at first appeared to be a disaster of a visit produced liberating hindsight. I chuckled as I juxtaposed in my mind the parting words of our manager from Arkansas on my previous week's trip, with the ones from Felicity in southern California.

Virginia Anne had hugged me soundly upon my departure from Magnolia Mall and slipped a packet of my favorite M&Ms to me for the trip back to Richmond.

"I hate that you're gonna get home so late, bless your heart. Are you sure we can't persuade you to spend the night here in Little Rock? It would be such a treat for us."

The warmth of her smile and the hospitable hyperbole of the South I was so comfortable with almost made me stay. As I left, Virginia Anne stood at the front of her store until I looked back from the mall exit between Cathy's Country Curtains and the Whistlestop Deli. Then she blew me a kiss goodbye.

Felicity had given me a decal promoting clean air to stick on my car. When I asked where I could get a Coke on the way out, she suggested a nearby kiosk that sold specialty water and blended juices. As I gathered my things for departure, Felicity said, "Ciao," from behind her desk and flashed the Hawaiian "Hang Loose" sign. A pretty Latino woman, who was adorned with the flashy bling of most of Corannado's customers, clip-clopped in on her backless spike heels. Felicity greeted her in the fluent Spanish she had not proffered earlier in the morning. The visit had been a mind-bending concoction of multiculturalism from the Valley Girl with the oddly old-fashioned name. I walked out into the mall past an ultra-hip nature store named Rock On.

* * *

While I continued my personal journey of growth, people of every color, religion, education and upbringing joined our ranks, and I realized that goodness was not born of only one class, creed or circumstance. My previous life supported the socio-economic rubric that the best people hailed from families of culture and learning and embraced the ethos I had been taught. I began to realize by using that censorious philosophy I had become insensitive and meagerly observant of those who were not cut from that familiar cloth. I came to know only portions of many individuals, and the wholeness of people escaped me.

As a young adult, I had been convinced that certain categories of genetics and environment would produce predictable behavior. While I moved through my career, however, I saw evidence that, in the grand scheme, we were all amazingly similar. What people had in common certainly provided comfort and continuity, but the infrequent homage paid to human differences seemed to be what created tolerance and dignity.

I was glad for my new respect for diversity. It had not been easy to come by. That prying open of my soul was a gift that our customers and employees unwittingly gave me during my time at This End Up. This expanded personal philosophy flourished and served me well in business and in my personal life. I thought it was secure in my heart until 14 years later when that belief was squeezed and almost expropriated.

* * *

It made sense that, as the company grew, it would have a proportionate increase in people problems, but it seemed like ours was exponential. We had a longtime employee who fought off an attempted rape after she was abducted leaving her store in Delaware. In Kansas, a muscle-bound father backhanded his tiny daughter as she sat on the top of our bunk beds. He yanked her down by the neck of her jumper and dragged her screaming, out of the mall by one twig-like arm. On several occasions, we dealt with abusive husbands and boyfriends, and in one case a girlfriend, who stood yelling and throwing things at their terrified partners in our stores. One night, Stewart received a call from a mall manager who said the gate to one of our New Jersey stores was down and locked. He could see a person lying on the couch inside whom he was unable to rouse. Stewart was up for hours talking to police who finally broke in to find a part-time staffer in a diabetic coma.

Stewart and I counseled on abortions, divorces, miscreant children, suicide, alcoholism, theft, anorexia, death, drugs and emotional and physical mistreatment. Our employees endured more types of human misery than we realized were possible. In some ways, store expansion created an era of sad maturation for us, but it gave us a bit of gratitude for the safety of our own existence—a safety that would choose not to follow us into the next chapter of our lives.

A couple of times Stewart and I made the expensive error of opening far-flung stores just to see how we would fare in an area. The mistakes quickly became supervisory and financial drains that district managers tried to stem by handling the employees in those locations mainly over the phone. To keep the store managers in such places connected to the company, we flew them to seminars, and they attended our training workshop in Richmond as well as the awards ceremony at our annual meeting.

One store of this type was Silverhill Mall, 375 miles from its baby sister store at Fielding Center. They were the only two stores in Washington state. The national sales manager had become willing to accept middle-of-the-road sales in exchange for personnel reliability while we debated our decision to expand the territory or cut and run.

The manager at Silverhill was Demi. She was a plain woman except for her almond-shaped, limpid green eyes, full of intelligence. On the one occasion I met Demi, I had the unsubstantiated feeling that she had been bounced around in life.

Demi's manager, Rosalie, often reported low sales figures at that store, but Demi was steady and trouble-free, under the circumstances a profile we could live with over the short run.

Over the phone one Monday morning, Rosalie delivered a shocker.

"She *what*?" I asked Rosalie.

"Demi slipped and fell last night as she was taking out the store's trash to the dumpster. She ripped off the end of her little finger on a jagged piece of metal at the doorway. By the time her boyfriend got her to the hospital, all they could do was clean it up and bandage it since he couldn't find the severed part in the dark." The nonplussed Rosalie sounded frantic with worry.

Two weeks later Rosalie called with an update.

"She WHAT?" I asked again.

"Demi's suing both Silverhill and This End Up. She's claiming she slipped in an unlighted hallway where we make her empty the trash. She's never complained about it before." Rosalie spoke in the angry tone This End Uppers adopted when they thought someone was being unfair to their company.

"She WHAAAT??" I screamed two weeks after the lawsuit conversation.

"Demi made the mistake of bragging at the bar where her boyfriend works about how much money she was going to get out of suing us. When someone asked her what had happened, she said she cut off her own fingertip with a knife. The waitress called the Silverhill office and turned her in." The barely suppressed glee in Rosalie's voice was hard to miss and easy to understand.

The fact that a seemingly decent person had put This End Up through a wringer with her wicked scheme rattled my optimism about the inherent virtue of people. I felt betrayed as I thought what might have happened to the company had Demi's deceit not been discovered. Our hard-won success was just that, partially because Stewart and I poured every cent we could back into our business after we paid ourselves modest salaries. The goal was to support our store growth without taking on debt. We had no rainy day fund to pay legal settlements.

Anger gnawed at me. A suit like this could have put us out of business, and hundreds of people out of work, their families jeopardized. I just could not fathom it. What happened to the Golden Rule? Was I entirely too naïve? I fantasized about retribution, but I knew better than that. I would simply have to make peace with Demi's double-cross.

CHAPTER 26: This Way Out (7)

I was already in bed when Stewart came home from work late one night. He and Lee were preparing for one of the mall audits that developers constantly required from their lessees to check the accuracy of reported sales figures. This End Up was in enough different centers now that we had one auditor or another with us on a regular basis.

Looking unusually whipped, Stewart sighed as he plumped his pillow and I knew that something was amiss. Had he discovered erroneous accounting? Was tomorrow's CPA an especially difficult one? Had he and Lee not completed the preparations for the inspection?

"What's wrong, Stewart?"

"I talked to David Rothenberg at U.S.B. Furniture today." U.S.B. was one of our three suitors.

"Are they ready to sit down yet?"

"Not really," said Stewart.

"I thought his team just needed that one last report. And didn't Lee send it out last week?"

"Yep."

Information would be dislodged from Stewart piece by piece tonight.

"I'd love to get to know them better. David's such a nice guy that I bet we'd really like that company, don't you?" I asked.

"I bet we would, but we'll never know."

"Why not? They said last month they were impressed with everything about our organization."

"They've changed their minds. They're out." Stewart's eyes closed with the exhaustion and disappointment I had seen on his face when he came through the door.

I would have to wait until tomorrow for the explanation, but I knew it was final.

And then there were two.

CHAPTER 27: Talk to Me

When the children were around seven and eight and could carry on a reasonable conversation, Stewart instituted a dinner table ritual. On the occasions we were all together for that meal, not as often as we would have liked, Dad went one by one and asked, "What was the best and the worst thing that happened to you today?" We each had to answer, and as the children matured, they learned the value of talking through feelings and the importance of appropriate reactions to anger, sorrow and joy.

In 1983, Stew and Ellie were 11 and 12 years old, and they started to show more than a passing interest in *our* answers. We told them when someone at work stole from us, when our mothers were sick, when friends were divorcing. And we began discussing our personal mistakes and how we sometimes felt confused or angry with ourselves.

Everyone's feelings were honored and not to be teased. In that way, we were able to get the children to tell us about their days and how events affected them. The "best thing" brought about congratulations and high fives. The "worst thing" received empathy, but the real focus was on solutions. Stewart and I were away from our children more than most parents we knew, and we wanted to make sure emotions didn't stay bottled up. We thought this open forum might give Ellie and Stew a key to success as adults. Honest communication became the watchword of our family.

Stewart and I could see no reason why this same know-how wouldn't garner positive results for our employees, both in their jobs and their personal lives. During our years in business, we had observed many employees who talked behind others' backs rather than have upfront, productive conversations about how they felt. The apparently teachable skill of honest communication could go a long way toward a remedy. But like many good intentions, pressed flat under the hustle of increasing responsibilities, it slipped out to the edge of our minds.

Approaching the end of a decade of growth during the mid-1980s, This End Up was spread over three-quarters of the United States and into

Canada. Each district manager had 20 to 70 salespeople in her stable; each distribution center manager had eight to 20 drivers and helpers in his. Because our sales organization was overwhelmingly female, the number of revolving-door employees continued to increase. It is a fact of life that even career-minded women often leave their jobs when family matters require a change. This turnover made it increasingly difficult for our management team to handle 200 stores, 12 delivery operations and thousands of customers. We came to grudgingly accept the employment cycle as a part of our company's makeup, even more reason for a reliable common bond.

The bricks of our management team were all in place, but we had to find the mortar to hold our spread-out people together. Stewart and I sensed a restlessness fomenting in our circle of growing diversity as the two of us became less available for on-demand instruction and mentoring. Geography made it imperative that we be able to endorse the individual judgments of our employees, and that condition called for a structured doctrine to use as teaching and measurement tools. Without that delegation of responsibility to our field staff, we might compromise our competitive marketplace advantages: an easy-to-build and easy-to-brand product, stores in malls, fast delivery, excellent customer service and well-trained employees.

The chance choice of some reading material from the Charlotte, North Carolina, airport bookstore barreled into This End Up like a hurricane. *In Search of Excellence (Lessons from America's Best-Run Companies),* by Thomas J. Peters and Robert H. Waterman, was the random book I picked up on my way home from a trip to our Hartford, Connecticut, store. As I thumbed through it, phrases with a familiar theme jumped off its pages. The name of the game is "rich, informal communication;" the prime ingredient is "open and honest communication;" excellent companies are obsessed with "widely sharing information and preventing secrecy;" and common in these businesses is "a vast network of open communication." The message was the same unifying one Stewart and I had made our family creed a few years before. I paid at the register and hopped on my flight.

Stewart and I devoured the book that highlighted the traits of "excellent companies." The management-consultant authors wrote of why firms lose their competitive edge, and about the commonalities of internal culture that create corporate stability. They listed eight characteristics that were shared wholly or in part by success-story companies.

Many of these habits This End Up already had. But we were not practicing one simple rule that all the superstar examples followed: the values by which organizations function should *always* be written down. When it comes to the core rules, the mission and heart of a company, nothing should be left to guesswork.

It made such sense. How could we have been so remiss? Most of our people worked alone, and by not having written guidelines for them, we were limiting our employees to learning by gut feel. Stewart called a meeting of our district and department managers, and asked them to read *In Search of Excellence* before they came. The participants knew the goal was to formulate a list of This End Up's core values.

On the appointed day, we began quite civilly. Once we started to put words to our beliefs, however, things went downhill fast. In retrospect, I know the reason this watershed meeting was so like a storm: we desperately needed a statement of shared values.

Our management team was made up mostly of people who helped start This End Up, and we were still as thick as the closest of relatives. How could the members of a family have respected each other for eight years, built the testimonial to loyalty that we had and not decided together what we believed in? How could we have sustained something as fortunate as This End Up without acknowledging the standards it was based on? How could we look at the expansion that was planned for this company and not fear for its health with such a lack of written principles of conduct?

Opening the floor for discussion on the book was like watching a storm gather in the distance and head our way. We disagreed. We argued. We pulled our hair and banged the table. We slept on it for a night. We yelled, paced, frowned. We slept on it for another night. We cried. We hugged and we smiled. At the end of three days, the list of This End Up's 10 Shared Values was complete. Stewart's penchant for honest communication and participative management won the day. Every person had a say. Every person had a vote. Every person was equal. Now, we had 100 percent buy-in on a written formula that would give employees what they needed to know to be able to accomplish our company's mission. The Shared Values formed a creed for This End Up, and they nurtured and steered us during the staggering growth still ahead.

As the voices of the storm quieted, the sun that replaced the clouds felt even stronger, and the air was clear and bright.

* * *

THIS END UP'S TEN SHARED VALUES:
(wording modified for this condensed form)

1. Sales: Selling our product is the most important thing we do. Use the following principles, no matter what your job, to create an environment where maximizing this goal can be accomplished by our sales force.

2. Happy Customers: A happy customer affects our income in three ways: he can buy from us instead of a competitor, he can refer other people to us, he can return to us for additional purchases. The greatest effort should be extended by every person in the company to keep this valuable human asset satisfied.

3. Honest Communication: Talk regularly to those whom you manage and those who manage you about what is right and what is wrong. It is not what you say that causes problems but rather what you don't.

4. Individual Growth: Strive to move forward in your career with us by performing outside your comfort zone. Resist being satisfied with the status quo.

5. Participative Management: Any person asked to fulfill a goal should be asked to participate in setting it.

6. Teamwork: Your job is closely linked with many others in the company because of our vertical integration. Focus on the solution of shared problems, not differences.

7. Minimal Red Tape: We have few set rules in this company. If a decision cannot be postponed about making a sale or keeping a customer happy, take action on your own, even if you cannot reach a manager.

8. Flexibility: Adjust your behavior and actions to individual circumstances in whatever way will achieve the best results for our customers.

9. Results: Allow good judgment to override policy in the achievement of sales and cost control. Our company will remain viable by the profits created from the judicious use of this adaptability.

10. Commitment to Excellence: This document is a statement of our standards. We will strive and sometimes miss these goals, but we will be better employees, friends, children, parents, spouses and human beings for seeking them.

CHAPTER 28: This Way Out (8)

The field of three suitors for marriage with This End Up had narrowed when Company No. 3 said, "No thanks." Now we felt the other two wobbling when Melville said, "We're still thinking," and Wolverine said, "That's all it's worth."

Stewart and I, Randy and Steve were 44, 40, 39 and 36 years old. We had worked flat out for nine years. Our individual dreams were similar: to come away from a sale with enough funds to allow latitude in our future choices of careers. And it would be glorious to buy a cruising boat, a farm and an airplane, respectively. We hadn't allowed ourselves to be too optimistic because our dreams might outstrip a modest sales price.

The courtship was an uncomfortable time. Stewart and I had to act normally, run the business and keep fudging the truth to our employees. The struggle to keep the covert yo-yo of developments from family and friends exhausted us. We seemed to hover between living our lives and not living them, and we wondered if our good luck had finally run out.

Deep into updating training manuals, the buzz of my intercom seemed to belong to someone else for a second. But, no, it was mine.

"Can you come up to my office for a minute when you have time?"

Such an unusual request from Stewart got my attention. We didn't talk much at work. It saved time in the workday to wait until we were home to discuss problems, not very healthy but the only way we could fit everything in.

I popped three Advils, a handful of M&Ms—the medicine's label said to take food with ibuprofen—and refilled my giant cup with Diet Coke. A class of new store managers waved shyly as they passed my office on their way to see the original This End Up couch. Grabbing up the latest customer service questionnaire to show Stewart, I hustled down the hall to his office. He asked me to close the door.

Most times, Stewart was slow to get to a point. Sometimes he talked and I had to give a little nudge like, "And so-o-o that means..." Today he dropped a bomb without so much as a preliminary breath.

"Melville is ready to make an offer."

Stewart and I met with Peter at a hotel in New York City to prepare for the final negotiations for the sale of This End Up. We expected a deal to be struck the next day, and we kicked around a few ideas about how things might go. Randy and Steve had given us their opinions to add to the mix, and all of our thoughts were framed by Peter with his buyout expertise.

Peter was his usual natty, polite, confident self that night. For the five months we had worked with him, he had never raised his voice, uttered a curse word or failed to stand up for my comings and goings. He had an air of quiet assurance when he gave me a hug as I headed to bed. In the soft voice I had become used to, Peter wished me happy dreams and said I had been a pleasure to work with. He sounded like it was a done deal, but sleep was elusive for me that night.

CHAPTER 29: You Bitch

The company was making quite a bit of money by the end of 1983, and for 1984, we projected opening 15 new stores for a total of 90, and revenues of $31 million. This End Up was able to bank a large portion of the profit, and we were going to need it, because manufacturing was running non-stop almost every day. The factory had grown from one building to a complex, spreading like kudzu over the 24 acres The Boys owned.

I laughed when I came across an old quote Steve had made to *The Philadelphia Inquirer* when he was interviewed at the opening of our 15th store in 1977.

"We don't want to be a whole lot bigger. We just want to keep the company really small."

Our 10 initial locations generated revenues of $2 million in 1976. At the end of our eighth year, 100 stores would rack up $40 million, the sales per store having doubled.

Several established This End Up stores were bumping against the high-water mark of $100,000 of sales in a single month, but none could quite make it over that line. The sales managers ran contests, the district managers offered additional weekend staff and extra sales tips were published in the company's weekly letter. Month after month, different stores would miss the target by a few thousand dollars. Everyone was discouraged.

At a meeting during that period, Stewart and I were bemoaning the failure to break the barrier when The Boys offered to take the winning store manager to lunch anywhere in the continental U.S. in a private jet. The next month, Lori, the longstanding head of one of the Richmond stores, flew off to New England in a Citation with the two bachelor owners of This End Up. Almost immediately, another store went over the magic number, and the $100,000 level was never hard to reach again.

When Lori ate lobster with Randy and Steve in a Nantucket seaside restaurant that day, she had a look of unabashed glee on her face. I saw it in the photo she brought back to the office, and it sent a small shiver of personal reward up my neck.

But little could my partners and I have dreamed of any reward like the glittering prize that was headed our way.

As This End Up continued to boom, Stewart and I concentrated on ensuring that the Shared Values stayed firm in our management team. With approximately 1,800 employees working for the company by the end of 1984, talking about our philosophy at any opportunity would help those Shared Values stay alive. Did our key people have the skills to carry them out? Did they have the desire to carry them out? Could we keep finding others who would buy into them? We worked on those three things every day.

This End Up needed a strong district manager in the Midwest, someone experienced who could deal with heavy travel. All of our original managers had their hands full with growing territories of their own. Annie was a highly skilled manager for a nationwide specialty store chain when we lucked into her. Her references were superb and she gave an excellent interview. She also lived in Chicago, the hub for this area. We snapped her up.

Early in her career with us, Annie was a standout, handling massive amounts of work well, and we promoted her to regional manager in record time. One of her greatest strengths was her consistently positive attitude. Nonetheless, like most strengths, when it was overused, it had a way of becoming a weakness.

At our quarterly sales managers' meetings, we often discussed what improvement was needed for every individual in attendance—Shared Value No. 3, Honest Communication. Most of us were careful how we said it, but it got said.

"Annie, can you give your report next?" asked Stewart.

"I'd be happy to," replied Annie with her Miss America smile. "I've just hired a darling girl for Clover Station, and I'm positive those sales numbers will take a real leap with her at the helm. Last Saturday I subbed for the store manager at Marshall Place so she could go to a concert she had been dying to attend. It was really a good thing for me to do, because I learned a lot about our weekend customer demographics in that store.

Now, last progress report I talked about Maria, who refuses to do performance reviews with her staff. We've made good role-playing progress on that, and I expect to be able to move on to more sales training with her in the next few weeks."

Because time was tight and Annie's reports focused on the good side of every issue, Stewart asked her to talk only about the problems in her area. She seemed genetically unable to pull off her rose-colored glasses even though we teased and coached her at every meeting.

One day, Annie reported on trying to change someone's behavior in her usual sweet, gentle style, to no avail. Other managers gave suggestions and she wrote them down dutifully.

Unable to contain himself in the cocoon of female sensitivity, Stewart finally yelled out, "Dammit, Annie! You've got to learn to be a bitch. Now write that down on your goals. Hold it up so we can all see it. Now DO IT." Such a sharp directive was a rare reaction from Stewart. We all called them his Spunk Speeches.

Three months later, Annie gave the familiar report about a district manager named Edith who had become increasingly problematic to manage. Annie said she was going to "give it to her" when they next met. I nodded in agreement but privately thought Edith would stay in place. Stewart asked Annie if she had turned into a bitch yet.

"…And last but not least I come to Edith," said Annie at the following quarter's meeting. "She has grown progressively worse and her terrible attitude has spread to her store managers." Hearing Annie use "worse" and "terrible" in one sentence was as mind-blowing as if our drivers had decided to wear dresses to work.

"So I flew down to Columbus unannounced and asked her if she could convince me that she should keep her job. When she said, 'Get me a new regional manager and I'll stay,' I told her it was her last day. And do you know what she called me?" threw out Annie with her color high. "She called me a *bitch*."

The room erupted into applause and cheers.

CHAPTER 30: This Way Out (9)

Peter, alone, would do the final negotiation on *This End Up's* behalf. On our own in Melville's corporate boardroom, Stewart and I were placed at the end of a long, lustrous table which shimmered under the brilliant downlights in the ceiling. Feeling somewhat like we were auditioning before an unseen panel of judges, I wondered if we would ever get a chance to meet the powerful people who occupied the now-empty chairs around that shiny ellipse. A number of distinguished old gentlemen who must have sat there at one time gazed down at us from gilt frames on the wall. On a small side table, a phone sat ready for quick contact with Steve and Randy, who were waiting in Raleigh like expectant fathers.

At the far end of the room was a set of double doors through which one of the most pivotal events of our lives was taking place without us. Stewart paced. His only other visible activity was a twitching jaw muscle. I fidgeted, my emotions perched on that discomforting edge I seem to seek. Excitement danced up and down my spine.

Time dragged by and a secretary popped in to see if we needed anything. The scent of her White Shoulders perfume muddled the stench of stale cigar smoke but didn't displace it. I wondered if she had any idea what we were doing there.

The second hand on my watch trudged forward; like a sailboat in irons, the next hour struggled to pass. We called The Boys.

"Nothing yet."

I felt like I might throw up.

Finally, one of the double doors in the conference room burst open and slammed into the wall. The only other noise was Peter's breathing, a sound that Stewart and I were devoid of just then. He was wide-eyed and clenched some papers to his pink oxford cloth chest.

"Well?" said Stewart. That single word was so weighted with meaning that it could have registered on a scale.

"I… It's… He," Peter, our smooth operator, had lost his cool.

We had a stock deal. The amount of shares that Peter had accepted on our behalf, and the price per share, finally tumbled out of his mouth. The words floated around disconnected in the silence of that gargantuan room.

I don't know why I said it. I know how to multiply. But I don't do well with long silences, so I fill space with words while my mind is sorting. It flew out of my mouth like a cork shot from a champagne bottle.

"Is that good?"

"Good? Is that GOOD??" Peter shouted in a tone of voice I had never heard from him. "That's what you call a goddamn, fucking home run."

So much for social graces.

CHAPTER 31: Nobody Does It Better

From the beginning of our company, Stewart and I hosted a yearly gathering that included every full-time person on the sales side of the business. At these events, we did three things. First, we shared specific information important to everyone in attendance, like how much gas mileage should be paid when we delivered furniture with our personal cars. Second, we held an educational discussion, like how to overcome the customer objection that the couch was too heavy when it *did* weigh 182 pounds. Last, we had a party where we told This End Up stories, drank and ate. This End Up was always big on parties.

At the outset, seven or eight employees came to our house. The size and sophistication of these get-togethers grew from modest to mammoth. Over the years, we added the full-time distribution, manufacturing and support people to the sales people from our ever-increasing stores, and in 1984, our largest annual meeting to date numbered about 500. Our program that year included professional speakers, awards, a slide show and, unbeknownst to Stewart and me, a presentation of X-rated ads, a joke our management team was in on. *(Photos 1.11 and 1.12)*

During the general meeting, the same three original sections were on the agenda, but they were all more ambitious. Topics affecting everyone might cover why tripling the size of the stores wouldn't pay off in triple the sales.

The education workshops often included a role-playing session on handling angry customers' calls: "Don't you tell me they forgot to load my couch on the truck when I'm having a huge dinner party here tonight for my boss. You solve it." Slam.

Equally ambitious, the revelry.

As I rode the elevator at the hotel, I marveled at how big This End Up had become. I didn't know any of the four employees I encountered even though they wore nametags in the familiar shape of our logo. Heading to my room to change into a costume that was part of the meeting's opening scene, I was inconspicuous in my street clothes and no I.D., and unrecognized by my fellow passengers.

"Hey, Jeanette. After the meeting, why don't you and Mary come to our room for some margaritas? Charles and me got all kinds of good stuff at our place."

"Well, I want to hear the band. Did you hear they're having karaoke?"

"Oh, come on, girls. You ain't never gettin' another decent delivery out of Charles or me if you don't swing by Room 519 tonight," threatened Flint.

"We could probably do it real late, after the bar closes down. Change out of our party clothes, you know, so we'd be comfy." Giggle. Ding. Fifth floor.

"Here you go, ladies. Catch." Flying room key #519 settled squarely before our three pairs of feet as the elevator doors swished shut.

"Man! That Charles is a juicy hunk." Ding. Seventh floor. "You want to keep the key, Mary, or you want me to?" Not even a cursory glance back at me.

Ding. Eighth floor. Temporary home to the star of the opening show. It would be fun to see the faces of Jeanette, Mary, Charles and Flint when they put two and two together. Maybe Stewart and I would stop by 519 later. We loved margaritas.

During the meeting, the sales team presented Stewart with a coat of many colors, a gift that had been in the works for months. Nothing would do but to strip off his blue blazer and don the present—a jacket made of most of This End Up's original fabrics. The expression on the president's face told how touched he was at the gesture. *(Photo 1.13)*

The top prize at the annual meeting was called the President's Award. A simple pin of jade and gold in the shape of our logo, it wasn't showy or expensive, but oh, how it was coveted. This End Up had tapped into a group of people who were driven to distinguish themselves. Stewart presented that tiny piece of jewelry to the one person out of those 500 possibilities who was the best example of the Shared Values. Earning it was like winning an Olympic gold medal. It brought the house down as Carly Simon's "Nobody Does It Better" played in an endless loop.

CHAPTER 32: This Way Out (10)

Things moved fast once Stewart and I could locate our voices. The top three men from Melville came in to congratulate us after Peter's shocking "home run" comment stopped reverberating in our ears. We listened to the main elements of the agreement, signed letters of intent and called an astonished Steve and Randy. With so much work still to be done by the lawyers before the final signing of the contract, we all agreed to keep it quiet until that part was complete. Holding that secret turned out to be one of the most difficult things we did in our entire careers.

As the president of Melville walked us to the car for the drive to the airport, he asked me how I felt.

"I—I'm not sure. It happened so fast." Fast? Funny how my perspective had changed in only a couple of minutes. A few breaths ago I thought I would explode from five months of waiting.

He put his arm around my shoulders. "It's not the whole answer you know. Your tires will still go flat, your roof will still leak and your children will still get sick."

I folded the corner of that comment for my memory. I will always be appreciative of the kind man who said that to me. My faith in being able to work with Melville took another step forward. That confidence was a good thing, because Stewart and I would be staying on.

The two of us held hands on the plane ride back home that night. We practiced keeping our faces straight. It wasn't easy.

"Can you believe this?" Can you BELIEVE this?" "CAN you believe this?" No matter how many times we whispered it on the way back to Richmond, neither of us could believe it.

At first the legal process went along smoothly, but after a few weeks, the part of the contract that stated, "subject to all legal and accounting matters being in order," took on real meaning. Melville's attorney called to report a complicated problem with our profit-sharing program. This End Up's plan did not conform with the guidelines of the retirement format used by the big company's other 12 divisions. Melville wanted *that changed before the final sign-off. With that single glitch, we started seven anxiety-filled months, with Stewart spending much of his time working on the solution. The distance between "close" and "there" gave new meaning to the word eternity.*

Peter encouraged us to find counsel that specialized in buyout proceedings. Once we chose a firm in Atlanta, Peter left us. His job was over.

CHAPTER 33: Winners' Circle

Today would be the culmination of a year's work. As Stewart, Steve, Randy and I flew into LaGuardia Airport to close the deal, we talked the whole trip about the remarkable people who had helped bring us this far. The partners already had decided to give away more than $1 million of the proceeds to those original employees who had been instrumental in This End Up's success. I still couldn't believe we had the ability to do such a thing.

The law firm representing Melville's interests was in New York's financial district. The four of us took a taxi into the city with a cabbie who spoke in an opaque accent we couldn't understand but couldn't shut out. His babble impinged on my solemn thoughts about the closure of this installment of my life, but nothing could dampen my excitement.

We pulled up to a towering glass monolith, took a warp-speed elevator to the top and, by the end of day, This End Up no longer belonged to us. Just like that, we stood in the winners' circle. On top of Melville's copies of the final contract, Randy laid the small, worn-out vinyl checkbook he and Steve had used for a decade to pay company bills.

In exchange for 10 years' work, the shares of Melville stock we had agreed upon seven months earlier were finally given to us May 30, 1985. While we had been frightened every minute of that time that the deal would blow up, our stock had *appreciated* six million dollars in those 210 days. The choices about the rest of our lives would be frighteningly and gloriously broad.

The partners walked out of the law office together and The Boys returned to Raleigh. In the elevator Stewart and I took down to the lobby the talk was of normal Wall Street things, interest rates and bond prices. How could that be? Didn't the people inside this lift look at my state of suspended animation and know the world had stopped?

Once we stood at the building's main steps, Stewart said in his regular voice that he'd like a Diet Coke.

"Yeah, me too," I squeaked back. But I felt as if I might spring apart like an old clock, flinging my body parts into the wild blue yonder.

* * *

Staring out the window during the quiet cab ride back to Midtown at the harried, withdrawn faces that mark so many people in big cities, I wondered about the unpredictable manifestation of fate. Why me and not them?

Perhaps the answer lay in a determination to cultivate my life the way I wanted. Or it could be luck. Or maybe it was the guts to choose risk when I didn't need to. Even at the zenith of my career, I was never quite sure why me.

What I knew for certain was that a life preserver too few women possessed now belonged to me. At age 40, I had secured total financial autonomy without the restrictions of a divorce settlement, or the luck of inherited wealth, or the renown of a famous family name. I earned that security the old-fashioned American way: hard work and dogged tenacity. I was a proud and blessed woman.

* * *

Stewart and I had a reservation that night at the Ritz-Carlton Hotel. We didn't talk much as we unpacked our beat-up duffle bag, and I suspected Stewart was busy thinking about what investments would protect and grow our bounties. A celebration never crossed our minds; after all, it was just the two of us. We didn't want dinner, but we decided to go to the hotel lounge for drinks. Two rowdy groups, one amorous couple and a single man were already there. We sat on the burgundy velvet banquette near that gentleman.

Zoned out, we were oblivious to things around us except when a police car passed with its whooping siren. I niggled the button in the tuft of the couch seat as we sat close together and talked intermittently. Neither of us offered a toast; the smile between us said it all.

The bar began to clear out. For one last salute to the day, Stewart signaled the barman. As we waited on the round's delivery, the person one seat down from us asked quietly where my Southern accent was from and what had brought us to New York. Although we tried to condense and play down the story, in our excitement we told him more than he bargained for with his casual opening gambit. The three of us clinked glasses. "So young, and so fortunate," he said and wished us continued happiness. With a tug to the knot of a red silk tie, he left for his room to prepare for a meeting the next day, nodding his head as he disappeared without an exchange of names. His departure left Stewart and me alone in the Ritz-Carlton Lounge.

As we drained our glasses and talked of bed, Stewart and I were surprised to see two waiters approach us. One extended a silver tray of cheeses, pâté, fruit and foil-wrapped chocolates, and the other man carried an ice bucket that contained a chilled bottle of champagne.

"What is this?" we asked.

"It's compliments of the gentleman sitting next to you earlier. If you would prefer, we can deliver it to your room."

Stewart and I were stunned. "How incredible! We don't even know his name."

The waiter smiled. "Really? That was Mr. Carlton."

CHAPTER 34: Paying the Price

In a few days, Melville would need to report its acquisition of This End Up to the business press, and the partners were eager for our employees to hear the story from us. Preparing to break the news felt like we were about to tell our children we were putting them up for adoption. Stewart and I flew the sales managers into Richmond and told them and the department heads about the buyout. The group was dumbfounded and worried about what would happen to their lives. They wondered how we had chosen Melville and wanted us to detail the reasons we thought the companies were a strong cultural match. Nervous acceptance settled on their faces.

"But what about you two? And Steve and Randy?" they wanted to know.

"Don't worry. Libby and I are staying on. I'm going to head up both parts of TEU because Randy plans to leave right away, and Steve will leave once he completes a design project he's working on."

Thundering silence. While some of them looked down at the table, others looked straight at us without so much as a blink.

"We wanted to tell you before, and I hope you understand why we weren't able to," I said. My heart hurt. "Now we have to ask you not to leak this to anybody until it becomes public. Just for a couple of days."

Stewart and I were asking a lot from people on whom we had just dumped a load of uncertainty. The urge to say "I'm sorry" was like a lozenge stuck in my throat.

We all knew This End Up would never be the same again. I don't think the managers felt set adrift exactly, but that meeting was a bittersweet moment for all of us who had learned to run the company together. Before we adjourned, the group toasted Stewart and me. In a typical example of their generosity, they subdued their uneasiness long enough to hug us and say, "We're happy for you."

Forty-eight hours later, we were jet-setters for the first time in our lives as we boarded a chartered Citation for stops in Washington, Boston and Chicago. We gathered as many support staff, store managers and drivers into those cities as possible to tell them the story in person. The logistical orchestration for that one-day trip, on such short notice, was as frenzied a task as we had ever tackled. By the time Stewart and I reached the Midwest, Stewart's assistant had left a message to contact her ASAP. The Richmond and Raleigh newspapers and the *Wall Street Journal* wanted us to call. The news was out.

The publicity made it tough to be low-key about our good fortune. I remember sitting at a stoplight thinking the person in the next car was staring, and I wondered if he recognized me from the Richmond spread. The story had been featured prominently in the Business section, complete with old pictures of the two of us in the Strawberry Street store. Stewart hated that. Our children were occasionally confused by some remark about our windfall, repeated at school by a classmate who had probably heard it at home. One older boy told Stew that he should ask for a bigger allowance. By the time This End Up and the Browns were old news, our whole family was glad for the limelight to move somewhere else.

Melville made no secret that it wanted the company to become larger. A conglomerate like that wasn't in the business of running little companies, and we were already looking for land outside Raleigh to build a giant new factory when the 100th store opened in late 1985. Although This End Up didn't belong to us anymore, Stewart and I felt more responsibility than ever to keep it healthy and growing.

Stew and Ellie, now 13 and 14, seemed as settled as any kids that age. If it hadn't been for our house manager Susan, I could never have traveled like I did in 1986 when Stewart was managing his double workload. During that year, we opened 52 This End Up stores for Melville. The set-up of every one took a massive degree of preparation, and our support and sales management people worked monstrous hours, as I did. With that much travel and a new store a week, it wasn't long before I was strung like piano wire. Trying to keep up with such a fast-paced organization wore me down faster than it did Stewart. We had different types of personalities; I was driven by details and closure while he focused on exploring options for the health of This End Up's long-range vision. Fifty-two stores in one year, responsibility for our home and children, the declining health of my mother and my internal drive for accomplishment created a hurdle I was barely clearing.

I had no time for anyone who wasn't on my schedule and no tolerance for anyone who had opinions other than my own. When I looked in the mirror, the lines of my face were sharpened by pressure and the search for perfection. My head pounded much of every day and occasionally my heart thumped in an erratic rhythm. Advil became my constant companion. I skipped medical and dentist appointments because they took too much time and lived on M&Ms because I could stuff them in my mouth on planes and in rental cars, giving up the time-consuming ritual of meals. I developed insomnia and often stayed awake in my hotel rooms into the early morning hours, writing countless follow-up notes full of harrowing judgments from my store visits.

One afternoon in my office, I thought I was about to lose consciousness or even have a stroke. Every nerve ending tingled and felt as if it were sitting on top of my skin. A loud sound roared in my ears. I was in trouble and called Stewart to take me to the hospital. Before we reached help, my hands and feet bent into abnormal positions while my breathing raced. As we screeched into the emergency room driveway, my eyes rolled back in my head and a black void settled over me.

With the battery of tests not yet complete, I was frantic to get back to my desk. Dr. Fleming pulled his chair close to the bedside. He took both my hands in his.

"Libby, you are in fine physical shape. But you have got to get hold of your life and put your emotional self back in order."

"What do you mean by that?"

"You are working way too hard, and the level of stress that it's creating in you has caused this problem today. I suspect it's not the first time you've had these spells."

"Nothing like this. Can't you just give me something that will keep me level?"

"Stress doesn't work that way. You have to do this for yourself. And for your family. I've read all those articles in the papers about what you and Stewart have accomplished. Congratulations. But I am telling you that you are not going to live long enough to enjoy that success if you don't slow way back. What happened to you today gives you a chance. Take it."

It took three miserable months to achieve the balancing act between the company's needs and mine. Even though the next two years were ones of continuing fast growth, This End Up had to share me with family and friends. We both did just fine.

In September 1988, 15-year-old Stew left Richmond to attend a Connecticut boarding school. His father and I were sad to think that our kindhearted son would never again live full-time within our family. Or so we thought. Ellie continued her education in Richmond. I felt lucky that she and Stew had turned out to be sensible and loving people with the easygoing nature of their father, but I wished I hadn't missed so much of their childhoods.

CHAPTER 35: Casting Off

The time for Stewart and me to leave This End Up had come. Deciding to quit wasn't easy, but it wasn't too hard either. We knew the business was at a crossroads that needed to be charted by new blood. The distribution process was antiquated, our manufacturing operation needed a shake-up and the whole company was a technological dinosaur. For the near future it would be strong and healthy, and we would be leaving it on the shoulders of capable and steadfast people who could carry it through to new heights.

This End Up had operated with Scrooge-like frugality for 15 years. We were leaving behind virtually no debt, 253 stores, six factories, 12 distribution centers, approximately 2,500 employees, and almost $100 million in sales for the year of our exit.

In January 1990, Stewart and I were 49 and 45 years old. We told Melville officials of our wish to leave at the end of December. They understood and thanked us with generous stock options for our five years in their service. Stew had been in school in Connecticut for one-and-a-half years and Ellie would leave us in September, headed for college in Chicago.

The refrigerator door came alive with pent-up dreams, made real with old photos from our island vacations on charter boats. Yachting magazines that had stacked up on our kitchen counter for years became our primary reading material. We pulled out the file from a 1989 visit to the Fort Lauderdale Boat Show, pouring over the information we had collected. Free weekends turned into scouting trips, and with Steve's years of cruising experience as a guide, we were able to identify good yacht manufacturers and tour several of their factories.

By February, the order was booked, our captain was hired and the itinerary for our yearlong trip was taking shape. Completion of our boat was scheduled for December 31, 1990, the day we were to leave This End Up. The children were thrilled and entertained visions of Thanksgiving, Christmas and spring break in exotic places. Once again, except for Ellie and Stew, we parked a secret down inside us and told no one of our plan for eight months. When we finally let our managers know the date and method of our departure, they weren't surprised. They knew all about our fascination with boats and islands.

Our last day was New Year's Eve, and the headquarters had closed at midafternoon. Stewart was in his office packing up and I was alone in mine with my memories. The immediacy of leaving made the company and all that it stood for unspeakably sacred all of a sudden.

This End Up freed me from the torpor of conformity, taught me to motivate, manage, create and organize something of worth, and fostered in me a love of exploration and intellectual stimulation. In many ways, the journey was a spiritual one that made me a stronger, better, more fulfilled person. In accordance with my belief in the justice of give and take, I hoped once again that I had delivered as much as I had received.

Stewart and I walked out into a cold and cloudy night. Sharp and fresh, the atmosphere had shifted and the pressure was falling. When we turned at the far corner for a last glimpse, the bright light by the front door had already receded in the New Year's Eve mist, and a cleansing rain began to fall.

POSTSCRIPT

S tewart and I had been gone from This End Up for five and a half years when Melville sold it to Citicorp Venture Capital. Three years later, in 1999, a newspaper reporter called asking what we knew about the current state of our old company. We could offer nothing since we were living outside the United States 80 percent of the time, but the inquiry alerted us that things had splintered in the land of crate furniture.

Home on New Year's Day in 2000, Stewart and I received a number of phone calls from past employees and friends who worried about rumors that This End Up was in trouble. Randy called from outside Raleigh. He and wife Susan lived on a farm with their pet Newfoundland Hannah and were planning their gift of a heart center in Hannah's name to N.C. State's Veterinary School. Steve called from Wyoming. He and wife Lisa had worked there in wildlife conservation and research since the early 1990s.

The four old partners pooled information—not one of us knew anything good. Inside the organization, where we still knew people well, nobody was talking, and the silence sounded like a death rattle. *(Photo 1.14)*

In February, a former employee and good friend called us in the Bahamas to say that Citicorp Venture Capital had filed for Chapter 11 bankruptcy protection for This End Up. Stewart and I had a somber supper and talked late into the night about how such a thing could have happened.

We were in Richmond the week before the liquidation of This End Up's assets began. It was May 2000. Eager to have the original This End Up couch come back into our possession, Stewart called the man in charge of the auction, explaining who he was and that he'd like to buy the couch since the office was being shut down.

"Get in line with everybody else," he was told. We didn't have the heart to do it.

The night after the auction, and shortly before we left to return to our boat in the Bahamas, Stewart and I went out to dinner. When we returned home, we couldn't believe what sat on our front porch.

The original crate couch had been bought for us by a small contingent of our former employees. The note said simply, "For all you did for us."

During the next couple of months, This End Up's stores, factories and distribution centers were closed, and most of its employees were dismissed. By the time Stewart and I returned to Richmond several months later, This End Up was gone.

* * *

A few days after Stewart and I found the couch on our front porch, the phone rang, pulling me away from visions of palm trees and turquoise water as I packed to return to the islands.

"Libby, this is Nick Austin. Do you remember me?"

Nicky was one of the first drivers we had hired for This End Up, probably late in 1975. My last sight of him had been in the downtown office about three months before I left TEU.

"I just took a chance that you still lived in the same place. I wanted to tell you and Stewart something."

I was shocked by the coincidence of Nicky's contact at the exact time of This End Up's demise.

"Well, I'm leaving TEU today after 25 years of working for y'all."

I was touched that Nicky still equated Stewart and me with the company since we had been gone for nine-plus years.

"I couldn't walk out without thanking you both for giving me a job back then."

The conversation recalled the sweetness we had seen in the traumatized young war veteran we had interviewed so many years ago.

"I don't know if you remember hiring me, but I was just back from Vietnam with my leg not totally healed. I was still fighting depression and nobody else would even see me. My family and my girlfriend had sort of given up on me. I was about to give up on me, too. And then you and Stewart gave me a chance."

Before I could utter a word, Nicky barreled forward, as if he might not get it out if he didn't say it all at once.

"Now I have a beautiful wife and three terrific kids. I've had a wonderful career with people who trusted me when nobody else would. I was afraid you might never know how much you helped me if I didn't call to tell you."

I barely choked out, "Good luck and keep in touch."

Nicky probably never thought about what a kind act he performed that dismal day, but he was a good example of the type of person who took This End Up to the moon, once upon a time.

* * *

In September 2003, a new friend with whom I had had lunch the previous day called me. Nell said how odd it was that I had told her the tale of This End Up just 24 hours earlier.

"I had to call to tell you something I saw this morning while I was driving carpool in Sleepy Hollow. I might not have noticed it before yesterday. A yard sale was going on and the people had painted a huge wooden sign to advertise it."

I couldn't imagine how this story could relate to me.

"What did it say?" I asked.

"It said, 'THIS END UP and OTHER GREAT THINGS.'"

Photo 1.1 ~ Stew and Ellie were 2 and 3 years old when This End Up was founded.

Photo 1.2 ~ Stewart and Libby in their first This End Up store, Richmond, 1975.

Photo 1.3 ~ Libby took her sales training program nationwide, eventually covering 253 stores.

Photo 1.4 ~ Vendors often overlooked our factory in the woods north of Raleigh.

Photo 1.5 ~ Two co-founders, Stewart and Randy, celebrate the successful opening of the "real" factory.

Photo 1.6 ~ One of our first shopping mall locations, late 1970s.

Photo 1.7 ~ A This End Up storefront, early 1990s.

Photo 1.8 ~ Another reason to celebrate: the arrival of the first This End Up tractor-trailer.

Photo 1.9 ~ The original This End Up couch, circa 1974.

Photo 1.10 ~ Steve on one of his many sailing trips.

Photos 1.11 and 1.12 ~ A couple of pranks uncovered by our shameless marketing department.

Photo 1.13 ~ Employees surprised Stewart with this coat made entirely of TEU upholstery fabric at the 1984 annual meeting.

Photo 1.14 ~ The four original partners, Steve, Libby, Stewart and Randy, at Fowl Cay, Bahamas, 2005.

PART TWO

CROSSROADS

"Mother, Mother Ocean,
  I have heard you call.
  Wanted to sail upon your waters
  Since I was three feet tall."

  A Pirate Looks at Forty
  — Jimmy Buffett

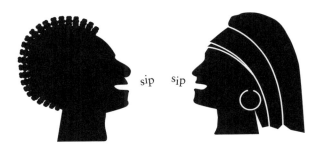

sip   sip

TALKIN' BAHAMIAN

I offer in advance my apologies for inaccuracies in explaining or portraying the Bahamians' delightful, melodious/cacophonous, fast-talking/slow-talking island dialect.

At times, visitors to the Bahamas think the locals of the cays do not speak English, so different is their colorful patois from the language heard in other English-speaking parts of the world. Below is a guide to the basic rules of the out-island Bahamian sister language used in this book.

Other than the word *is*, the present tense of the verb *to be* is used seldom.
(*I is mad. She mad.*)

The future tense of the verb *to be* is usually stated by attaching *guh* or *gern* to the main verb, and *ing* is used rarely.
(*We guh take her to school.*)

The past tense is not employed, generally.
(*I plant my flowers las' week. She take my bike from de yard yesterday.*)

Th at the beginning of words becomes *T* or *D* in most cases, and *th* at the end of words is pronounced as if the *t* stands alone.
(*Dere's beer on dat bar. Dem fish is mine. He gat a lot of good t'ing at Christmas. I in here takin' a bat.*)

Sounds are dropped in the middle and at the end of many words.
(*She diff'ren' from me.*)

The plural is generally omitted.
(*Dat mamma gern to buy t'ree dress.*)

Frequently, the letter *v* is pronounced *w* and the letter *w* is pronounced *v* at the beginning of words or dropped from the middle of a word. (*Dat lady is wery ogly. Vut you gat in dose box? She eat nuttin erry day. Dat why her boonggy stringy.*)

Additionally, Bahamians make words of their own from pieces and parts of Standard English. (*She big up.* = She is pregnant. *I all confuddle up.* = I am confused. *Dis place is jam up.* = This place is crowded. *He cascate he dinner.* = He threw up his dinner. *Sip sip gat it he kerpunkle up las' night.* = Rumors are that he got drunk last night. *De boat reach?* = Has the boat arrived yet? *Don't put mout' on it.* = Don't say it or it might come true. *Boonggy* = Buttocks. *Stringy* = Skinny.

CHAPTER 1: On the Hook (1)

"*Seventy feet? What do you think? Too big?*" *I ask Stewart. The boat takes on Amazonian proportions from where we stand. We had been looking at pictures of cruising models around 50 feet in the boating magazines. For the one-year trip Stewart and I are preparing to embark on, that seems a generous size. But since we arrived at the Hatteras plant in North Carolina to view our options, both of us have been edging our way from mid-size vessels to queen-size ladies.*

"*We'd need a good captain to handle this girl with only the two of us as crew,*" *I say. "But between vacations bare-boating and time on Steve's boats, we'd be quick studies.*"

"*Somewhat,*" *Stewart offers. He frequently answers my questions with words that mean nothing to the untrained ear, but we've been married 24 years and experience has given me a partial grip on their meaning.*

"*Doesn't a year to build her sound like a long time?*" *I ask.*

"*Not necessarily.*"

Along with my two brothers, I had been born into a boat-loving family. When our father stopped being transferred to a different place every couple of years, we circled back to his coastal hometown in Wilmington, North Carolina. Shortly thereafter he bought a johnboat. We kept it moored to a piling in the shallow tidal flats of Greenville Sound where we lived, using a pulley system he had rigged up to haul it in as needed. By the age of 12, I could pilot the boat with a handle mounted on the small outboard motor. When the family upgraded to a larger boat, it was a cinch to navigate with a steering wheel.

By the end of our first year in Wilmington, my dad built me a wooden Pram—eight feet long, gaff-rigged sail—and painted it turquoise to match the color chip I picked off the revolving display at the paint store. I named her Lollipop, *and I raced with a fleet of 10 identical boats. Every girl won a prize at the end of the season. Mine was for being the bravest sailor. I had almost caused the fathers a collective heart attack one day when I sailed* Lollipop *across the bow of an oncoming commercial* shrimp boat, screaming, "Sailboats have the right of way!" Playing by the rules was important to me even then.

When I turned 15 and was allowed to go out on the Intracoastal Waterway with my buddies, we did nautical things like ski 20 miles non-stop from one beach town to the next. Where we lived you begged for a boat far more than a car, and at 16 we took them out at night and raced from one channel marker to the next, a case of beer banging around in the iced-down engine well. The following summer I got lucky. I survived riding in a boat that my friend flipped while running wide open, and lived through skiing over a barely-submerged oyster flat that somersaulted me onto the razor-sharp shells.

"Stewart, remember when we were dating, and we went out for a sail in Blue Belle during that awful storm? Didn't we have to be towed in because the mast broke in two?"

Blue Belle was the 16-foot Windmill I had upgraded to after I outgrew Lollipop.

"I'll bet I'd never be that scared in a boat like this," I said, eyeing the 70-foot Hatteras.

Stewart's mind was on more practical matters. "Do you like having the galley on the main level instead of a few steps down, like that boat we chartered in Greece?"

Once I married Stewart, he was an easy convert to boating with his love of the outdoors, easy touch on the wheel of boats under sail or power, and intuitive understanding of the interaction of wind and water. An excellent swimmer, he was more comfortable in the water than I.

When we moved to Richmond in 1968, we missed living on the ocean and as soon as we were able, we bought a beach house near Wilmington. Our children could drive the 18-foot motorboat we kept there by the time they were 13. On the occasions we vacationed somewhere other than North Carolina, we usually spent time on my brother's boats in the Exuma Cays or bareboating a charter vessel in the Virgin Islands or the Grenadines.

"Are you OK with this one, Libby?" asks Stewart.

"OK?" I think. "How could anyone possibly not be OK ordering a dream boat to motor around in for a year of rest and relaxation in some of the most beautiful cruising spots in the world?"

I pinch myself. (Photo 2.1)

CHAPTER 2: The Name Game

Five and a half years had passed since Stewart and I finalized the agreement in 1985 to sell our business. Once the deal was closed, many people were astounded that we returned to the company rather than jumping into full-time leisure. Between mid-1985 and the end of 1990, This End Up Furniture Company tripled in size. In December 1990 we retired from a monstrous workload of 15 years' duration. At 46 and 50 years old, we bailed from the safe harbor of home and job into an uncharted life of exploration and considered ourselves inordinately lucky.

Our plan for 1991 was to cruise between the Florida Keys and the Virgin Islands on our new boat. Life on a yacht seemed like the ultimate fantasy, but with years of experience on boats we knew our itinerary would take courage and serious on board equipment to survive incidents I didn't want to think about. In the cruising world, peril keeps watch around the clock. Risk would prove a steadfast companion, always on board and watching for its opportunity both to excite and to frighten me out of my wits.

Stewart and I fed off adventure more than most people we knew. But we weren't nuts. Although we had motored and sailed boats for years in the Intracoastal Waterway, ventured into the ocean for deep-sea fishing and cruised among nearby island chains, the two of us alone could not handle this kind of bluewater boating. A knowledgeable captain would make it possible to play during the day and sleep at night, but experience was only one of the qualifications we would need on the résumé.

Technically capable boat captains were not hard to come across, but many carried extra baggage: unreliability, insobriety, troubled family relations or loud personalities. Living inside 70 feet of moving real estate with someone outside my immediate family was hard to imagine. It might be difficult to do with someone in my immediate family.

Unsettling images crossed my mind—eating every meal with a stranger, vetting every remark and moderating every mood because of his presence. Although I had learned to mind my tongue during my years at This End Up, I much preferred the freedom of unrestricted speech in my private life. Stewart and I had settled into the loving but headstrong relationship of many long-wed couples, and our humorous bantering was laced with the ever-present static between opposites who attract. Bringing a third party into that routine could turn our sparks into fireworks. But we couldn't globetrot without finding a captain, and I knew who could help.

When we were young, my brother Steve and I sailed competitively and for pleasure, each in his own boat. Steve raced *Banshee,* his 11-foot Moth class sailboat. His bedroom swelled with trophies; mine was bereft of a single prize. Later, as This End Up grew, so did the size of Steve's vessels, and Stewart and I became addicted to the nautical adventures we took on them. During some of our trips, Steve's captain, Gregg, was at the helm.

Gregg was a tall, muscular man with the quiet, contented demeanor of someone equally happy to be with others or alone. He spoke with a soft southern accent and had good experience at the wheel of mid-size boats. As guests we found his knack of being on the spot when we needed him, and invisible when we didn't, made for easy company.

What are you doing about a captain for your new boat?" Steve asked me over the phone one night.

"Don't know. We need to find a Gregg. Got any recommendations?"

"How about Gregg himself?" Steve asked.

"Why would you ever want to give up Gregg?"

Steve said he was taking a sabbatical from full-time boating to concentrate on flying, but wanted to make sure Gregg had a good job after all their years together. I knew that boats, islands and oceans would always be high on Steve's priority list though, because the two of us had been born sea babies. In February 1990, we had the obligatory interview with Gregg. He took over as full-time captain even before our boat was built, our eyes and ears throughout the construction process.

We had been tinkering with what to call the boat for months, to no avail. Naming a vessel that would be a full-time address took on similar importance to christening a child. Stewart and I had stringent requirements.

It couldn't be too cute, so *Brown Sugar* and *Great Crate* were scratched. We wanted to cruise incognito, so there went *This End Up,* although it had some technical merit. The name had to be easy to pronounce over the marine radio, which eliminated foreign words, a string of words and those with a lot of vowels. In the cruising community you became known by your boat's name before anyone learned your given one. As you wandered around a dock, you might hear, "Oh, there's the couple off *Oui, Oui.*"

"People live on a boat named *Wee Wee?*" someone would inevitably ask.

On a trip back from our beach house one day, Stewart and I talked about what we were doing with our lives and why. We had sold our company and retired early; we were stepping into a scenario where we would spend with abandon while we created nothing of value; we were moving away from our hometown of 23 years onto a boat to navigate dangerous seas to places where we had no connections. And while we motored through the Caribbean for a year, we were leaving our children in the United States—one 18-year-old freshman in an Illinois college and one 17-year-old senior in a Connecticut boarding school.

The choice to follow the path that led to This End Up was the first big crossroads of our lives. The decision to live full-time on our boat was the second. When we returned to our hometown where we would soon be visitors, Stewart and I had reached rare agreement—"Crossroads" met every criterion for the name. Mission accomplished.

As we pulled into the driveway, I said, "Great! I'll call the Hatteras factory and give them our decision. Now they can paint *Crossroads* on the boat's transom."

Never one to close out his options too soon, Stewart said, "Let's sleep on it."

CHAPTER 3: A Home with No Mailbox

As Hatteras models of that day tended to be, *Crossroads* was sturdy and somewhat blocky in shape. My crate-designing brother jokingly called her "the This End Up of boats." He agreed, though, that she was exactly what we needed for a combination of bluewater cruising and stickybeak exploring in and out of the islands. At 70 feet, she was a floating palace, and the boat drew wolf whistles as she cut through the water with her long profile.

On a temperate day in January 1991, the boat Stewart and I had commissioned 12 months earlier left the factory in North Carolina a nearly naked girl, heading to finishing-school in south Florida for conversion to a grande dame. Electronics, anchors and lines, canvas top, furniture, housewares and recreation equipment were only a start. The marine industry's Madison Avenue and Rodeo Drive all in one, the strip between Fort Lauderdale and Miami was where boats became yachts. Gregg arranged for a fully-outfitted, 17-foot inflatable dinghy to be waiting for us. It would be our family vehicle and we named her *Roundabout. (Photo 2.2)*

The trip down to Florida was a good one. Stewart, Gregg and I started our little team during this first voyage together, a team that would live through physical dangers beyond my imagination. Our captain made it clear from the beginning that he considered his No. 1 priority to be our safety, even if it meant overruling us on an occasional decision. I couldn't imagine then why he would even bring that up.

If the companies that specialized in finding yacht captains needed a person to put on the front of their brochure, they should have known Gregg. Tall, with a perfect physique, a patrician nose, and a steady gaze when we first met him in the '70s, he still looked the epitome of a strong and capable captain 20 years later. And his résumé was equally impressive: a degree in marine biology, 12 years of experience maintaining sail and power boats while he made numerous trips as a delivery captain between the Virgin Islands and North Carolina, six of those years as a fully licensed captain of 50- to 60-foot power vessels. *(Photo 2.3)*

Once we had *Crossroads* securely in the Fort Lauderdale boatyard, my mind reeled, thinking of everything I had to buy to outfit her. The food and household supplies alone took four trips to the grocery store. We were provisioned as if we were setting off on an ocean crossing instead of a four-hour, 50-mile trip to Cat Cay in the northern Bahamas.

When the building plans for the boat were being drawn up, Stewart and I asked Hatteras to build a big freezer under the floorboards of *Crossroads'* stern cockpit. Where we were headed, it could be months before we could replenish necessities like coffee ice cream and Ball Park Franks. I expected to eat different things, but I didn't want to be deprived of my favorites.

Storage on boats is tricky. There is usually one place and one place only that many items fit, sort of like a jigsaw puzzle. Often that single place on a boat makes as much sense as storing your iron in the refrigerator.

The place for the extra toilet paper, for example, was through a hole in our bed's platform where it would roll into the dark corners under the king-size space and have to be retrieved with the fishing gaff. The spices had to live in a plastic bucket that fit only inside the galley banquette, and the fishing rods hung from the ceiling of the aft deck overhang. After I removed the hatch cover from the five-foot-deep lazarette that held the big freezer, climbed down the ladder from the cockpit and put the milk, butter, cheese, o.j., bagels, ice cream, coffee, nuts, and meat for a year down inside its frigid walls, I wondered how many times a week I'd make that chilly descent for food. After finding a place for necessities, there seemed no spot to store anything extra on the boat, because some piece of essential paraphernalia sat in every cavity and on every ledge.

My new surroundings would be a world apart from my old neighborhood, so familiar and secure. Starting soon, days would be filled with constant vigilance for the path of other boats, for the approach of unknown people, and for signs of weather that couldn't be ignored by ordering a pizza, closing the front door and sitting in front of a fireplace. I was about to embark on an adventure where I would live in countries that spoke my own language but had deep differences in culture. Away from the buffer of work and friends, I would reside 24/7 with my husband and a man I barely knew. I wasn't sure which part of the journey would enlighten me most.

CHAPTER 4: On the Hook (2)

C rossroads *pulled into the boatyard here in Fort Lauderdale late yesterday afternoon. As much fun as the trip down from Wilmington was, I'm glad to be here finally, where we can start equipping her. Hatteras said to count on the boat being here at least three months, maybe more. This morning, when Stewart and I arrived at her assigned slip, No. 71, workmen were swarming all over the boat, and Gregg was standing on the bow with a clipboard.*

Stewart and I are going to function as Gregg's crew during docking procedures, and we practiced several times before we left North Carolina. My assignment is the bow line, since the front of Crossroads *is the easiest for Gregg to power to a dock. Even if it takes me several tosses to get that heavy line to the dockmaster, the bow can stay in place for a minute or two. Once the tether is secured, Stewart will handle her spring (side) and stern lines. Gregg says the boat will weigh about 110,000 pounds when it's fully loaded. That tells me how frightening and dangerous it would be to have her tossed up against a dock by wind and current and inexperienced crew. But the three of us got it down perfectly before we left Wilmington and brought her in smooth as silk here in Fort Lauderdale.*

I'm trying to learn a little bit about the navigation equipment that Stewart and Gregg discussed last night at dinner. Amazing what's available for yachts these days. One thing I know, we'll really need a good radar system when we're underway in the rain, although hopefully we won't be on any long passages in a storm. That's one reason the guys want a weather fax on board, too, so we can plan around bad weather.

The three of us have been working together on an itinerary. After our first night at Cat Cay to clear Customs, we decided we'll cruise on into Nassau. We never really spent much time there when we were on Steve's boats. I expect Nassau is where we'll really start to get into the Bahamian culture. But that's three or more months off.

CHAPTER 5: Central Casting

We snapped a final salute to the boatyard on a sun-drenched April morning, and *Crossroads* glided south as the last pale rays of the sunrise faded over the horizon. The maiden voyage was the very picture of our tropical fantasy at sea: Gregg in his snow-white captain's shirt, a custom-designed *Crossroads* burgee snapping in the breeze, glasses of fresh-squeezed o.j. in the cup holders and Jimmy Buffett singing about changes in latitude. Fate smiled brightly upon us.

The water was perfect as we pulled off the Miami coast and headed east into the Atlantic Ocean. The day's weather forecast sounded superb, but Stewart and I knew the maritime highway leading to the Caribbean could change its personality with the slightest wind shift. Common sense made Cat Cay a prudent first stop after crossing the irascible current of the Gulf Stream.

As Stewart steered *Crossroads* on a southeasterly course under Gregg's watchful eye, he tuned in the VHF marine radio so that he and I could reacquaint ourselves with this vital instrument. We knew it functioned as a combination telephone and public-address system in yachting communities worldwide, and boaters generally left it on all the time except late at night. The radio wasn't difficult from a technical standpoint, but personal technique was open to scrutiny because everybody within its range could listen.

Gregg's personal rules for radio use were to repeat the name of the boat you were calling two times, keep the information short when hailing on the central Channel 16, and switch immediately to a lesser-used channel once contact was made with the other party. And be verrry careful what you say. Since it had taken a year to decide on *Crossroads'* name, Stewart and I liked to hear other mariners' choices over the VHF, and for the next hour or so we delighted over the colorful names of the boats as they called each other on the radio.

The first conversations we followed provided a lesson on privacy.

"You tell that son-of-a-bitch Harvey Blaine on *Seashell,* if he ever lays a finger on me again I'm calling the cops," raged the woman.

"Now, Marlene, you know you just have to chalk last night up to Harvey being blind drunk," said Harvey's friend.

"You're no better than he is, taking up for that creep. He told me he wasn't married and you agreed. You're as big an asshole as he is."

"Well, MIZ Farley, I'll give him the message when I see him at Walker's Cay."

Stewart and I figured half the boats at Walker's Cay that night would know who did what to whom if they happened upon Harvey Blaine or Marlene Farley.

The dinghy for *Daddy's Toy Box* checked in. "*Daddy,* this is *Babydoll* calling."

Son of a Beach tried to raise *Toodle Lou* at the same time *Sailbad the Sinner* called *The Office*. That caused the kind of stop-and-go confusion on Channel 16 that you find at a four-way stop sign.

And in an example of oxymoronic self-analysis, the owner from *Placid* was a woman whose gusto blasted from the mike like a carnival barker.

As we pulled into our 3A slip assignment at Cat Cay's marina, Stewart and I handled our first docking. The world could have blown up around us and we wouldn't have noticed, focused as we were on being the perfect novice crew. When Gregg turned the engines off, I glanced at the stern of the boat in neighboring slip 3B. Her name was printed in big, loopy black and purple letters: *Placid,* with a winking eye painted on each side of the name and a Jolly Roger flag rippling atop the mast.

CHAPTER 6: New Bran' Adventures

After the smooth tie-up, we cleared Customs and Immigration in the afternoon. Sunset slipped away to a night delirious with stars. Sitting on the flybridge, sipping Bailey's over ice, we declared there could be no room in the heavens for an additional twinkler. Later when I opened portholes by our bed, a warm sea breeze ruffled my nightgown. Stewart's mouth was full of goodnight mumbles as my eyelids shut with the rocking of the boat. Richmond already seemed like a distant memory, and, like the time when we sold This End Up, I imagined it couldn't get any better than this.

When *Crossroads* pulled out of Cat Cay the next morning, the sun bloomed above the horizon and the air was cool enough for long sleeves. The palm trees near the marina reflected the glow of sunrise in their fronds, and the boat moved past them with the low rumble of her big Caterpillar engines. Gregg, Stewart and I marveled in congenial silence at the sky that was turning, just at the rim, from the purple of early dawn to the yellow-gold of day.

Our destination was Nassau, the capital of the Bahamas, on the island of New Providence. I sat on the flybridge the whole trip, eager to turn my winter-white skin to a tropical tan in one day. Without sea legs yet, my stomach rolled in protest of the big boat's movements.

Gregg steered *Crossroads* into Palmetto Marina, where we had a reservation for several nights. We were eager to see what the hype was about regarding this famous hub of cruise ships, casinos and shopping, the city where almost two-thirds of the country's population lived.

The dockmaster deftly palmed his tip and welcomed us with a smile. Then, dipping his chin to signal a confidential message, he suggested we tie off and lock *Roundabout* at the bow of the boat, up by the marina's concrete bulkhead. The request was unusual; dinghies were almost always secured to the stern of their mother ship. "Dat way, I watch out mo' better for de tiefs what cruise aroun' lookin' for a small boat to take," explained Palmetto's chief guard.

The next day, Stewart and I hopped into our dinghy to go look at the huge cruise ships docked just north of our marina. The scene around those floating cities was crazy. People moved like ants to and from unknown destinations. The well-publicized Nassau Straw Market was nearby, and one swarm of sightseers headed in that direction. We pulled up to the quay to see what the stir was about.

"Hey, mon," said a small boy, speaking directly to me. That greeting was my first personal experience with the Caribbean hello we would hear almost daily. Apparently it made no difference that I was a woman. "You gimme five dollar, I vatch yo' boat."

We were unprepared for the throngs of tourists that the four massive cruise ships disgorged, but the Bahamians weren't. Passengers filed in and out of casinos, duty-free shops and American fast-food joints in a frenzy of consumption.

The humanity that overran the maze of the Straw Market's stalls was no problem for the purveyors of native products. Even after years of teaching sales skills in the States, I could learn a thing or two from the Bahamians. I watched as a woman in a simple red cotton shift enticed a bejeweled princess in a low-cut Diane von Furstenberg dress, her platinum-streaked pageboy bobbing in agreement with the vendor's every word.

The saleswoman's slightly damp skin glowed a rich, dark-brown, with a thin overlay of black, the color of a chocolate truffle. Red roses on her extra-large batik dress shook as she laughed, like flowers bouncing around in a breeze. Fortified by its oscillating backside, her solid body blocked in her prey by wedging into the open end of the aisle of pretty hats. Sphinx-like in her quiet composure, Minnie wore a broad-brimmed one, her name stitched on the crown.

Push-up breasts a-wobble, the American diva gushed over Minnie's hats in a thick Dallas drawl, a black grosgrain headband outlining her makeup, which was melting in the sun. She and her shipmates, piling up straw goods of every sort, could hardly wait to unload their cash, happily ignorant of Bahamian bargaining customs.

A bored-looking man named Bert from Dubuque, flushed with sun and liquor, struck up a conversation with Stewart and me. The top of his shiny warm-up suit was zipped only partway up, revealing his morning's conquest. The solid gold anchor hanging from the chain around his neck was worthy of any pirate's chest.

Just as the tourists began to settle into their island pastimes, the ships' horns began to bleat their roundup calls. Hordes of people trudged slowly over giant gangplanks to exhaust themselves at shuffle-board, groaning boards and gaming boards, retiring with distended stomachs as the ships cast off for the next scheduled port-of-call and another island's shops and eateries.

As we motored back to our quiet vessel, Stewart and I knew how lucky we were to have no itinerary at all, to be responsible to no one's schedule, and to settle for no one else's adventures but our own.

Just over the bridge near the marina, a number of locals were selling seafood from tiny shacks. They wore a variety of original headgear. The best was a small white towel, plastered tightly to the skull, which was secured with a bungee cord above the salesman's ears. He looked like a sheik on the Sahara as the terrycloth ballooned out over his shoulders in the breeze.

"Hey mon, try some Basil conch salad. I t'ink you like it." Basil was chopping tomatoes, onions, green peppers and conch faster than my eyes could follow. Drenchings of sour orange and lime juices, along with a bit of fiery bird pepper, completed the preparations. I wandered down the dock.

"Great," my ever-game husband said. "I had some down in the Turks and Caicos a few years back and it was wonderful."

"You ain't had none since DEN? Oh mon. You really need a special serve-up. I fix you somet'ing put glide in your stride, lead in your pencil."

Stewart and the conch salad chef were laughing conspiratorially a few booths away, drawing me back toward where they stood with two plastic cups of the delicacy, one for Stewart and one for me. Basil was adding a final touch to one cup—a small item that looked like a piece of gristle.

"Das for YOU mon. Sumt'ing special. You be a new bran' person now." Chuckle. Wink.

"What about Libby?"

"OH NO MON. NOT FOR HUH! You do all de work. She jus' LAY DERE," he said in a going-deaf voice.

We received our first, but far from our last, lesson about the Bahamians' belief in the aphrodisiac power of this native gastropod. I doubted if Bert-from-Dubuque would eat a piece of eroticizing conch gristle on *his* trip.

As Stewart shot craps that night in the casino, I savored peerless people-watching opportunities. A strikingly gorgeous woman, even at her towering height, was rubbing her hand in the crotch of an obese man who sat on a stool playing $100 blackjack. When the waitress happened by, the woman ordered drinks in a deep voice, and I realized he was a transvestite out to earn his evening's wages. A nonchalant Asian man lost thousands of dollars at a roulette table that had been cleared especially for him. Another cruise ship crowd pushed their sleeves up to show off a plastic bracelet printed with the name of their boat, a dog tag in case they got snockered or snookered between the Tiki Bar and the slot machines.

A woman was sitting on a couch in the lobby, smoking a cigarette while she nursed a baby. Her friend painted two-inch nails bright red on the young mother's uninvolved hand. Paper umbrellas and cherry stems were all that was left in the glasses set before them.

While my husband lost his last three chips, I chatted with a woman who said she was a native of Nassau. When I asked why she wasn't playing a game of chance, she said it was against the law for Bahamians to gamble inside their country. Although I was a proponent of my government staying away from individual rights, after a few hours at the Coral Casino, I could see the wisdom of such an edict.

CHAPTER 7: On the Hook (3)

Not a good week here in Fort Lauderdale. First, Ellie wrecked her Jeep in the snow in Chicago—thank God she wasn't hurt. I guess people from Virginia aren't too good driving in those conditions. Stewart told her he wants her to deal with the insurance company and repair shop herself and to call him if she has questions. That seems a little heavy for someone 18, but I guess she needs to learn to be independent with us going so far away.

Then Stew's school called to say he broke his wrist in wrestling practice and needs to spend the night in the hospital. He'll be back in class before I can fly from Fort Lauderdale to Hartford, rent a car and get out to a remote corner of Connecticut. I guess it'll be a good trial run to see how he handles it on his own, because soon Stewart and I will be cruising farther and farther away. He'll be off at college next year, and he's already been in boarding school for two years and spent a summer working in Mexico in between. Being away from us never seemed to bother him then, and he sounded fine a while ago when I talked to him on the phone.

I hope Stewart and I aren't overplaying the importance of independence for 17- and 18-year-olds. But it won't be long before we see them. I've already blocked off the dates for their spring Parents' Weekends; we'll fly up for those no matter where we might be on the boat. And they're coming to spend spring break with us too. We're only leaving for a year, after all.

CHAPTER 8: Umbilical Cord

C rossroads moved smoothly out of Nassau Harbor in the late morning with *Roundabout* bobbing along at the stern. Heading to the Exuma Cays, we planned to spend the next few months cruising in that area. Recently I had read a poem by Bliss Carman that generated vibrant memories about the water there.

> *Look out your door*
> *and tell me now*
> *the color of the sea.*
> *Where can I buy*
> *that wondrous dye and*
> *take it home with me?*

As if it couldn't bear to exert itself in the day's heat, the sea had hardly a ripple. On that calm water, *Crossroads* maneuvered cautiously among inter-island supply vessels, the lifelines for outlying cays. Gaudy day-tripper boats and dive vessels loaded with gear cut in and out of our path like souped-up cars on highway 95. Just before Rose Island, the party boat *Cap'n Twilly* passed us in the opposite direction with reggae music blaring. A bare-chested girl danced inside a circle of tourists while the M.C. encouraged her antics. Some of the guests on the Early Bird Booze Cruise yelled over to us, "Need some crew?" and "I do bathrooms."

Later during our time in the Bahamas, we met some of the long-standing local residents who showed us lovely restaurants, took us to their clubs and introduced us to their families and friends. Stewart and I were glad to find that other side of Nassau, although its bawdy surface didn't seem to bother the easy-going, accepting citizens of this country. They were champions of an oft-repeated phrase: "What is, is." I understood the advantages of such a philosophy in the islands, but my entrepreneurial soul snickered silently when I heard that expression. I tucked away a secret belief that I would never belly up to that attitude.

On the 40-mile trip to the Exumas, I sat on the flybridge again and allowed my mind to reel out some conflicting feelings. I realized Ellie and Stew weren't kids any longer, but no other parents I knew were doing anything like this with a child still in high school. Stewart and I had placed them on the edge once before by risking what we did to build This End Up. Was I just allowing status quo to unsettle me again? Or had personal desire gotten the best of my judgment? Leaving my children in the United States was not something I could take lightly. My mind wandered back to the earlier trips Stewart and I had taken to the Bahamas.

Centered in the chain of islands known as the Bahamas, the Exuma string rises from the Caribbean Sea about 200 miles from the U.S. mainland. We had enjoyed it on week-long jaunts from the early 1970s to the early 1980s. Memories of those trips were vivid with contrasts: fresh fish fried almost inedible in local restaurants, laid-back spots where frenzied mosquitoes gorged themselves, small quaint locales overrun by hordes of loudmouth tourists, water and electricity and phones that ran out, gave out and cut out. But the most dazzling recollection of all was the color and feel of the turquoise sea that surrounded Stewart and me as we island-hopped across the scattered pearls of the Exumas. I knew our love of all things tropical had sprung from visiting the cays that dot that glorious part of the Bahamas.

But a week-long trip and a yearlong trip were two different things. Was this snip of the umbilical cord too soon and too final? Stewart and I were placing ourselves way out of easy reach. Great adventures might liberate me but would they frighten my children? I didn't want them to foot the bill for my pleasure.

When we approached Highborne Cay at the northern end of the 140-mile-long Exuma chain, Gregg dropped anchor in the lee of the island for our first sleep riding the hook. A veiled light from the stars shone down on us as darkness gathered and the sky filled with dipping constellations. Bedding down to the cradling swells of the tide change, Stewart and I fell into the sleep of the oblivious, and the unindoctrinated.

In the morning, we swam along a stretch of the island's western shoreline and then dinghied out for a long snorkel at Octopus Garden. Hand-size, luminescent red starfish littered the bottom under the shallow sea; a majestic spotted eagle ray, wider than it was long, fluttered by me with no regard; in the distance, a large school of drum swam just above the floor of the Bahama Bank. The divisive undercurrents of the world on top of this aquarium were nowhere to be found in the peaceful kingdom below. When we got back to the boat, I started my lessons on marine life with a book that eventually wore out, giving up the particulars of the magnificent fish of the Bahamas.

Our first month, we drank in every detail. Stewart's way of easing into experiences was a good governor on my preference for plumbing the depths of each new happening. My skin got tough as a turtle shell and the part in my hair glowed red where the sun fried me every day. The vastness of the sea, furrowed with currents, had a grandeur that landlubbers could never dream of. I tried in vain to capture its majesty on roll after roll of film to show to our friends back home. I dared Stewart to name a place where the sea could be more sparkling or crystal clear. Not a chance. Drizzling the water's surface with grape, peach and raspberry colors, sunsets turned it into a solid sheet of liquid gold, day after day. Even my low-key husband gushed superlatives.

CHAPTER 9: Yes, We Have No Bananas Today

Many evenings, just as the sun completed its job for the day, the haunting sound of a conch being blown from one boat or another echoed over an anchorage. The tradition was somewhat like the end-of-work whistle at a factory, only far more alluring. The smell of a grill being fired on the boat's deck, the sight of fish being prepped for supper, the taste of a sundowner and the feel of aloe on sunburn—then, the first star in the night sky.

Occasionally, the moon shined so bright I could have read a book by it. The darkness melted away and the light silvered everything on shore. On nights when the moon flickered in and out through gaps in the moving clouds, lambent light caused the peaks of the wavelets to glitter. Amazing, we thought, to know that this orb in our little piece of the sky was enchanting half the world.

If there was no moon, we sat on the flybridge as Gregg pointed out every constellation in the star book. "Watermark," the haunting ballad by the Irish folk singer Enya, played on the stereo as we sat speechless in admiration of the boundless stars in the Milky Way. Its path looked like a piece of black velvet on which a saltshaker had turned over, marking a luminescent trail across the heavens. On those occasions, my life in Richmond seemed far away and my anxieties small in the magnitude of God's work.

At dawn, the windows of *Crossroads* blazed as red as rubies when the sun seeped into the blue-black sky. Faint early-morning light shined through our open portholes while the boat swung to and fro on its anchor chain, and the rosy glow lulled me back to sleep for a few more minutes before I got up to see the spectacular final rays of the sunrise.

For the most part, my thoughts were calmer at sea, free from the responsibility of work and the pressure of leadership. Yet I was discovering that years of such intense work were not possible to push aside like a bite of too-rich dessert. The elimination of stimulating problems made me uneasy. I felt I should be contributing to something bigger than myself; I was concerned that I had become a parasite.

My motor still ran faster than nature's machinery. Even with all the beautiful options at my disposal, some mornings I awoke with my heart pounding because I didn't know what my day would bring. Shouldn't there be a goal, not just the random unfolding of the next 12 hours? Although many boaters thought true freedom came when one stopped heeding time, I put on my watch first thing every morning so I could be efficient in whatever activities presented themselves. Six weeks into our trip, I wondered if I would be able to stay on *Crossroads* for a year with such a long way to go to adjust to my radically-altered circumstances.

When Gregg cut the engines after a long day running the riprap angles of the Exuma chain, silence was almost spooky. In a protected harbor called Big Major Spot, we dropped anchor in hopes of restocking the pantry at a nearby island called Staniel Cay. As we swiveled our heads in reconnaissance that afternoon, Stewart and I never guessed how familiar we would become with the area.

Two months had passed since we left the United States, and we were learning not to expect things to occur on an American time frame, trying to adjust to the fact that that would be light speed in the islands. I came to expect the grocery store to be devoid of fresh grapes, pears and cantaloupes. If milk was there, I learned to count on it being past its due date. Once the shock of an inverted law of supply and demand wore off, I mostly went to the market to hear the local gossip. Should a perfect avocado be for sale, it was like finding the golden Easter egg. You weren't surprised when you didn't get one, but you were thrilled when you did.

Having to tamp down my fervor for immediate gratification, I learned that the difficult procurement of provisions was one of the things that warded off the development that might otherwise spoil the natural beauty of these out-islands. With that realization, I came to know the goodness of mango, soursop and breadfruit and to realize that box milk was just fine.

Our American habit of taking plenitude for granted blew away in the wind of the Bahamian out-islands and was replaced by an increased sense of indebtedness to our native land. Simultaneously, I began to understand how spoiled I had been in the days when I thought I deserved what I wanted when I wanted it. In an attitudinal U-turn, I began to lose patience with people like the old me who spoke as if the American way was the only way. Every person should live in a foreign culture once in his life.

A storm marched in to pay a call one night. Our weather fax hadn't mentioned one word about it. The day had been a long one and Gregg, Stewart and I were bushed. Rough water had made for poor fishing, and we were scraping the bottom of the larder. On Staniel Cay, I found a withered green pepper, sweet potatoes, mac and cheese, pigeon peas, black bananas and rum raisin ice cream. And that was the combined largesse of the Tip Top Grocery Store and Shanda's Supermarket.

In addition, we had been plagued all day with small breakdowns. Stereo parts had come loose and washing machine parts wouldn't turn. Two natural enemies, saltwater and moving components, kept Gregg hopping all day in an effort to make peace. He headed to bed early after checking the anchor's scope.

Stewart was securing things on deck when the first thunder echoed off the water like cherry bombs exploding in a tin can. Gregg appeared just as the anchor chain gave a mighty jerk in the squally wind, and we pulled free of the sandy soil of our crowded anchorage. *Crossroads* slid untethered into the inky darkness toward our much smaller sleeping neighbor. The first of a number of uneasy nights to come troubled our sleep until almost dawn.

CHAPTER 10: Cruising Tingums

Soon after our close encounter in the harbor, Ellie and Stew arrived for a short summer vacation on the boat. We discovered some wonderful spots to explore on reefs, in caves and at island bars. Bars were big on their 18- and 19-year-old agendas. Stewart and I were comfortable using nautical charts by now, so the four of us would launch off in *Roundabout* for a full day of adventure right after breakfast, returning just at sundown. *(Photo 2.4)*

To the south of our anchorage, scuttling iguanas and ospreys diving for fish shared quarters on a frangipani-scented island. We discovered a snorkeling place at a tiny cay to the north where the coral arched and braided to form spirals and cups, columns and fans like we had never seen before. A big stand of fire coral reached out for us as we swam by, but we knew its sting could land us in the hospital from barely a touch—that is, had there been any hospitals.

The water wherever we floated was clear to 30 feet. One sand spit gave up more sand dollars than I found in all my summers on North Carolina's beaches. While we drifted in an inlet, 5-foot, 3-inch Ellie widened her eyes as a barracuda, almost as big as she was, maneuvered alongside her with its outthrust lower jaw and razor teeth.

In the cave of a giant sea-hollowed boulder, we swam around and looked up to the sky as the clouds winked in and out of view across the jagged opening of its ceiling. The shallows nearby offered conch for a snack, once Stewart figured how to remove the animal from its home. A squeeze of lime, and we ate it under casuarina trees bearing a half-rotted hammock full of old dreams.

On a tiny cay, we came across an old, rundown bar with a sand floor. The sign on the lunch table said the choices were cheeseburgers, grouper fingers or conch bits. The kids wanted frozen daiquiris, and I thought I'd try to derail midday liquor for teenagers until they were back on *Crossroads* at cocktail time where we had more control over the proportion of rum to mixer.

"Vut you guh have?" asked the waitress, sporting one pink sponge hair curler just above her eyebrows.

"These two want daiquiris, but I was wondering what the drinking age is in the Bahamas," I said with a conspiratorial twitch of my eyelid.

"Drinkin' age?" The confused waitress looked at Ellie and Stew, then at me, then back at them.

With a snap of her cornrowed head, she said, "Honey, if dey can walk, dey can drink. Strawberry or banana?"

"One of each," said the newly minted adults.

Stewart, Ellie and Stew ordered cheeseburgers but I thought I'd try the grouper fingers.

"Dis ain' de day for grouper."

"Then I'll have conch."

"Dis ain' conch day neither."

"What do you mean?" I asked.

"Dis *cheeseburger* day. Grouper and conch, dey later. It say right here on dis card, 'Cheeseburger, Grouper OR Conch.' Today is cheese-burger."

"Well, then, I'll have a cheeseburger."

The bartender, who answered the phone on the wall, yelled out to our waitress, "Get Tingum and tell her dat Tingum on de phone for her."

Stewart and I were fond of the Bahamian word *tingum*. A handy term that meant "whatchamacallit," it could refer to things or people and we had adopted it into our everyday vocabulary.

In a few seconds, out from the kitchen came Tingum #1 who picked up the receiver and carried on a short conversation with Tingum #2. Like magic, our waitress knew exactly whom the first and second Tingum referred to.

We thanked our waitress for the tingums we'd eaten, paid at the bar and returned to *Crossroads* for our last night at anchor before heading back north.

We cruised up to Nassau where Ellie and Stew left us, Ellie to work at Wrightsville Beach until her classes started in the fall, and Stew to live with a family in the Dominican Republic, building latrines for their tiny village.

CHAPTER 11: On the Hook (4)

After a great dinner tonight at Charley's Crab on the Intracoastal Waterway here in Fort Lauderdale, Stewart called his friend Jake, with whom he'd grown up in Pennsylvania. He asked Jake if he and Helen would like to be our first guests aboard Crossroads once we got to the Exuma Cays. It's a long way for them to travel, and he wasn't sure they would think it was worth flying down for a week on the boat, but they accepted right away. We told them we'd let them know once the date firmed up.

Both of them had lots of questions and I probably gave them too many details. But I feel like they'll have a good idea of how things work on a boat before they arrive. That's a point in favor of full disclosure—no surprises.

CHAPTER 12: Jake and Helen

Once we put the kids on the plane in Nassau, we made a pro-visioning trip to prepare for friends' arrival in one week. The trip had been scheduled for months. Our guests would land at the Staniel Cay airstrip, which had broken plastic chairs in an open-air hut serving as the airport terminal. No phone. No water. No porter. No taxi. Tropical bathrooms were available though: ladies in the bushes to the north, and gents in the bushes to the south.

Stewart's childhood buddy, Jake, said in the last phone conversation, "Don't worry if you're not right there when we land. We'll be fine wait-ing in the air conditioning at the terminal." *(Photo 2.5)*

It sounded like our friends had a perfectly laid-back island under-standing about time, if not conveniences.

"Oh, we'll be there. But it's a hike to the dinghy so pack light and in duffel bags. Can't wait to see you."

We took a shopping excursion by taxi to Nassau's largest grocery store to stock up for Jake and Helen's visit. Stewart and I had no idea it would be the most expensive goods we had ever come across in a market of such low quality and meager choice. Just as I was checking out with the food, Stewart arrived with his load of wine and beer. By the time we had paid the driver to take us to town, wait, return us to the dock and help carry the boxes to the boat, the trip cost more than $1,100.

And us with no paycheck.

We had seven days to play in the northern half of the Exumas during our run between Nassau and Staniel Cay, where we would pick up our friends. Sights and sounds of the labyrinth of small islands were heavenly for the first three days. Then, the smell of weather coming.

Waking on choppy water the fourth morning just off Warderick Wells, we knew from the swollen gray clouds and plunging barometer that we faced a couple of bad days on a rolling boat. *Crossroads'* water-making machine, which converted saltwater to the fresh water we used for drinking, cooking, laundry, bathing and flushing, heaved a sigh and shut down. Gregg disappeared into the boat's rocking bowels to see what was what.

Time for an early lunch. When I opened the pantry, a can of tuna bounced off a pitching shelf and slammed edge first into my shin. Another bruise bloomed on my battered body, still unused to working in such tight quarters. Just as my temper settled, a small rat ran out of the still-open cabinet and disappeared under the dining table.

When Gregg surfaced for a tool, I told him about the rat.

"Oh yes. Sometimes they crawl off a dock, up the lines and through the hawse pipe onto the boat decks. We'll get a trap at Staniel," he said to me as nightmares of rodents skittering while I slept crept up my spine.

A continuing series of bothersome boat snafus wore down my mood even more over the next few days. As the boat moved into the harbor at Big Major, though, four hours before the excitement of our first company, I wanted to be of good cheer for this long-awaited visit. But the usually gentle, prevailing southeast wind blew 17 mph from the southwest, and *Crossroads* kept time with a discordant tune.

You never knew what the next boat entering a harbor would bring to the community. Part of the interest in cruising was the daily changeover of your neighborhood. Variety might include a 160-foot boat with a movie star and uniformed crew of 10. Maybe a 70-year-old single-hander with a patch over one eye, just in from a transatlantic crossing in a 38-foot wooden sloop. Or perhaps a young lawyer-couple disillusioned with such hardball careers, bareboating a ketch named *Sweet Freedom* through the Caribbean with their three-year-old son and a black Lab.

Hooker had a personality all her own but one we'd rather have avoided. Not slowing a bit in recognition of our presence, the 45-foot sport fishing boat passed within spitting distance of our stern. *Hooker's* wake would have rocked a cruise ship, and *Crossroads* erupted into motion. Onions and oranges flew out of the basket on the counter and bounced down the steps to the lower level. The small TV fell out of its cabinet and landed on the chair below. Books thrashed to and fro in their case, and Gregg's navigation charts took wing. After a run around the large and mostly deserted harbor, *Hooker* decided the only place for her was next to us.

"JEREMIAH WAS A BULLFROG...."

Music from *The Big Chill* blasted from outdoor speakers at a volume loud enough to be heard by a passing airplane. The fishermen screamed at each other over the music as the liquor came out and the guts of the fish they cleaned floated under our boat. A bit of the cleavage on one angler's backside stood exposed, lily-white, to the noon sun as he urinated off *Hooker's* swim platform.

I turned away to focus on the cruise with Jake and Helen while I got a jump-start on dinner. Within a few minutes, the last of the potato peelings was securely in the disposal. Switch. The god-awful noise sounded like a hippopotamus belching when the gadget hurled its half-eaten contents onto the low ceiling over the sink. I felt the hot flush of hostess duties around my neck.

At Bar 'n Bites, a watering hole on its own tiny coral rock a half-mile from the runway, we waited for the island hopper bringing Jake and Helen. Wish Air was running an hour late, not far from its norm on the once-a-week flight. I thought back to the delayed arrival of that same plane when the children had come two weeks earlier. The pilot had said he was late that day because, as he was taxiing to the terminal to pick them up in Nassau, he realized that that moment would be his only chance to vote the whole day. So he pulled the plane over to the side of the runway, jumped the fence and took a taxi into town to discharge his civic duty. Today's explanation might be just as colorful.

The old salt next to me confided that Bar 'n Bites was where Jimmy Buffett wrote "Cheeseburger in Paradise." Slide, the bartender, rolled his eyes, served up hot conch fritters and pushed another Kalik, the Bahamian beer, across to Stewart while we waited for our company.

Two and a quarter hours after the plane's scheduled arrival time, we were on the way to *Crossroads* with our excited friends and their two bags, big enough for a month's travel in Europe. They asked where the control tower was, and I asked why Wish Air was so late.

"Well, we flew over Staniel Cay more than an hour ago heading south, but the pilot said he had to get some government official down to Farmer's Cay before he could drop us off," said Helen. "Then after we started back this way, he landed at another island where a kid ran out on the runway to give him two lobsters. Jake passed them up to the empty co-pilot's seat and then we took off and came here to Stanley Kay."

Unloading our city friends onto *Crossroads*, we secured their monstrous hardback suitcases on top of the workbench in the engine room and sat down to Gregg's Crossroads Coladas. Helen presented us with gifts — monogrammed linen hand towels for the boat and a beer-making kit for Stewart. It was very sweet of her.

As we headed off toward George Town, Helen asked if there was a place she could buy vitamins on the trip — she'd forgotten to bring hers.

No big deal if not, because she knew George Town was the capital of the Exumas, she said, and she'd just get them at the health food store there. Uh-oh.

Stewart figured on three days of island hopping on the 60-mile trip down to George Town and then two days spent there. *Crossroads* needed to cover a lot of water and we would have to hustle. Six days from now, Jake and Helen had to be on a flight back to the States.

The wind had ratcheted down to 13 mph, so Gregg guided the boat out into Exuma Sound. Within 45 minutes Jake was throwing up in a plastic trashcan on the stern cockpit, and we had to pull into an anchorage only a few miles from where we took off. After lunch he felt better so we puttered around in the dinghy.

"I thought tropical islands were covered with hills and palm trees," Helen said. Stewart's jaw muscle jumped.

She and I each made a dish for supper, and Helen wondered if I had any low-fat, instead of whole, sour cream for her recipe. Of course, I was lucky to have sour cream at all. When she asked for Hellmann's mayonnaise because she'd never liked Duke's, I gritted my teeth. The guys grilled fish and we all went to bed early.

We woke up to a light sprinkle and while I made coffee, I heard Helen and Gregg whispering in the forward hallway. I asked Gregg privately what that was about.

"Well, we had a little toilet-flushing problem last night, but it's all fixed now."

After a calm run of 30 miles, the rain was pouring from a windless sky, and we pulled into a spectacular harbor about three o'clock. Stewart tried to engage Jake in backgammon, but he didn't know how to play. Bridge was a no-no because neither of our guests knew that either. I wanted to lie on my bed and read a book.

"What do you two like? Hearts? Poker? Chess? We have dice too," tried Stewart.

Jake said, "You know, my family never played games when I was little."

The rest of the trip was calm and rain-free, and except for our guests asking, "What are we doing next?" the minute an activity was over, we had a pleasant time. But never again did Stewart and I invite anybody to stay on *Crossroads* for seven days.

CHAPTER 13: On the Hook (5)

There aren't too many things I'll miss whenever we finally leave here, but this town's restaurants are one of them. I'm sure there will be charming little island places in Nassau and George Town, but having eaten out almost full-time for the months we've been living in a hotel has spoiled me because I hate to cook. One thing I can count on in the Bahamas, I know, will be fresh fish and lobster. M-m-m.

Speaking of food, I know I'll have to make some changes. They won't have the brands I'm used to in grocery stores in the States. Even in Miami and Fort Lauderdale, I can't find Mrs. Fearnow's Brunswick Stew, so I probably won't find Honeycup mustard and Charmin toilet paper when we get into the small cays. That's OK. Part of the adventure.

I wonder where I can get my hair cut in the out-islands. And where to take my dry cleaning. It won't matter much. It's really only my silk shirts, and I won't be wearing them except when we're invited to go on other yachts for cocktails or dinner.

CHAPTER 14: Folkways

Stewart and I wandered the lunchtime streets of George Town munching grouper fingers and familiarizing ourselves with the place we expected to be our home base for the next four or five months. Strolling into a teeming open-air food market, we made a friend of the owner, Mercy. She offered a sample cup of conch salad to Stewart. He ordered a quart of it to pick up later in the day. The gold-toothed proprietress cocked her turbaned head and favored him with a knowing look through sensational false eyelashes.

Upon our return, the little stand was still bustling. Darting eyes and whispered conversations had the air reeking of arrangements other than homemade food. We sidled up to collect our conch salad.

"Miz Brown been fix?" boomed out Mercy in the crowded lean-to as she handed over Stewart's conch.

"Been *what?*" he asked.

"FIX. FIX. You know, her parts?"

"No. Why?" asked Stewart, disclosing my medical information without shame to half of George Town.

"Well, you gern get mo' babies shonuff, you eat all dat conch."

On the way back to the dock, Stewart and I noticed a "Prevent AIDS" campaign in the Exumas' capital city. Official signs appeared everywhere, explaining how to avoid this scourge. No one stopped to read them.

Just outside the liquor store, though, on a post by the front door, was a pointed message with visual assistance. A group of giggling teenagers was looking at it. Two stick figures held hands: a boy, conspicuous because of a slash between his legs vertical about 120 degrees, and a girl, discernable by a bow on her head. A savvy marketer of condoms had distributed this one-line, heart-shaped poster—"Got a STIFFY? Use a JIFFY."

One day, Stewart lined up a local bonefishing guide named Cecil. I struck up a conversation with him while Stewart gathered his equipment, having spent $200 and half a day so he could release four small fish back to their habitat, thereby securing nothing for dinner. *(Photo 2.6)*

"Cecil, are you married yet?"

"Yes, um. I got five chirren."

"Really? Boys or girls?"

Cecil gave me the lineup. "Two inside boy and one outside boy and t'ree outside girl."

Huh? Wasn't that six? What did that mean, "inside" and "outside?"

Uneasy about addressing unfamiliar terminology since I was just learning the Bahamian culture, I switched gears to focus on George, Cecil's twin brother whom we'd met earlier.

"George told me he was looking for a girlfriend. Has he ever dated Joyce, that cute waitress from the dining room at the Frangipani Hotel?"

"Oh, no. She too stringy for him."

"I thought she was cute yesterday when she helped us at lunch."

With uncharacteristic verbosity, Cecil spilled the details. "No. George, he like women wit' a little sumt'ing in de back. Not dose big asses, but enough to grab aholt to. And, you know, a good size in de front too," said Cecil with demonstrative hand motions for my complete understanding.

I was speechless and Stewart had difficulty containing his laughter. Cecil sensed that he might have offended me.

"Well, really, George and me like women wit' some meat on 'em. Kind of fluffy. You know, Miz Brown, jus' like you."

A couple of nights later, Stewart and I decided to take Gregg off the boat for a little R&R. Rumor had it that Harborside was a fun place for dinner so we tried it. For no apparent reason, we were seated 25 minutes later than our reservation. Appointment and reservation times in the Bahamas were quite fluid.

We ordered cocktails from Della: a glass of wine and two Kaliks. The three of us watched four serving people laugh, flirt and ignore the guests. After 10 minutes, the beer arrived but it was room temperature, so Della put one cube of ice each in Stewart's and Gregg's glasses to solve the problem.

"Refrigerator broke," came the typically brief Bahamian answer to our inquiry about the beer's temperature.

"Hope they get it fixed soon," said Stewart.

"Me too. It two day already. Vut you gern eat?"

"Grouper would be great if it's fresh," said Gregg.

"Outta grouper."

"How about lamb chops?"

"Dey ruint in de freezer."

The two men finally settled on ribs. I ordered chowder and a Caesar salad and hoped that Stewart and Gregg wouldn't get trichinosis.

The ribs were cooked to leather, the men got applesauce instead of French fries, and Della could only be found for help if Gregg pushed through the swinging door to the kitchen, where she was dancing with Frank the salad chef. And the loud music over the speakers was *not* Jimmy Buffett.

The bill came to $70 with a 15 percent tip automatically added on top and another five percent if we used a credit card. Bringing up the subject of a deduction for the glass of wine I never received seemed more trouble than it was worth.

We motored at a snail's pace in *Roundabout* as silver blobs of bioluminescent plankton radiated in the water. The full moon laid down a wide stream of light that led us right to slowly swinging *Crossroads*, which was anchored close to shore. Gregg went in to finish his book.

Ignoring marine night dangers, Stewart and I shucked our clothes and floated unfettered off the stern in the warm water. As small waves slid against the beach, we could hear the sound, like a cat lapping milk, and in the perfect saturation of moonlight we could see their foaming tops deposit a white lace mustache where the water met the sand. The scent of the sea that night was of salt, but also of chance and of adventure.

For another couple of weeks we poked our noses into George Town's corners. I wandered into Sheena's Threads. "Finest Clothes for Ladies in All the Bahamas," it said on one sign, and "Downward Payment Accepted" on another. A rack of sundresses stood in the middle of the floor. Soft blue and green ones, lavender and rose ones, all made from the dreamy Androsia fabric produced on neighboring Andros Island. A grape-colored cover-up with soft green fish was irresistible. Next door was Cashmere and Axcel's Unisex Hair Salon. I was invited to "Take a Walk on the Wild Side" but didn't have time. Also, I feared my regular hairdresser would throttle me if I went savage.

CHAPTER 15: Almost Heaven

A few days later, Stewart and I packed a picnic supper and motored out to Mariah Cay. If we had ever wondered why islands utterly seduced us, this one gave all the answers. We were alone in Eden.

Stewart worked on his casting in a wide ribbon of water that wound into the island from the north side of the cay. When I wasn't tucking away astonishing shells, I read books from the Sailor's Exchange and had time to look up unrecognizable words in a little dictionary, heaven for a bibliophile who had been too busy for years to indulge in such leisurely pleasure. We snoozed and walked and talked and snoozed again on the perfect angle of the shoreline, and I was lulled to near inertia by the hypnotic sinking sun.

When we were hungry, we squeezed lime over fat lobster chunks and discarded civility to savor the juice of an Eleuthera pineapple and let it run past our chins and down our necks. We washed the sweet nectar off in the silky, turquoise sea—hedonists for the day.

Later, Venus sat like a diamond hanging below a gold moon pendant as the two of us puttered the six miles back to *Crossroads* on flat water, iced bronze on top. I thought about my choice to go instead of stop at this second intersection of my life. What continued to galvanize me was having creative control over the design of the road and not having to follow someone else's rules about how to drive on it.

Snorkeling became an everyday event. I learned to be comfortable with evil-eyed barracudas that hung in the fringe of my sight, just below the surface. Occasionally, I saw a shark with a knife-like dorsal fin and black beady eyes that swam by without apparent interest, and my grateful heart slowed to a dull thud. But it was the antics of the smaller tropical fish inhabiting the reefs that lured me into the silent world of marine animals.

Tiny iridescent blue chromis flitted together like a pack of Tinkerbells when I entered the water, and turned with a precision flap of 30 little tails to regroup at a safe distance from me. Their lozenge-shaped bodies glowed as if they had stuck their wet snouts into an electrical outlet, and they darted around with a flash from their mosaic scales.

A shy yellow, green and blue queen angelfish shimmered like colored chain mail as she moved her foot-wide, spade-shaped body in and out of coral passages on the sea floor. Apropos of her name, she was marked with a black spot encircled by a brilliant blue ring on the top of her head, giving the appearance of a royal crown.

Girdled with a dark centerline, a cigar-shaped bluehead wrasse heckled a pair of butterflyfish that sported Lone Ranger masks across their eyes.

A triggerfish turned sideways when it swam near me to show off blue lipstick that must have come from a theatrical makeup box.

Some aquatic signal beckoned a jailhouse-striped sergeant major to a jagged coral head where an orange squirrelfish with enormous black eyes seemed to be hiding from underworld bullies.

A Nassau grouper, the color of a frothy cappuccino, cruised within three feet of me, and I felt like a clumsy interloper in an other-worldly place of grace beyond my ken.

With our minds and hearts initially sated by the beauty of the Bahamas, we began to feel the pull of home. When Gregg, Stewart and I took Big Al's Taxi to the George Town airport, I knew our captain was anxious about leaving the boat. Stewart's preoccupied manner told me he was anxious about something too, but the Bahamas would see snow before that worry had a voice. My eyes were bright with the thought of my children, and only having them in my arms could fill the emptiness that I felt after three and a half long months away from Ellie and Stew.

CHAPTER 16: Two Sides of Risk

Once most of hurricane season was over, Stewart and I decided it was time to venture farther afield. A trip down-island sounded perfect for the holidays. We could be in the Virgin Islands by early December to celebrate our first Christmas on the boat with Ellie and Stew.

Crossroads set out for an intermediate stop in the Turks and Caicos on a mid-November day. She was filled with fuel and supplies for the 240-mile trip from George Town, Exuma, to Providenciales, the largest island of the T&Cs. The trip would be our first substantial bluewater passage, and Gregg estimated it would take 26 hours dock-to-dock, and 54 hours more to St. Thomas, U.S. Virgin Islands. The weather fax issued a report with nothing but good things to say about what we could expect over the next few days. We had been boating for seven months though, and I had witnessed the tendency of that weather fax to prevaricate on several occasions.

Gregg prepared us for operating overnight in three-hour shifts with a caution about the captains of large oceangoing vessels snoozing at the wheel, deaf to the VHF, and secure in their belief that the Big Boat Rule would keep them safe. We were not to pass too close to the stern of these behemoths since they sometimes towed unlit boats on cables as long as 300 feet. The last frightening tip was a comment about how many containers fell off freight boats and floated barely submerged, waiting to rip the guts out of poor *Crossroads*. Thank God I was returning to Richmond before the boat left on the long stretch to the Virgin Islands.

Uneasy the whole trip into Providenciales, I hardly slept at all. My preference not to make the long delivery voyages turned into a rule on that run to the Turks and Caicos. From then on, my plan was to meet Gregg and Stewart, or Gregg and the hired crew, wherever and whenever they arrived safely. I was never able to overcome my fear of bluewater cruising. Even though our maiden open-ocean voyage on *Crossroads* was capably handled and moderately comfortable, I knew it was impossible to be completely sheltered from the dangers of water and weather.

But it didn't occur to me then that terrifying moments on boats happen on short hops, in calm water or even while tied to a dock. Safety wasn't only a matter of crew skill, boat condition or trip preparation. Safety required luck.

Before Stewart, Gregg and a crewmember hired for the passage left the Turks and Caicos, they heard from another captain at the dock. He wanted to follow the better-equipped *Crossroads* on the journey in his smaller Hatteras motor yacht, *Sea Ducer*. His vessel's autopilot had failed, and Captain Chuck was going to hand steer the boat throughout the trip.

The weather turned dire underway. The bow of our big Hatteras, tunneling through the underside of the ocean's surface, caused seawater to stream through the interior recessed lights of the forward half of the boat. Gregg unstrapped the life raft and removed it from its case in preparation for the disaster that threatened but never came to pass for *Crossroads*. *(Photo 2.7)*

But Captain Chuck, his mate and *Sea Ducer* were lost in the 16-foot waves of the violent storm. Stewart was shaken to the core when I finally received his "safely here" phone call from St. Thomas, and I was nauseated for hours at the thought of how close my captain, crew and husband came to their own watery graves. How close we came to paying risk's ultimate price.

My first errand when I got home to Richmond, blithely tended to while my seafaring husband was praying for his life, was a simple trip to the grocery store. I felt like a Russian émigré, staring at the choices in the cereal aisle. Twenty times the island selection of Rice Krispies, Cocoa Puffs and Corn Flakes looked back at me. Bran cereal alone took up half a shelf. I'd forgotten how to choose among so many options.

An acquaintance rolled by in a short white skirt and visor with a country club monogram. She said she bet I was glad to be back in civilization. "What are you looking at?" she asked me.

"I was counting the number of cereal choices," I mumbled, still surprised at something I took for granted during my former sporadic homemaker duties.

"Oh. Well. OK. See you around."

I knew our decision to live full-time on a boat was unfathomable to many people. My behavior in front of the breakfast foods probably didn't do much to encourage my fellow shopper to consider a life outside of team tennis and the world's most bountiful and convenient food supply. Why would anyone give those things up?

At the hors d'oeuvres table during a Thanksgiving cocktail party, Stewart and I gobbled long-missed goodies as if we had been ship-wrecked for the 11 months we'd been away: shrimp, pâté, crab dip, Camembert, baby lamb chops. People seemed fascinated with our new life, mostly the fact that we loved it.

"*Re-a-lly?* You live on a *boat?* That's so interesting. How long do you want to do that?"

The two of us were delivered fresh drinks, and Stewart lifted the napkin that came with his glass so we could read its printed message.

"To be a Virginian, either by birth, marriage, adoption, or even on one's mother's side, is an introduction to any state in the Union, a passport to any foreign country, and a benediction from the Almighty God."

Oh, my.

The New York Times. A pound of Boar's Head turkey breast. A catalog order that arrives in two days. Grass in my yard. Mail in my box. Pressure in my shower. After two weeks of home's comfort, convenience and clarity of purpose, the siren song of wanderlust lured us once more.

CHAPTER 17: On the Hook (6)

The workmen at the boatyard are finished with Crossroads' *interior wiring, so we're beginning to work on buying the household and recreational equipment. I've finished choosing the fabrics for the furniture and the pieces are on order.*

Today we drove down to a dive shop in Miami that's supposed to have the best snorkel gear around. Gregg needs a mask that has his eyeglass prescription in it and Stewart wants extra long flippers for diving. We bought equipment for the children and a variety of sizes to outfit guests.

The sales person spent a lot of time assuring me that a really good snorkel set gives tremendous confidence to even a modest swimmer like me. I mean, I'm perfectly fine when it's calm, and I'm not scared of deep water, either. But we might be swimming for quite some distance from time to time, and I want to be ready.

CHAPTER 18: Double Jeopardy

On our trip to pick up *Crossroads* in St. Thomas, Stewart and I stopped in South Carolina to spend a day with a boating friend who had been a federal judge for years. Over lunch, Stewart asked Taylor if he carried a gun on his own boat when he cruised down the island chain where life was a bit less civilized.

"Absolutely. I keep it loaded and on my bedside table every night. And so should you," Taylor implored.

"I'm not sure I could shoot somebody point blank. Maybe at their feet or something but not right at them," Stewart said.

"Stewart, you buy a gun before you start traveling to all those deserted anchorages. Learn how to use it and shoot anybody who comes onto your boat at night right between the eyes. Dump the body overboard in deep water and never tell one soul about it. Otherwise you'll spend a long stretch in a hellhole of a prison."

After that shocker, we decided to get a gun for Gregg and one for us. If a federal judge thought it prudent, we would arm ourselves, but I could tell Stewart was uneasy with the decision. A few days later, we left for St. Thomas packing heat.

Two weeks later, Stewart and I were in one of St. Thomas' marinas on *Crossroads,* waiting for Gregg to return from a trip back to the States. Water was sloppy in the harbor, and wind sang through the rigging of nearby sailboats, causing their halyards to ding-ding against the masts. I was glad to be tied to the dock.

Earlier in the day, we had met the crew of *Nefertiti,* a 150-foot Feadship in the slip two spaces down from us. She belonged to a real estate developer who had just approved plans for a 280-foot yacht that would take three years to build. Since the owner was not on board that night, the captain asked Stewart and me to dinner and gave us a tour of the boat. She carried more equipment and toys in 10 square feet than *Crossroads* had in total, and Captain Brock had permission to use them.

The next morning, Stewart returned from a tour of the dock saying he thought something was wrong on *Nefertiti.* She had police guarding her and none of the usual crew activity. With several hours' downtime before our departure for the British Virgin Islands, we set out to see if we could help our new friends. When Jean-Claude, the chef, walked by, he whispered to meet him in the nearby supermarket.

"Just after midnight one of our camera alarms went off, meaning someone who shouldn't be was on *Nefertiti's* deck. When the captain went out, he took the pistol. A native was rifling through our lockers on the bow and he ran when Brock shouted at him. Brock told him again to stop or he'd shoot. The man kept running with a bag of our gear. When he wouldn't hold up, Brock yelled and fired the gun into the ground next to him. The thief lay down and we called the police."

"What happened?" Stewart and I asked.

"When the cops came, they found our goods in the man's possession, handcuffed him, escorted him through that gate over there and released him. We watched it all. An hour later they came back, arrested Brock, handcuffed him and took *him* to jail. He's still there. *Nefertiti's* owner is in Chicago and hasn't been able to get anybody to talk to him about letting Brock out. The police haven't charged him with anything because the gun is legal, registered properly, and the thief was caught in the act. But they won't let him go."

My mind turned to our new stainless steel, pump-action shotguns. Fear, which always stood at parade rest inside me, was on the march.

Stewart and I returned to our boat to await Gregg's imminent arrival. The VHF was chattering with island patois and promised to be as amusing in St. Thomas as in the Bahamas.

"*Eppie-Fanny, Eppie-Fanny.* Dis is de Git-n-Go calling *Eppie-Fanny* on Channel 16. Come on in *Eppie-Fanny.* I got to confirm yo' dinner reservation for tonight."

"*Eppie-Fanny,* I know you 'round here somewhere. Answer de Git-n-Go."

A distinctly British accent responded to Channel 16. "I am calling back to the, um, Get and Go Restaurant. Would you by chance be trying to hail the sailing vessel *Epiphany?* Over."

"Roger. Das you. Let's switch to 14 so I can git your order, *Eppie-Fanny.*"

My skin turned the color of sunrise over the next few weeks, somewhere between the Dogs and Virgin Gorda. Searching out wonderful places where we would bring the children once they arrived for the upcoming holidays, Stewart and I researched our way through snorkel spots, frozen drinks and steel bands, sunning ourselves between assignments on beach after beach. The British Virgin Islands were perfect for boating with their clear water, trade winds and compact layout of easily navigable islands. At Cane Garden Bay, we stopped for a day of relaxation and went in for a beer at Stanley's Welcome Bar. Ellie and Stew would love this one with its tire swing hanging from a tree out front.

"You know, Jimmy Buffett he wrote 'Life is Like a Tire Swing' right here at dis bar," said the waitress.

"That Jimmy Buffett really got around bars," I said to Stewart.

We motored over to Jost Van Dyke to anchor for the night, exclaiming at how the landmasses vaulted out of the sea. At Foxy's, the dreadlocked proprietor asked what state we were from as he sat on a picnic table and strummed his guitar. He delighted the crowd with a clever ditty about Virginia, and every other state from which people hailed.

At the Flying Cloud on Hollis Cay, Stewart and I had a terrible dinner and a wonderful time. The owner gave a risqué musical performance about the hazards of charter boating, which was topped only by a donkey that cruised the open windows near the dinner tables. Patootie gulped beer and snatched paper napkins off tables and laps with a toothy munch. Gentlemen needed to have their body parts in the right place when Patootie was on the job or no amount of conch would help them ever again.

From Norman Island we could get to blue-chip places by dinghy so we stayed anchored in the bight for several days. Some of the best snorkeling around was at the Indians, just a short hop in *Roundabout*. The only seahorse I ever saw was there. It stared at me over the top of a purple sea fan like a character out of *Nemo*.

Once false confidence was built up about how much we thought we knew of the vagaries of the sea, Stewart and I took off in the dinghy to snorkel the wreck of the *Rhone* one day. The 310-foot ship met its demise in the hurricane of 1867, a mile and a half from Salt Island. Much of its skeleton still lay in about 40 feet of clear water.

With the wind increasing on the 20-minute trip from *Crossroads*, the water became choppy but tolerable. As we slipped into the ocean above the *Rhone*, we felt lucky to have the wreck to ourselves because it was a popular tourist attraction. Since the sea floor was far too deep to anchor, Stewart pulled *Roundabout* behind us, and we oooed and aaahed at the spectral sight. A light current flowed past, but not enough to concern us, as we drifted apart on our own paths. I had never seen a big shipwreck since I didn't scuba dive, and the chance to be so close to one intrigued me. From time to time, I spotted Stewart under the water, diving 20 feet as he held the bow line of the trailing dinghy.

It didn't seem like a half hour had passed while I snorkeled over the iron ghost. I was busy trying to imagine the horror of the people who lost their lives in it during that storm, watching the big fish that preferred to swim in deep water and thrilling to another novel experience.

When I raised my head, Stewart and *Roundabout* had vanished.

Choppy waves broke over me, and no matter how hard I tried I couldn't get above them. I screamed Stewart's name as loud as I could, but the slapping of the chop overpowered my voice. A cloudbank slid across the sun and the day turned more threatening. My resolve not to panic wilted and shriveled to nothing as the alluring lines of the wrecked steamer became gray and macabre. Thoughts of drowning caromed around my mind, and I wondered if my husband had already been swallowed up.

By now used to snorkeling independently, Stewart also failed to realize we had separated. The height of the waves had almost doubled since our arrival, and he had difficulty getting into the boat since we had neglected to attach the swim ladder. When he finally managed to do that, he was 150 feet away, too far to see or hear my plight. Only by driving in widening circles was he able to locate me. His calm-under-pressure manner, so opposite from my style in times of crisis, was the salvation of a terrifying episode.

"Oh, there you are," he said when he found me. If I hadn't been so frightened, that thrifty phrase would have caused me to lose it. But, right then, right there, those four words were as welcome as a Coast Guard helicopter. Days later, as Stewart described his version of the predicament, I realized that his fear had been as great as mine.

CHAPTER 19: Treasure Islands

Four friends flew down for a visit at mid-month. Everywhere, the sights and noises and voices were so different from home. One evening, heaven's exuberance produced a watermelon-colored sunset and 11 hours later a cantaloupe-colored sunrise. Hummingbirds helicoptered around a hibiscus thicket. Salt flavored the air, leaving a rime of fine granules on our skin. The flurry of compliments from our friends made Stewart and me feel ridiculously proprietary about those intoxicating islands, and I fear we might have acted as if we had created them for our guests' enjoyment. Racing to fit in the pleasures of here and now, we left breathless on their third day with us for Anegada Island, a 14-mile trip to paradise. *(Photo 2.8)*

After a ride there in the back of a hinky old truck, our group snorkeled Loblolly Bay. We feasted that night on lobster, the best we'd ever had. They were cooked on the beach at the Anegada Reef Hotel, where the rum punch seemed extra smooth as we watched daylight lapse in one final explosion of color. A nutty Frenchwoman brought a blow-up doll to sit beside her at the outdoor bar. She called him Herb, said he was her fancy man and danced with him under the moon.

Having friends with us brought back to mind the contrast between the life I was leading and the lives of others I knew. I lay in bed at sunrise and wondered what people back home were doing this morning. I envisioned most of them steering their courses with the joystick of convention. It seemed I had spent my life crossing borders, both literal and figurative, and along with those expanded territories I had had a range of galvanizing experiences, not all of them amusing. My stateside buddies might be toasting their toes by a popping fire, making a shopping list for things unattainable at my out-island Bahamian market: crunchy granola, sun-dried tomatoes, Pepperidge Farm Whole Wheat Bread. Maybe they were making plans to see a great movie, or scheduling a date with the hairdresser.

Was it guts, genetics, fate or simply personal choice that made people turn in such different directions? I recognized that I might never find the answer and that knowing it mattered less and less to me every day. "What is, is." The Bahamian gospel seemed to be making its way into my own philosophy.

At the Baths on Virgin Gorda the next day, our group jumped off the boat to climb the gigantic rock formations that looked as if they had been casually tossed on the white sand beach. With no dock available, Gregg would keep *Crossroads* moving parallel to shore while we swam in for a quick hike of the natural playground.

Our plan was to gather on the beach in an hour to return to the boat. Stewart and I had done this before and knew that the return swim could be dicey. It required us to dodge bareboaters, mega-yachts and dive craft while stroking against the incoming waves. Once we were back on board, we would leave for a laid-back lunch on Cooper Island and an afternoon of deep-sea fishing. *(Photo 2.9)*

The swim in to the Baths was easy. After exploring the rocks, the six of us sat down in a shallow pool to cool off. As Henry leaned back on his straightened arms, hands under the water on the sand for support, he pushed one of them into a full-grown sea urchin that sported six-inch spikes. Two of the brittle spines broke off in the fleshy part of Henry's hand just below his thumb.

"You have to pee on it," said Stewart.

"What??"

"No kidding. Urine draws poison to the top and slows its entry into your bloodstream."

"I can't do that," Henry said.

"OK. Then I will," said Stewart. "Anybody's pee will work."

By the time the rough and ready medical procedure had been completed, we were late returning to *Crossroads,* and I could see Gregg pacing outside the pilothouse. Waving at him, we started our 60-yard swim so we could leave to find a doctor to remove the urchin spikes from Henry. The wind had freshened and incoming rollers were sizeable as we swam through unpredictably staggered waves in the busy boating lane. With all his charges back in the heavily rolling boat, Gregg sped off in search of the nearest clinic in Spanish Town.

"Whoee! You really *got* some needles in you," said the nurse who was prepping Henry for the doctor who would dig them out. "You want Novocain or are you a real man?"

"I'll take Novocain," Henry told the wisecracking nurse.

"That's too bad. We ain't got any."

The children came for Christmas break. We anchored in Virgin Gorda Sound, where Santa arrived on water skis, throwing candy into every boat's cockpit. At sunset one day, we spotted Ellie through our binoculars, driving the four-piece local band from its afternoon gig at one waterside restaurant to its evening gig at another. *Roundabout* was loaded to the hilt, and our daughter could barely be seen at the wheel, struggling to control the overloaded boat. Stew was nowhere in sight. Most parents worried about having their teenagers leave the house for an evening out in the family car.

In an endless dome of bright blue sky, the cumulus clouds were stacked like twist cones from the Dairy Queen. All four Browns, plus Gregg, went for a long snorkel on New Year's Eve day. Afterward, we lay on a postcard-of-a-beach to dry, and silver jet contrails shimmered in the sky. While we speculated on their exotic destinations, not one of us could think of a single place on earth he or she would rather be.

On New Year's Day 1992, we pulled anchor in a warm rain. We had been gone from This End Up exactly one year. I still missed it, but the languid beauty of the islands was addictive. With so much else to see, to do, to learn in this world, we couldn't go back yet. Gregg signed on for an open-ended job on *Crossroads*.

I wanted to collect memories that we could revisit in our hearts when the time came to end our wandering. When we returned to our point of departure, by choice or by circumstance, our broadened experiences would help us appreciate the peculiarities of home instead of slighting its limitations. I stored those mental souvenirs away in a treasure chest inside me, and I hoped they would give us the vision to look forward with courage, and backward with gratitude, during the final leg of life's journey.

"How long have you guys been cruising?" asked a man we met on the beach at Bitter End Yacht Club.

"Oh, about a year."

"I can't wait to get back home where I can count on what'll happen in my life," said his wife. "You must be going crazy after a year. Aren't you ready to get off that boat yet?"

No way, I thought to myself. It was one of many similar questions I fielded from women over the years, and I was becoming accustomed to the contrast. Rarely did I meet a woman who *wanted* to work, who *wanted* to live on a boat, who *wanted* to have out-of-the-box experiences. Every time I heard someone voice discomfort with what I felt so compelling—a life philosophy based on risk and reward—I was puzzled anew, and sorry that those of my gender who were able to choose that path so often dismissed it with a shuttered mind. I knew what they were missing.

CHAPTER 20: "No Problem, Mon"

Stewart and I were different people from the ones who had lived in a white Georgian house that stood politely mid-yard from its peers. The longer I was on the water, the less I could imagine returning to Richmond full time. I wondered where we would land whenever we quit living aboard the boat.

Back from the Virgin Islands in September 1992, *Crossroads* was boatyard-bound in Fort Lauderdale for additional electronics and small repairs. Gregg made regular trips to check the progress and hired a delivery helper to assist him in getting her back to Great Exuma. The start of our next cruising year was around the corner, and the mere whisper of winter had us itching for shores carpeted with powdery sand.

The TV told of fog and pouring rain back in the States. All over the East Coast, planes were grounded. We anchored near Staniel Cay with friends who were supposed to leave on a charter coming in from Miami. CNN showed airports from New York south running hours late. We called Vincent. He was the local contact for the charter service, Winged Taxi, conducting his business from Bar 'n Bites. Most everything of importance in the Cays happened in their bars.

"Vincent, will you call us when the plane lands at Staniel?" asked Gregg, who knew it would be hours before the little charter craft showed up.

"No problem, mon."

Few people lived so contentedly with a three-word philosophy, but most Bahamians we met found time and accuracy to be inconsequential notions. "No problem, mon," was not just a phrase, it was a philosophy. I decided their lack of specificity was a guard against having to bear proof about anything. Without that burden, they had the leisure to operate when, where and how they wished. What fabulous freedom.

Our friend Jack, who was flying out with Stewart and me from Nassau the next day, came with us to see our guests off from the airstrip. The weather had not been perfect for them, but partly cloudy with temperatures in the 70s would look pretty good as Tricia and Sid worked their way through icy, aerial gridlock back to their Monday morning meetings in New Hampshire.

On the return ride, we cruised near the shoreline of the little village so Jack could take photos for his watercolor hobby. Laundry hung limp among some of the colorful cement houses and their scrubby trees, trying in vain to shed moisture under a blanket of dark clouds. Partially finished buildings were crumbling back into their foundations, abandoned for lack of money or tenacity. Window openings regurgitated railroad vine, which didn't know its place in the Bahamas, and animals made a home under the leaves in the structures' dark corners. One house had a stubby besom by the yawning doorway, waiting for its mistress to take charge of the dirt floor. *(Photo 2.10)*

Jack was tickled by a sign at a "T" in the road. "This Way" pointed one arrow, and "That Way" pointed the opposing one. As *Roundabout* slowed for the camera's advantage, a native woman strutted by with a stack of tiny purple braids piled on her head. The sound of her flip-flops against her heels was like water slapping a lazy cadence on a tethered boat. The slow roll of the rest of her reminded me of a wave lumbering over a sandbar at low tide. Headed at the same drowsy pace in the other direction, a bandy-legged old man muttered to himself as he drank a beer. Angling a toothless grin at the young woman, he lifted his crumpled hat. She nodded in recognition of the gesture and they passed on. The casuarina trees were left to converse with each other, as a soughing breeze blew across the empty path.

I thought how lucky that their distance from Nassau and George Town protected the pristine beauty and peace of the Exuma Cays. I also thought how lucky I was to spend so much time there, since I didn't have to sprint through airports anymore to make a Monday morning meeting. Fat drops of rain splattered, and Stewart gunned *Roundabout* in a dash for *Crossroads*' shelter.

The next morning was blustery and cool. Jack, who had dived all over the world, was eager to see Thunderball Cave. Gregg came along and the four of us jumped in for an early snorkel in one of the prettiest spots around. Conditions were far from ideal, but Jack, Stewart and I were leaving for Nassau at noon, and we didn't want our guest to miss such a renowned Exuma attraction. Within seconds of entering the water, all of us were slammed against the razor-sharp limestone face of the cave by a ferocious current and stiff wind at our backs. The inflatable dinghy had been anchored 35 feet away to avoid a chance meeting with the shards of pointed reef near Thunderball's sheer side.

Because I was only a moderate swimmer, Stewart and Jack had to hold me off the sharp rock by turning their backs to the tide and pushing their feet up against Thunderball's wall. That created a human block between me and the meat grinder that was the cave's exterior side with its rows of jagged coral teeth. Although the three men were all strong enough to get themselves back to the boat, they couldn't do that if they had to pull me the whole way. Gregg swam to *Roundabout* and brought the dinghy's bow line toward me. Even though it came within 15 feet, I was unable to cover that distance, because the second I started stroking away from Thunderball, the tide slammed my body into the cave's serrated outside wall.

The water was tinged pink with blood from our arms, legs and backs. I instantly lost whatever little peace of mind I had about sharks and envisioned them schooling below in preparation for a feeding frenzy. Panicked when saltwater poured in through the top of my snorkel tube, I sucked it in and choked off breathing altogether. Gregg struggled to hold the end of the line near me in the rushing water, but since I was consumed with violent coughing and had lost one flipper, Stewart and Jack had to drag me like dead weight to the rope's frayed tail. Gregg tied the line to my T-shirt and hauled me over the high gunwales of *Roundabout* just in time to keep us all from being snatched by the roaring current and flung out into the open water.

Smeared with Neosporin, I barely pulled myself together enough to board the six-seat Piper for the 40-minute flight to Nassau. After such a scare, I wanted nothing more than an uneventful trip up the Exuma chain. As the plane buzzed over Big Major Harbor, Gregg stepped out onto *Crossroads'* bow and flashed the "V." "Safe trip, don't worry," it said to me.

The weather had cleared, and tufts of the Exuma Cays appeared beneath us in Rorschach inkblots. The islands rose out of brilliant turquoise water that matched Jack's mirrored sunglasses. As always on this ride, my mind played its games.

One island looked like a writhing snake with a forked reef at one end, just where its flicking tongue would have been; it reminded me of the cobras in baskets I saw at the Casbah as a child living in Africa. Another was shaped like a plume with sand that fanned out in wispy strokes; it made me think of the times my childhood friend Betty Gray and I had contests to see who could stay still the longest while we tickled each other's face with a feather. A wavy cay was shaped like a mountain switchback with blue Creamsicle water in all the coves between the switches and the backs. Three others looked like a family walking in a line: a big daddy with sloping shoulders, a curvaceous mama blessed with a tiny waist and a big chest, a wiggly baby tagging along behind.

The cobalt blue of the deep inlets that separated oceanside cays, one from the other, wore white ruffled crosscurrents like crinolines. A few clouds cast pewter shadows on the water, and I confused them with the gray-green islands until they dissipated like a dream. As if the Lord had poured out uncut diamonds onto a piece of spotlit aquamarine velvet, the Great Bahama Bank twinkled up at me as it wound around the crenelated shorelines of the Exuma Cays.

After we entered the main terminal, I walked down to Specialty Air in the domestic flight area to make a reservation for Stewart's cousin, who was visiting a few weeks after our return to the boat.

"Yeah?" said the man behind the counter. He bore the protective sheath of apathy.

I told him what I needed.

Without any response to me, he turned his head. "Altea," he screamed at typical Bahamian volume. "Some lady, she needin' a seat."

I waited and listened to the hands tick-tick on the big clock behind the counter. The door to the office finally opened and Althea pushed through with lilac stilettos clopping. Her claw-like nails were scratching thick green braids crowning her head. She yelled over her shoulder to someone still in the back room.

"Girl, don't you git your nails done at dat salon. Dey don't know SHIT 'bout nails...May I hep you?"

The service levels at Specialty Air reflected no hint that tourism was the biggest business in the Bahamas.

Althea did know something about fingernails, though. I marveled as I watched her maneuver all 10 of her dragon lady ones over the computer with lightning speed, even though they curved in toward her palm like a jai alai basket.

At one of the newsstands, I bought a *USA Today*. The "50 cents" was marked out and nearly quadruple that price was written in its place. In line to pay, I noticed a sign in a prominent spot at the cash register: "We don't change money. We don't have bathrooms. We're nice once in a while, but today's not it."

Booming flight announcements bounced around the high metal ceiling at ear-splitting decibels. The words were so distorted it was impossible to understand them. On the way to the plane, I took meager refuge in the long line for the ladies' room where most of the stalls wore "Out of Order" signs and paper towels were long gone. A mother with her toddler came close to punching an elderly woman who tried to beat her to the next available potty.

I couldn't wait to get home.

CHAPTER 21: Tobago Torch

The islands of the Caribbean form a long arc that curves between Florida and Venezuela. After two years spent getting acquainted with the stretch from the Bahamas to the Virgin Islands, Stewart and I wanted to see the Leeward and Windward Islands, which lay off the northeastern tip of South America. That became our destination for an extended cruise in 1993-94. From Fort Lauderdale to Grenada, the round trip was 4,500 miles, a voyage roughly equal to the distance between Detroit and Honolulu. At an average speed of 12 mph, we felt that six months was a reasonable amount of time for the journey.

By the time we arrived in the Tobago Cays one evening, the all-day 35 mph winds had pummeled *Crossroads* and her family to exhaustion. I was weak from bracing myself against the vaulting seas and fluky currents. A potted plant, a basket of lemons, the entire CD collection—things that had not been put away or secured with a bungee cord—became a battery of missiles, but I was too seasick to clean up the mess. With such strong headwinds, our arrival time was much later than estimated and night was moving in fast. Gregg said we would have to drop anchor wherever we could since there was no marina in these cays.

The sky developed the color of a bruise and storm clouds glowered. Thunder and lightning erupted around us and Gregg fought to keep the boat in position to allow Stewart to lower the anchor. In *Crossroads'* spotlight, rain jetted sideways like a wide-open fire hose. Stewart's foul weather gear ripped open and flapped behind him, flinging hood, zipper and pull cords into a fury against his body. Unable to maneuver the boat against the heightened maelstrom, normally soft-spoken Gregg screamed from the flybridge against the oncoming wind.

"Drop it! Drop it!"

Gregg's command vanished in the howling storm, and Stewart heard nothing. Unanchored, *Crossroads* slid farther into the open water as if seeking a rendezvous with the encroaching tempest.

Even with that memory still vivid, words wilt and inadequately describe the sizzling arc of lightning that cleaved the sea only a few yards from Stewart, who held the anchor chain in one hand and the metal bow rail in the other. From my vantage point inside the wheelhouse, his body turned the blue of a blowtorch flame. He released the anchor, fell sideways onto the deck, and covered his head with his hands.

A tornado-like wind, rife with ozone, whipped into the boat as I ran out into the rain.

CHAPTER 22: Pirates of the Caribbean

We were spending a few days in one of the easy anchorages of the Grenadines, which lie south of Petit St. Vincent in the Windward Island chain. My brother, Bill, and his wife Amy were cruising with us through Martinique, St. Lucia, St. Vincent, Bequia and Mustique. Sunny but windy for the past five days, the relative calm of steady 22 mph winds had sent the men out in search of provisions. In the tiny, deserted bight, Amy and I luxuriated on *Crossroads'* aft deck, enjoying an all-girl afternoon of reading, sunbathing and reminiscing about the beauty of the previous night's sunset. *(Photo 2.11)*

The nearby island was like one that a child might draw; two fullfronded palms stood joined at the base in bowlegged sentry, swaying on a deserted crescent beach. The deep register of far-off thunder faded into rumbling drum rolls. Amy dried her freshly washed hair in the sun, and the vanilla scent of her shampoo wafted through the air. I drizzled ice water through a straw over my hot skin while the boat, floating in the lee of the land, moved back and forth in the meandering backwash of the tide off the shore. It was a slothful moment abnormally unencumbered by conscience.

The throaty sound of well-kept motors signaled a speedboat rounding the corner of our bight. As a sleek, black "go-fast" with white trim thundered straight toward us, I counted four shirtless men, two with machetes in their belts. *Black Power* was painted on the side in gold script.

"Give us money," said the thieves, nearly ramming their boat into ours.

"We don't have any," I answered.

"You give us money now or we comin' on your boat," said the biggest man as he hung onto *Crossroads'* side.

It's odd how your mind can allow a ragged memory to pop up crisply just when you need it. I hadn't thought of my self-defense class in years, and there, right in the middle of a crisis, was my teacher's voice, clear as could be: "Try not to show you're scared. Don't be timid."

"I'll give you food and a bottle of liquor, but you have to leave then."

"We want money," demanded the spokesman.

Piracy, a word most of us associate with legends of old, was alive and well in the 20th century.

"Only food and liquor. Take it or leave it," I said.

My bowels were mush, my heart a 10-pound weight. I was too frightened to get our rifle. If the pirates turned more menacing, I'd give them whatever they wanted.

Before I handed the bounty over, I repeated, "You promised you'd leave."

And they did, although one of them drew his weapon and shook it at Amy and me. The driver, laden with jewelry and attitude, gunned the engines, causing the cigar-shaped boat to stand on its tail in a final "fuck you" gesture. With two defiant high-speed circles around *Crossroads,* the thugs split, leaving us to pick up the broken, spilled and displaced jumble inside once the boat stopped rocking in their hateful wake.

CHAPTER 23: Cheeseburgers in Paradise

"Burgers!" said the sign outside the bar on Union Island in the Grenadines. After a long morning of wandering the island's quiet hills, we couldn't wait. *(Photo 2.12)*

We flushed the owner out of a dominoes game so we could place our order, and I left to find a bathroom. On the outside of the "GULLS" door was a sign: "Bulla say, 'If it's yellow, let it mellow. If it's brown, flush it down.'" Inside was a poster titled "Why a Beer is Better Than a Man," a stack of paper towels for toilet paper and an utterly defeated commercial deodorizer.

I chuckled to think of certain friends using Bulla's bathroom. That would be my friends whose powder rooms were dressed with mono-grammed linen hand towels, a choice of French soaps, a beveled gilt-edge mirror and a pretty lamp with a silk shade that gave off a flattering light. Maybe even fresh roses in a vase and an oil painting over the john's tank.

I forgot Bulla's flushing directions and the blue "Johnny Maid" flowed out over the rust-stained bowl. Neither tap at the sink had water so I swung through the door to lunch.

Even nestled between two pieces of stale white bread, the burgers enticed our beef-deprived palates. They came with chips and pickles on the side, a slice of onion and watered-down French's Mustard. Two old hounds chuffed around us in hopes of a morsel.

"Does it taste kind of weird?" I asked Stewart.

"Seems fine to me," said the most non-discriminatory eater I've ever known. "Another Carib beer, please."

The owner flashed gold front teeth as he made his third pass to check on our pleasure. "You want carrot cake now?"

"No, thanks, but the cheeseburgers were great."

"Oh, dey special," said Bulla.

Here we go again, I thought. That shifty Jimmy Buffett must have spun the same cheeseburger-in-paradise tale to every island bar owner he came across.

"Yessir, dey real special. Mos' folks say dey like my goat burgers better den de reg'lar kind."

CHAPTER 24: On the Hook (7)

C rossroads *has only got about three more weeks in the yard.*
That's good news; if I have to stay in the Holiday Inn many
more nights, I'll go nutty. I think I've been in every store
between Stuart and Miami looking for something or another that we
need on the boat. I'm provisioning like we're off to the moon where
there aren't grocery stores. We're only going 50 miles over to the Bahamas.

A man on a boat in the slip next to Crossroads *cut his finger off this*
morning with a saw. I've never seen so much blood. But the Fort
Lauderdale EMTs were here in a couple of minutes. They stabilized the
man and whisked him off to the hospital.

That incident has made me think about our first aid kit—it had
better be really complete. I wonder if the three of us ought to take a Red
Cross course on CPR. There must be clinics on most of the Bahamian
islands and certainly on the Virgin Islands, but it wouldn't hurt to know
the basics. Just in case.

CHAPTER 25: In Stitches

Heading back north through lumpy seas, we called in at St. Lucia's Rodney Bay, low on fuel and food and full on garbage. The three of us divided the duties: Gregg would fill *Crossroads'* big tank with diesel, Stewart would find a place to dispose of our three trash compactor bags, and I would head to the market. Once we put ourselves to rights, we planned to explore the old Creole buildings of Soufriere and later to dinghy to the base of the island's most famous landmark, the towering Pitons. The twin volcanic peaks rise one-half mile straight up from the sea and distinguish St. Lucia from her neighbors for miles. *(Photo 2.13)*

At first, I didn't hear my name being called, so unlikely it was that I would be known here. I was absorbed with how to make dinner from the sparse offerings.

"Miz Libby Brown? Miz Libby Brown?"

"Yes?" What could this elderly St. Lucian man want with me?

"You Messa Stu-art wife? Come quick wid me. He 'bout to bleed hisself to deat."

I found Stewart slumped onto the fender of a rusty old pickup. At the same time blood was pouring out of a long gash in his calf, some of it was trying to clot around Stewart's fingers while he attempted to squeeze off the hemorrhaging. A circle of seven men squabbled at the marina's trash dump, staring and pointing. Only two of them wore tops; a barefooted teenager finally relinquished his ripped T-shirt so I could wrap the leg. The rag looked like the one we kept in *Roundabout* to wipe spilled gas and oil off the engine.

On the way to the hospital, the taxi driver said he needed to stop and pick up his kids at school. I dissuaded him with a tirade, after which he floored the rattletrap over bottomless potholes while Stewart explained what happened.

One trash compactor bag was cut through with a jagged piece of a crushed wine bottle. Without noticing that, he had swung the bag with great force to get it up onto the piled dump truck for its trip to the garbage pit. The deep, four-inch-long cut had resulted from a shard of a nice bottle of Kendall-Jackson chardonnay.

"Sit down." The grouchy receptionist at the local hospital had no sympathy for the only white faces in the waiting room. She had no sympathy for the other faces either.

A woman in hard labor screamed from a gurney in the corner while an ancient man whose sheet had slipped to the floor sat bent over and naked in his wheelchair as urine pooled below it. Against one wall stood a pile of bloody linens with flies crawling among the folds. Stewart continued to bleed.

"You need a tetanus shot? Not sure? Put your arm up here."

"I want to see the needle come out of the packaging please," said Stewart.

"Harrumph," said Nurse Ratchet.

Next came the doctor, a young woman, overworked and brief with words. She pulled out the Novocain bottle.

"I want to see the needle come out of the package please," said Stewart for his second injection of the hour. Drugs and AIDS were said to be prevalent in this part of the world.

With a scathing look of affront, the doctor held the package three inches from Stewart's face and slowly ripped the syringe free of its wrapping. Then the already-prepped suture tray with its grubby liner was brought in and Stewart's leg swiped once with alcohol. The doctor picked up her weapon.

"I'm sorry, but I didn't see that particular needle removed from its wrapping," said Stewart.

"*Mister* Brown, we are a one-needle-per-patient hospital, and I wish you not to insult us again."

With that, knowing the Novocain could not yet have taken full effect, the physician started her stitching. Stewart could have used some of that chardonnay.

There seemed to be an inverse relationship between the cleanliness of needles and the rest of the hospital. At least we hoped so.

CHAPTER 26: An Embarrassment of Riches

The States seemed half a dozen planets away. Almost every day something "tropical" happened, forcing me to live with inconvenience in good humor and to enjoy moments of bliss in the midst of maddening complications. For someone who craved sharply defined answers, questions starting with "Why," "How" and "When" could bring on a heart attack in the islands. "Whatever" was my goal for adapting to the Caribbean attitude.

Accepting the "No problem, mon" philosophy was a daunting process for me. Of all people, Type A Americans wrestle with it most, and I was a perfectionist to boot. That unusual mixture, precision on island time, was the cause of bedeviling angst. For me, subscribing to the "Whatever" viewpoint seemed almost impossible, but unless I wanted health problems of the ilk that had sent me to the hospital in my This End Up years, my need for information and efficiency had to give way.

One of the other things that took adjustment was making friends along the way. I wasn't doing so well with my "Whatever" when it came to that. We met a steady stream of people on our voyage, but the transient nature of cruising always had us saying goodbye. Occasionally I was sorry that our acquaintance had been so short; many times I was not.

Too often, rich, self-satisfied people seemed to believe they were entitled to pleasures as if the sky rained supplies and servants just for them. Some were in such a hurry to have fun they butchered animals and reefs, dropping anchors carelessly onto coral heads and throwing live starfish in the bottom of their dinghies to suffer a torturous death in the sun. With blinders drawn tight around their eyes, these selfish travelers passed by most of the things worth knowing in a search for the most famous bar or the toniest gift shop.

The ones who really raised my hackles were the overbearing men who prattled on, with a presumption of superiority, about how the locals needed to change their outdated ways to fit into today's world.

"It would be so goddam easy. I could turn this place around in a heartbeat," said in the smug verbiage of the unwittingly fortunate.

Mr. Two-Weeks-Vacation on a charter boat where a uniformed staff of 10 catered to his every whim lacked a scintilla of sensitivity. I learned during my years in other people's countries that Americans seem hardwired to think we know how to make everything better. This attitude often prevails where there is a lack of education about the area.

The difficulty of making friends was an unanticipated disappointment with life at sea. I wasn't exactly lonely, for I had the good company of Gregg, Stewart and a steady stream of visitors. And I wasn't bored, because unscripted encounters inspired me with what I didn't know. Yet when I returned for a visit home, people there seemed disconcertingly similar to the way they were years ago, and sometimes I felt isolated by our differences.

Restlessness came more from lack of a specific challenge. The children would both finish college in the next year, graduating with an extra measure of independence. Showing little need for advice, colleagues from This End Up had forged ahead without me. Friends at home flew off on trips, upgraded houses and planned weddings. In the past, I had derived happiness from a stiff yank on my brain and energy. Now, the most rigorous tasks of my day were choosing what number sunblock to wear and snorkeling against the current.

What exactly *was* my purpose?

CHAPTER 27: Sleepless in St. Bart's

Back-to-back incidents near the French island of St. Bartholomew created a couple of scary nights. The first occurred at late dusk in Colombier, a small, secluded bay with a deserted shoreline. A steep, craggy hill rose above our cove, its ridge dotted by the ubiquitous goats of the islands that roamed from a tiny village located over its crest. In February, occasional large wintertime swells crept in late in the day. The floor of the sea inside this marine reserve was not a secure anchorage, so yachters in the harbor tied their craft to mooring balls.

By the time *Family Matters* entered the anchorage, the distant sky unfurled a wide, gray curtain of rain. You could smell it coming. A swollen tide exploded through the narrow opening of the bight as the storm rolled in behind it. Bone-rattling waves swelled and thrashed the beach — whomp, whomp, whomp. Boaters scurried about on wildly swinging decks to snatch loose objects as the line of squalls approached, and we heard a man's voice calling into the dusk on the VHF.

"To all boats in Colombier. This is *Family Matters,* a 46-foot Grand Banks trawler with no anchor available. I have three young boys on board and need help securing the boat for the night. Over."

There was silence from the captains as they ran through their options. The rollers were big and a shared mooring could damage both vessels. Lending an anchor was not the answer because the bottom of the bay was untenable. To raft up to another boat would be impossible in the up-and-down ride of bulges and clefts in the sea. And any thought of beaching *Family Matters* was dashed with the explosive power of the waves that slammed into shore. The last vestige of light disappeared in a downpour. We knew our community of yachtsmen was the only hope for help in this remote location for the man with three little children in fast deteriorating weather.

"Have you got plenty of fuel, *Family Matters?*" asked an anonymous captain.

"Yes, we're good on fuel."

"You're going to have to motor around inside this harbor all night. Mind the underwater rocks on each side of the harbor," said a voice from who-knew-which boat. "And don't get closer to the shore than 75 feet or these big waves will eat you for dinner."

Quiet fear was all that could be heard from *Family Matters*.

Gregg gave direction and support. "Put the boys in life jackets. We'll leave plenty of lights on. Call *Crossroads* if you need to talk. I'll stand by overnight on the radio."

"This is *Scotty*. Let's split shifts monitoring the VHF, *Crossroads*," said a man with an accent we couldn't identify.

"Yeah, me too. This is *Ocean Commotion*."

"My sons and I are very grateful, everybody. God bless. I'll check in during the night."

He did. And they made it. But it was a sleepless night for many of us.

The remarkable sea. Its capricious light and impulsive wind might intertwine to form a day that's marvelous or a day that's rotten, but it rarely creates a day that's dull. The next evening, in the same anchorage, empty moorings abounded because many boats from the night before had left. One notable exception was a 53-foot Swan sailboat named *Blue Moon*, whose owners had not participated in *Family Matters'* trauma. Cruising offered myriad opportunities to help, but not everyone liked or was able to put himself at risk.

Conditions were perfect for seeing the famed green flash, so we sat on the bow with a sundowner and a fresh kiss of sunburn. This elusive sunset phenomenon happened just as the sun slithered below the water horizon, most frequently on a clear, cool winter day. The last remnant of the fiery ball turned bright green for a second or two, if you were lucky. Blinking at the wrong time could ruin it, and although live-aboard boaters had seen it numerous times, landlubbers often swore that looking for the green flash was similar to a snipe hunt.

The sea had shown us her wrath and her glory in just a few short hours. We retired exhausted but happy after another day in paradise.

"Help! Help! I need someone to come to *Blue Moon*. Is anybody awake? HELP!"

The call came in at 2:20 a.m. and Gregg, who left the VHF on all night when *Crossroads* was anchored away from civilization, was up and on the radio within seconds. He had a mother's ear for tuning out unimportant noises and for being wide awake at the first sound of trouble.

"This is *Crossroads*. What's the problem?"

"I can't wake my husband up. He's unconscious. I don't know what to do."

"I'll be right there," Gregg said.

By now, Stewart and I were up too. Grabbing the blood pressure cuff and first aid box, the two men jumped in *Roundabout* and roared off across the water to *Blue Moon*.

Through the night-vision glasses, I could see Stewart on the bow holding an I.V. bag in the air, its line snaking down through the open forward hatch. Then I heard Gregg over *Blue Moon's* radio asking if there was a doctor or nurse in the little harbor, or anyone within listening range who knew where the nearest hospital was. No answer.

Around 4 a.m., our captain returned alone to *Crossroads* to call for help over the single sideband radio. A U.S. operator patched him through to a physician in Washington, D.C. Thousands of miles away, a doctor listened to the symptoms and walked Gregg through treatment. The diagnosis was a vicious diabetic coma. A MedEvac seaplane was arranged for first light, and a hospital awaited the patient's arrival.

At dawn, a sliver of golden red ball inched its way free of the horizon to dispel the morning clouds. With the new sun spreading its colors, our captain motored us away from St. Bart's, acting none the worse for two sleepless nights. I wondered if the couple on *Blue Moon* realized how lucky they were that Gregg and Stewart answered their cry in the night.

CHAPTER 28: The Beat Goes On

The weather was beautiful in the Bahamas in early summer, 1994. I had broken my own rule and made the bluewater cruise from the Turks and Caicos back to George Town, Great Exuma. We had a considerable following sea, and I sat mesmerized by the seethe and froth of water that lifted *Crossroads'* stern and sent her sliding smoothly down its towering mass. By now though, I'd been through enough frightening incidents on the water to know how deceptive those gentle rollers could be.

With the last of the light, we approached our favorite part of the Exumas, where we had spent so much time in our first two years of boating. The anchor chain rat-a-tatted through its roller on the way to a lazy night at the bottom of the harbor. Isabelle, the wild pig that lived on Big Major Island, sauntered out to see who was making all that racket in the neighborhood.

After a daylong trip up the island chain, Stewart and I decided to dinghy over to Bar 'n Bites for supper. A faded Bahamian flag hung at rest as a sunset of gentian violet and verdigris unfurled. The Pepto-Bismol pink door with the tattered screens banged shut behind us. Stevie S's band blared from stereo speakers in a tussle for attention with the baseball announcer on TV.

"Hey *Crossroad*. You back." Slide's baritone welcome reminded me of *Cheers*, the place where everybody knows your name.

Our old haunt hadn't changed. Its steadiness was one of the nicest things about the joint.

Across the bar, Bahamian men were speaking to each other in a mystifying mix of shouting, teasing and daring that was hard for me to grasp. They repeated the same thing over and over, even when a half deaf person could have heard it the first time. The lingo of the locals made me smile, the part I could understand over the din.

Two women sat at a table talking with rare disapproval about an acquaintance.

"You know vut wrong wit' her?"

"Nah, vut dat?"

"She ain' got no broughtupsy."

When asked why he didn't respond to a note someone had written him, a grizzled old Bahamian man answered in the oblique manner of his countrymen.

"I read readin' but I don' read no writin'." Print, as in the Bible, versus cursive, as in a note, I presumed.

I heard an American ask a Bahamian what he was doing the next day.

With the most perfect *carpe diem* answer, he said, "How I know? Today ain' gone and tomorrow ain' touch." The guy with the New Jersey accent exhibited the confused look that I was used to seeing on foreigners' faces. It reflected the near impossibility of translating island dialect on a first visit. Or sometimes on any visit. Too bad, because there was wisdom there.

When Sadie came to take our order, her graph paper face was the same as it was when we left her months earlier. The humped vertical lines of her brow and the pursed horizontal lines of her mouth sent out the signal, "What is, is."

I ordered fried shrimp from the menu.

"Dat item in limbo."

Stewart noticed the old favorite #9 on the menu and couldn't resist the marketing come-on: "A Bacon, Lettuce and Tomato Sandwich made even better on our Bahamian bread."

"Sadie, I'll have the Bacon, Lettuce and Tomato Sandwich please."

"Vut dat?"

"Well you know, lettuce leaves, slices of tomato and bacon between two pieces of bread with just a little mayo."

"You mean a BLT?"

"Exactly," said Stewart.

"Well why you don' say so?" Sadie huffed off, no doubt puzzled at Stewart's stupidity.

Later, leaving to return to *Crossroads,* I called over the crowded bar to Slide.

"Thanks, Slide. See you tomorrow."

"God spare life," came the reply. For the first time since we left Richmond three and a half years before, I felt I had found a place where I belonged, a place that delighted and confounded and educated me at every turn.

Our trips back and forth from the States offered up a piece of culture shock and brought the need to adapt within a few hours to either the strange reality of living on a boat in the Caribbean or the remembered familiarity of living in America. Friends kindly gathered us back into their activities the minute we called to say we were home, but through no fault of theirs, Stewart and I sometimes felt out of step.

My feeble bridge skills seemed even feebler when the women had me to play. I didn't know how to use cilantro in a recipe because in the out-islands, they never heard of it. At lunch one day, a friend mentioned how well a mutual acquaintance was doing with her chemo; I hadn't known she needed it. And the neighbors at the top of the hill were people I'd never seen before. We felt like outsiders soaking up local chitchat. Life went on without us and sometimes it made me sad.

I wasn't much interested in the talk of clothes and where people bought them on their trips to New York. In discussing their travels, deluxe accommodations and the most famous golf courses were often the topics. I had little to add to the talk about the Mexican yardman's failure to speak plain English. At a cocktail party, one woman voiced her disappointment in the engagement of a girl we all knew: "She can do better than *that*." Yep, life went on without us and sometimes it made me glad.

Many people had become an imprint of circumstances that came their way, whereas I seemed bound to wrestle with fate. Perhaps each of us was born one way or the other, a genetic thing. I was awfully glad to be on Plan B, although the struggle to coexist with constant uncertainty sanded me dull some days. But I wouldn't give anything for the beautiful moments in between. I wondered what challenges Mexico would throw out for my continued education as I flew out to meet Stewart, Gregg and *Crossroads* there.

CHAPTER 29: Chicken Shit

Our welcome into Mexico was a little chilly, but Ellie and Stew, who joined us for a week of Thanksgiving vacation, said it was awesome. The epaulet-trimmed policia stood on our bow for an hour with Uzis aimed at our hearts while their co-workers had Gregg pull out every item in every compartment on *Crossroads*. We never determined why Mexico considered a family of four with clean-as-a-whistle passports to be a target for such a search. Perhaps it was the sure knowledge that they would find things like the Yamaha parts, the bottle of rum and the CDs they took for their trouble.

We cruised for a week in and out of the hot spots of the Yucatan Peninsula and said goodbye to Ellie and Stew at the airport in Cancun. Our children were young adults. Ellie and Stew had outgrown their need for us much sooner than we had outgrown our need for them, and we recognized that most likely the end of our family unit as we had known it for 21 years was right around the corner. Of all the times we had put the children on a plane that would carry them back to their own lives, I never felt quite so empty as when that particular loading door closed. I knew we would spend the winter without seeing them as Gregg set our waypoints for Belize.

Crossroads was based at a marina on an island not too far from the mainland. From there we had easy access to good fishing, diving and sightseeing. Ambergris Caye was big enough to have a vibrant boating community, a thriving tourist industry and a town with hotels, restaurants, a clinic, a bank and a grocery store.

Several weeks into our time in Belize, a group off the boat next to us asked if we would join them at the Drop. Off we went, listening to tales of wild times on Saturday nights at the big bar in the center of town. Our new friends sounded like insiders at the Drop.

Upon entering the packed bar, everyone paid a $5 cover charge. "Not too bad," we thought, but we weren't sure why I got a stub that said 71 and Stewart got one that said 33. Our friends just laughed when we asked. "You'll see."

At ten o'clock a horn sounded. A chicken was brought out onto a cement floor in the middle of the bleachers where the crowd sat. The playing field had 100 squares, numbered at random. The master of ceremonies screamed, "READY?" and the crowd cried back, "READY!"

Surely it wasn't what it looked like. The Drop's owner seemed to be blowing into the chicken's anus. For her part, the chicken flapped her wings and squawked. You could hardly blame her. *(Photo 2.14)*

Then the victim was placed in a spot in the middle of the floor and allowed to run around to her heart's content within the confines of the numbered squares. Suddenly the bettors roared their approval, or disapproval, I wasn't sure which, and the MC screamed into the microphone, "NUMBER 16!" A buxom woman shrieked and bounced her way down to center court waving her ticket. She was presented with $100.

"How did they choose number 16?" I asked from my back-row seat.

"That's where the chicken dropped her load," snorted the sweating drunk beside me. "Guaranteed every time within one minute of blowing her up."

As the lucky winner turned to walk off, the MC chuckled into the mike. "Oh, no you don't. Here's the pooper-scooper. Go to it!" The crowd went wild and bought tickets for the midnight show.

By the time we got back to the boat, my thoughts were about civility. I wondered if our gang in Richmond was having fun at the club. They probably were. Pink lamb chops and plenty of ice. Conversation about a good restaurant in London, a Broadway show and a daughter's graduation from law school. Maybe the capital campaign for the university.

Ambergris was a little rough for my taste. To me, it was uncomfortably primitive that some of the local men wore loincloths and machetes. Although there was reportedly little crime of personal violence out in these small islands, I was frightened sometimes. I thought both the natives and the tourists lacked a certain degree of what? Civility? Polish? Broughtupsy?

A middle-aged American couple was killed just down the beach from our marina as they walked from dinner to their hotel. The murders happened right after we left for a visit home. It was the main topic of conversation when we returned.

Several weeks later, after a daytrip to Guatemala on the most prayer-eliciting airplane ride ever, the three of us buttoned up the boat and she, Gregg and Stewart ran for the Bahamas a month earlier than we had planned, while I returned to Richmond. If we needed any more proof that our lifestyle was playing chicken with fate, it smacked *Crossroads* in the face on her way back to George Town.

"Mayday! Mayday!" The international call of life in danger came over the VHF the first afternoon of the trip on otherwise quiet seas. Stewart and Gregg listened as a terrified woman screamed in fractured English while a man on a vessel nearby tried to get information.

"We are hurt with a whale. The boat is falling down. You help us please to save us."

The French couple was in a sailboat but the woman didn't know where in the vast ocean they were located. After several more references about a whale, there was silence.

"Sailing vessel *Bienvenue,* come in. *Bienvenue,* what is your location? Over." Nothing.

"This is motor vessel *Plain Sense* calling the sailboat *Bienvenue.* Come back please. Do you copy, *Bienvenue?*" Silence.

Four days later, over our single sideband radio, came a request for help in finding a 38-foot Beneteau sailed by two French citizens. They were overdue in the Turks and Caicos by 48 hours. In a subsequent announcement we heard someone report that authorities thought a submerged container had sunk *Bienvenue,* which had a man and his pregnant wife on board.

CHAPTER 30: On the Hook (8)

We have a date when we can leave Fort Lauderdale—only four more days! Crossroads *looks beautiful, and so capable with all her electronic accoutrement. On Monday she gets a tank-full of diesel and a bath and final polish. Then we're off, finally, on our year's adventure.*

I hope this squally weather blows over before we pull out. A 22 mph wind doesn't make an ideal day for my first official try at casting off from a dock, let alone crossing the Gulf Stream. It would be different if we were just pulling into a harbor to drop the hook. That's much easier than throwing the heavy lines in bad conditions to a guy at a marina. You'd think after all the docking lines I've handled in my life, both from the boat side and from the dock side, I wouldn't be so nervous. I just need a little practice, I guess.

I have to get over being such a wimp. For heaven's sake, Gregg, Stewart and I brought the boat all the way down from North Carolina to Florida without any problem. After a year of building her, three-and-a-half months of outfitting her and years of dreaming about what it would be like to live on her full-time, let's get on with the fun.

CHAPTER 31: Foot Loose

In Great Exuma during the fall of 1995, Stewart and I awaited the arrival of a delivery crew that would help Gregg take *Crossroads* back to the Leeward Islands while we returned to the States. The trip had been delayed by blustery weather, and our captain would not depart even with the most experienced crew until he felt confident of a safe passage. The two of us would have a nervous wait, once we were back in Richmond, until we heard that the boat had safely cleared customs in Anguilla.

Young Stew had been in the Bahamas for a visit with us before *Crossroads* made the long trip south and had left just that morning from the George Town Airport on his way to a job in Buenos Aires. Although the worst of the weather had cleared, Stewart and I held our breath when his little charter plane rocked back and forth in the strong crosswind.

When we returned to the boat, the two of us joined Gregg on board as he maneuvered *Crossroads* to the dock for fueling in the strong easterly blow. The man who would catch the line I was set to pitch from the port side screamed at me.

"T'row it! T'row it!"

The Dockmaster at Exuma Docking Services yelled so that I could hear him over the gusting 35 mph wind that was pushing the boat away from the fuel dock. I wasn't used to handling the spring line. My job for four-and-a-half years had been the bow line, but Stewart and I switched places that day. He had a much better chance than I of getting the heavy front line to the dock on the first toss into the stiff oncoming breeze. But that meant I had only a few seconds to throw mine into the hands of a moving target. The conditions left no room for error.

Without thrusters, which would have kept the bow or stern tight to the dock, Gregg, who was steering from the flybridge, had a fight on his hands to keep the back of the boat from swinging out on Stewart's successfully attached front line. I had one end of the spring line on the port side loosely wrapped around a cleat with a few idle spools of it on the deck at my feet. The remainder of the 30-foot, 3/4-inch rope was in my hand like a lasso, ready to give it my mightiest heave against the wind. Usually I waited for Gregg's signal to tell me when to throw, when to secure, when to loosen, but in my new position under the overhang of *Crossroads*' walk-around, we couldn't see or hear each other.

"T'row it! T'row it!" I heard again.

I threw the line as hard as I could. Jamal caught its whipping tail and hustled to wrap it around one of the big pilings just as the stern of the boat slid away from the dock. When I stepped back to secure the other end of the tether to *Crossroads*, my foot landed in the middle of the streaming line, too late to avert serious injury. The uncoiling circle grabbed my foot, slammed it against the heavy cleat and popped it backward.

I saw it, I heard it and I felt it. From my hip down, everything was out of kilter. The snap of my mangled foot and ankle sounded too inhuman to be mine. And I probably yelled that vulgar four-letter word my mother said I should never utter under any circumstance.

On the bow, Stewart heard my scream. Only quick directions from him to Gregg on the flybridge caused the taut rope to slacken. A few more seconds would have taken my foot off.

Gregg carried me down the dock and put me in the back of a taxi van for the airport. I prayed that the pain pills I had taken didn't wear off before we got to Miami. Stewart called our doctor in Richmond to prepare for my possible entry into a hospital there.

The pilot of the small plane laid me out in the aisle since all the seats had passengers, and when we reached Miami, the taxi driver asked Stewart, "Where to?"

"The closest hospital," he said.

I must have looked odd entering the Emergency Room in a bathing suit and T-shirt, no shoes or pocketbook. The young doctor who first looked at my injury stuck his head through the examining room curtain and said to a co-worker, "You gotta come look at this one."

I asked for more drugs.

We spent a long night in a hotel near the airport before the US Airways flight to Richmond the next morning. I had two broken bones and numerous ripped tendons, a dislocated knee and a wrenched hip. The doctors didn't want to set my foot and ankle because of third degree rope burns, which they said could be the most problematic of my injuries. I suffered through four weeks of physical therapy and two additional weeks of home exercises before I could move from crutches to a cane.

I had boated most of my life. I knew not to step into a loose coil of line. In one second, that knowledge blew away in the wind. Even with a full-time captain and years of experience, even at a sturdy dock with capable help and even on a well-maintained boat with a team that had worked together for years, the bumper sticker was right. Shit happens.

CHAPTER 32: Another Crossroads

Hurricane Lili was headed into Cuba in mid-October 1996. *Crossroads* was docked in George Town again, and she seemed safely out of the storm's way. We breathed a sigh of relief from our armchairs in the States as Lili moved away from the Bahamas. Gregg, Stewart and I had agreed to meet at the boat two days later to begin our fall trip to Cat Island, San Salvador, Rum Cay and Long Island.

At 4:00 a.m. the day of our departure, our phone rang in Richmond. Gregg was calling to say the storm had taken a sharp easterly turn and was screaming directly toward the lower Exumas. The two men agreed to meet at the airport in Nassau to see what arrangements could get them into George Town the fastest. Air service was closed south of New Providence.

Hopping a ride out of Nassau with a U.S. film crew, they arrived after the storm to find *Crossroads* with a 3- by 4-foot view into the port side of one of the guest staterooms. The wind on the backside of the storm had driven the boat repeatedly into the dock pilings but we were still afloat, unlike many less fortunate in Elizabeth Harbor. The hurricane's sudden turn and 120 mph gusts had prevented many people from securing their vessels properly. The results were disastrous. With such limited resources in the George Town area, Gregg and Stewart felt lucky to find the Lowell brothers, who were makers of fiberglass "flats-fishing" boats, to patch *Crossroads* enough to get her back to Florida. Our cruising season was off to a bad start. *(Photo 2.15)*

By the beginning of 1997, Stewart and I were back on the boat, and we began to debate the pros and cons of buying a lot somewhere in the Bahamas. In spite of our frequent pleasure in meeting new people, we were tired of saying, "Goodbye. Nice to have met you," and moving on to the next strangers. We looked for land in Nassau and Harbor Island, Eleuthera. We visited Treasure Cay and Hope Town in the Abacos, and Rum Cay and Long Island on the far-eastern side of the archipelago. But they all paled after seven years of sailing in and out of the Exumas. Our first choice — hands down, no question — was those exquisite cays.

We found a lovely old house on Goat Cay in George Town but lost it to another bidder at the last moment. A large tract on a nearby island had been bestowed recently on a college endowment fund in the States. That group strung us along for a year after we put together a professional presentation at their request, only to have them nix our interest without hearing the bid. Norman's Cay was a spectacular island except for the spooky feeling we got as we walked around the infamous Bahamian drug-running base of Carlos Leder's former cartel. A 30-acre parcel on Pipe Cay, halfway down the Exuma chain, caught our eye and we placed a bid with a local agent. He usually refused to return our daily calls over a two-month period, and Stewart and I started doubting our decisions—both the one to buy that remote piece of land and the one to deal with that agent. We withdrew our offer and returned to days of riding in *Roundabout* in search of the perfect spot for a modest house.

Stew came back from Argentina in the summer of 1997 to start graduate school before he moved to São Paulo, Brazil, on assignment for Ford Motor Company. Ellie married Matt and moved to Boston. Gregg's family was eager to have him home, and after seven-and-a-half years with us, he gave his resignation with 12 months' notice. With that development, our bluewater cruising days were over. A 70-foot boat was more than Stewart and I wanted or needed to travel within the Bahamas. *Crossroads* would need to be prepped for sale. *(Photo 2.16)*

On one of our last trips to George Town before Gregg's departure, we were all enjoying a magnificent late spring day when we entered Elizabeth Harbor. We were tracking down a house we had heard was for sale on the south end of Great Exuma. Although weary of tilting at windmills, we were scared to let any tip pass us by in the event it was The One. The night's rain had evaporated and, by early morning, not a cloud could be seen. Approaching the inlet we had traversed innumerable times in *Crossroads,* our wind indicator showed 23 mph. Not calm, but certainly within an ordinary range for us.

That my day might be overtaken by fear on this short, peaceful jaunt was beyond my imagination. As I lay on the couch in the salon, catching up on sleep from our early start, our 50-ton vessel was slammed with a wave like a battering ram. She geed sharply to the right and immediately hawed back to the left in a motion that meant *Crossroads* was out of control. For the next few moments, she gave us a swerving, dipping, roller-coaster ride. I could see Gregg fighting for control, turning the wheel first right, then left, as far over as it would go. On the helm's third series of revolutions, the 70-foot yacht lay nearly over on its side, and I watched the sea rise to the upper level windows.

No amount of clutching could hold me back. My body rose off the couch, bounced over a table frame bolted into the floor and slammed against the opposite wall, coming to rest on the thick glass top that had flown off the coffee table in front of me. While I lay waiting for my first experience with a rogue wave to pass, I lost count of the oscillations *Crossroads* made before she righted herself under Gregg's unflappable competence.

As we continued our hunt for land where we would keep our family close, Stewart and I started the search for a smaller boat that we could be comfortable piloting alone in the Exumas. Dreams of idyllic days with future grandchildren whetted our appetite. Though boating had been an amalgam of contentment and fear for me, I didn't consider returning home. Richmond was like a box of candy, a special treat I anticipated with delight. But after I had enjoyed a few pieces, my wish was to return to a saltier diet.

The water lay turquoise, whooshing and winking, the one sure thing in most of my capricious days on the sea. Another early fall sunset flamed in the Exuma sky, causing the clouds to glow orange from within. In dusk's typical habit, the water was quiet as its blue-green color shifted on the slack tide. My skin was prickly and the late sun warmed a place on my back.

The scent of teak oil from Gregg's afternoon work floated on the sh-h-h of the breeze. SNAP. He connected the top back onto the can with two quick taps from the heel of his paintbrush handle. Before he left to shower, he set before us a pitcher of his trademark Crossroads Coladas in a bucket of ice. The frozen drink tasted like juice from ice-cold honeydew. I spilled a few drops of the green nectar on my sizzling fore-arm and licked them off in a slurp of coconut, sugar and salt. The moment was just short of inebriating.

Gregg rejoined Stewart and me as we sat on the bow mulling the lack of decent property on the market in the Bahamas. *Crossroads* was anchored in a tiny deepwater hole on the north side of the uninhabited island called Fowl Cay.

"I think I understand what you're looking for after watching you search for two years," Gregg said. "If I were going to pick a place in the Exumas for you to buy, it would be right there."

Gregg nodded his head toward Fowl Cay, which was fast fading into the shadows.

"But it's a whole island, not just a lot. And besides, it's not for sale," I said.

"How do you know? From the look of things, *somebody* doesn't love it very much."

In bed that night, Stewart and I talked about how our dream of living in the Bahamas seemed to be slipping away as months of no luck ticked by. Gregg and *Crossroads* were leaving us, our children were starting their own adult lives, we were happy in our hometown only on a part-time basis, and we wanted a place to lay down new roots for our old age. *And,* we both longed for another shot at a project. A private island in the heart of the beautiful Exuma Cays? Maybe, just maybe.

We could build three houses instead of one. That way Ellie and Stew and their families-to-be could come at the same time. Friends could visit for a house party. What better place to spend our retirement? Lush tropical flowers, a library of great books, the big one on a fly rod, frozen Crossroads Coladas at sunset, the stars of the Milky Way, an outdoor shower, a snooze in the warm Caribbean breeze.

Perhaps we'd rent the kids' houses when they weren't there, but just to friends. Well, and maybe to a couple of the interesting visitors who would inquire.

Early the next morning, Stewart motored in *Roundabout* the mile into Staniel Cay in pursuit of information about the run-down island with the funny name. I turned the page to a new month on the calendar: September 1997. As I watched my husband disappear into the sunlight, I never imagined that anything could threaten such a hopeful future.

CHAPTER 33: On the Hook (9)

When we woke up this morning, the temperature was 79 degrees and the early sunlight had that weird gauzy quality of a big city sky. The job superintendent dropped by to tweak one last thing and tell us "Good Luck." It's hard to believe that Gregg, Stewart and I will start our trip today.

Page 31 of my journal stares up at me over breakfast, white and blank. I wonder what I'll think about my entries at the end of our cruising year. And I wonder what my writing will be like from this point forward as I make the change from speculation to recollection. Will it overflow with enthusiasm, running up the margins of the page, or will it be terse and tight with disappointment?

So many people would give anything to have an adventure like this for a week, let alone for a year. OK, it's scary changing my whole lifestyle. But I'm the one who says I'm tired of the status quo, that I want to explore new places and meet new people. What's causing me to be so afraid? I have to buck up.

I flip to the coin's shiny side for an attitude adjustment: a journey with no timetable and no financial worries, a sabbatical from leadership, a chance to understand island culture from the inside, a life at the heart of Mother Nature's bounty, a year of doing things for the first time. Twelve months to focus on my spirituality.

Don't turn into a risk-coward at this point. You chose it, Libby—now you go with it.

* * *

When Gregg starts Crossroads' big engines as we prepare to pull off from the fuel dock, I close my leather-bound journal with its penned expectations. In twelve months, I'll see how they stacked up.

Goodbye, Fort Lauderdale. Wish me Godspeed.

POSTSCRIPT

Gregg got a job in Stuart, Florida, and moved his family there in September 1998. He offered to be on call for Stewart and me until we sold *Crossroads*. One day we had an engine problem, the same problem we'd tried to get repaired earlier in the Bahamas. The mechanic in Nassau had thrown in the towel, so we were faced with having to hire delivery crew to take the boat to Fort Lauderdale for a solution. Stewart called Gregg in a last-ditch effort.

Three days later, we had the part we needed, and, over the phone, Gregg talked Stewart through the process of installing it. A couple of hours saved us thousands of dollars and months away from the Exumas.

Sometime after that, I heard Stewart call him and say, "You know, Gregg, I don't think I ever told you what a great captain you were. I'm sorry it took me this long."

We keep up with our former captain on a regular basis. There is a void in our lives where Gregg used to live.

* * *

Crossroads was sold in February 1999. The day I unloaded our life from under her seats and her beds, from out of her cabinets and her lazarettes, from inside her closets and her pantry, I played my old favorite on the stereo: Carly Simon singing, "Nobody Does It Better."

And no boat could have done it better. She kept us safe over 61,000 miles of dangerous bluewater cruising, a trip equal to circumnavigating the globe two and a half times. She kept us comfortable in driving rain and blistering heat. She kept us happy while we chased our dream of exploring the islands from Florida to Tobago. She had been our home for eight years, one month and eleven days when we bade her farewell with one proviso on the contract—the new owner could not use the name *Crossroads*.

The man who bought our boat took her to Kentucky to live on a lake. I guess she deserved a rest.

* * *

Stewart and I came back to the States to await delivery of our new boat in March 1999. Without Gregg, we knew we'd stay in the Bahamas for the rest of our cruising years, and a 53-foot express trawler would be just right for us to handle by ourselves.

She cut a charming profile in a lovely, low-key way, trimmed with natty teak railings, her hull painted the blackest shade of green with a Chinese red boot stripe. Faithful *Roundabout* trailed behind as we pulled away from the boatyard where we had commissioned our new boat, with Gregg once again behind the wheel. He had agreed when he left us in 1998 to make the delivery of the new one to Staniel Cay. Gregg, Stewart and I motored on the path we had taken eight years before — Fort Lauderdale to Cat Cay — for our first trip aboard our second boat named *Crossroads*.

CROSSROADS COLADA

4 ounces melon liqueur
4 ounces light rum
4 ounces crushed pineapple
2 cups crushed ice
6 ounces cream of coconut

Toss it all in the blender and whir 'til smooth.

Garnish with salt air, a tropical sunset, and share with someone you love, or would like to learn to.

Tiny umbrellas optional.

Photo 2.1 ~ Stewart and Libby on the deck of Crossroads *with Captain Gregg at the stern.*

Photo 2.2 ~ Stewart at the helm of the family vehicle, Roundabout.

Photo 2.3 ~ Gregg Gandy, captain of Crossroads.

Photo 2.4 ~ Stew enjoying another tropical sunset.

Photo 2.5 ~ First class waiting room at Staniel Cay landing strip now has telephone service and benches.

Photo 2.6 ~ Stewart fly-fishing in the Exumas.

Photo 2.7 ~ Crossroads in heavy weather.

Photo 2.8 ~ Stewart and Libby entertaining good friends on Crossroads.

Photo 2.9 ~ Libby dolphin fishing from Crossroads' *stern with Stewart.*

Photo 2.10 ~ Laundry day in the Bahamas.

Photo 2.11 ~ Crossroads *at sunset.*

Photo 2.12 ~ *Traditional sugarcane harvesting on Union Island in the Grenadines.*

Photo 2.13 ~ St. Lucia's Pitons are twin volcanic peaks that rise a half-mile from the sea.

Photo 2.14 ~ A fowl kind of roulette in Belize, the chicken drop.

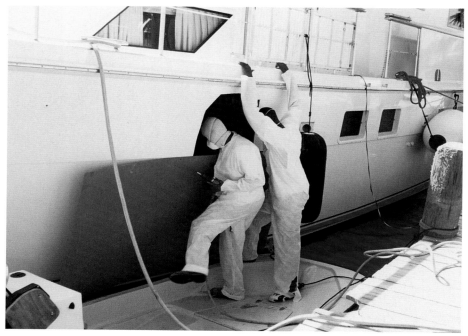

Photo 2.15 ~ Hurricane Lili pounded a 3- by 4-foot hole in Crossroads' *port side.*

Photo 2.16 ~ Ellie and Matt on vacation aboard Crossroads.

PART THREE

FOWL CAY

"Anything worth having
is a pain in the ass."

— an anonymous friend

CHAPTER 1: Misery

* * *

Phone service was down for the second straight day. Having lived with Batelco for two years, I figured it could be double that, or more, before the Bahamas' only telephone company was back up. The slam of the phone's receiver back into its cradle drowned out the plopping sound of leftover raindrops. At first, I couldn't speak, and then I couldn't stop.

"I don't think I can keep living in a place where I can't make calls or get medicine or have my hair cut, Stewart. It's too primitive. I'm too old. We're supposed to be retired and having fun, but we're both so exhausted after 10-hour workdays we eat cereal out of a box and fall into bed."

Unhappiness poured out of me unfettered on a warm day in February 2001.

"You've lost so much weight your pants hang in folds around your butt. We might as well be living in a Third World country. I feel trapped. And scared. I hate being scared."

A porthole on *Crossroads*, our 53-foot trawler, revealed a circular view of the world outside. There was a gauze of color over aquamarine at the start of another brilliant Bahamian sunset. *(Photo 3.1)*

"Well, OK, what would you like to do?"

Stewart weathered my second meltdown in two weeks in his practical way. Sometimes I wished his patience and equanimity would crack and fall into line with my agitation.

"We didn't almost kill ourselves building This End Up to live like this, did we? I'm not a prissy, pampered girl. You know that. But nobody we know, certainly no woman we know, could do this day after day."

The pride I had taken for years in being as tough, unemotional and independent as any man took a hit from my own chauvinistic remark. My family of brothers, entrepreneurial mother and pilot father had not encouraged prissy or pampered as desirable characteristics, female or no. Being perceived as hearty and able was the ticket. I suspected that upbringing had given me part of the mettle to live on a boat for nearly a decade.

"I can't find water to drink on that island half the time, and it's disgusting to have to go to the bathroom in the brush while I watch for a workman to walk up on me."

"I agree, it's rough, a lot rougher than we thought it would be," Stewart admitted.

Five straight days of vicious squalls had rocked us in a 360-degree circle as we jerked around on our anchor in the harbor at Big Major. Rain fell as if it were trying to pound *Crossroads* into the depths, and every reverberation of the waves in the enclosed boat met a resounding retort from the unyielding side of the trawler. The noise sounded like shotgun blasts.

During that stormy interval, covering the quarter mile from the mother ship to Fowl Cay in our open dinghy twice a day had soaked every pair of pants we owned. Our damp clothes hung on door handles and chair backs, showerheads and closet doors in the tight interior of *Crossroads,* emitting the fusty smell of saltwater and sawdust into the stale air.

"And if any more things on this boat break, we might as well move into those awful places on Fowl Cay where the carpenters stay. We agreed to return to *Crossroads* for lunch every day because the boat was supposed to give us a few minutes of peace. So we don't have to eat pig souse and johnnycake while we listen to earsplitting rap music. So we can try to call the children on the nonexistent phone and cool off in the nonexistent AC. What a joke. All we do for the hour is try to repair the air conditioner, the dryer, the stereo and the trash compactor. And when they're fixed, we have a list of five new things that are broken. Then our 'lunch break' is over, so we wolf down sour cottage cheese and rotten apples and tear back over to that hell hole," I said.

Having earlier made and eaten by myself two batches of chocolate chip cookies in a futile search for comfort, I was wired on sugar, mildew, cold medicine and self-pity.

"The TV doesn't even work in this weather. I can't take it anymore, Stewart. No kidding. I don't *want* to take it anymore."

The distinct smell of Stewart's Macanudo cigars trailed him, and silence, that old troublemaker between us, held its cards close to the vest. Stewart and I were polar opposites when it came to voicing frustration.

"TALK to me," I croaked, reaching for sore throat lozenges to defang the onslaught of laryngitis.

"Well, Libby, one reason we bought the island is so we can get off the boat and back onto land, so we can be more comfortable and not have to worry about keeping things working all the time." His eyebrows stood up in a hopeful signal that I would come around. "Things seem to me pretty much the same as the eight years we lived on the big *Crossroads*. Why is it so different now?"

Conversations like this always ping-ponged between us in a no-win pattern. If Stewart tried to be calm and reasonable, I ran him down with near-hysteria. On the rare occasion that he fell into doubt with me, I was terrified by his agreement. But where I really lost it was when he tried to offset my overstatements with his understatements. That was like throwing a match into a fuel tank.

"WHY? Why is it different? You're kidding, right? It's different because we don't see, and can hardly talk to, our family or friends. We have a grandchild and no telling what she looks like. We spend every day working from sunup to sundown in broiling heat or pouring rain."

I paused to breathe, my heart racing with the afterburn of anger.

"And in between all the problems on that cay, you're on the phone pleading, again, to get the lawyer to return a call or some administrator to give us a permit or some company to send a part for the boat that will take us weeks to receive way out here."

My husband's blue-green eyes were still, in perfect solidarity with his face.

"It's also different because we paid a huge part of our net worth for this island in 1998 and walked out of that lawyer's office without one thing to show that it belonged to us. No title, no nothing. We took the word of strangers from a foreign country in an incredibly stupid gamble. Now we can't get our money back, we're not even sure where the title is and we keep putting in more cash to develop it because nobody would want it halfway finished."

Then, the final furious wrap-up. "And after being harassed and ignored by this government for all that time, while you have been nothing but patient, polite and working to complete our side of the promise to make this a resort, we still don't have an extended land lease. They treat criminals better than they treat us. Work, beg, pay, beg, sleep, beg—that's all we do."

Stewart pushed aside three beer bottles at his end of the cramped dining table, crossed his arms and laid his forehead on them. Having beaten him up like that, I found I had done the same to myself, and I wept for us both.

* * *

CHAPTER 2: Seduced

I remember the first time we set foot on Fowl Cay. I had never seen so many termite tracks in one place. When Stewart picked up an old picture frame that was leaning against the wall, it fell to dust in his hands. The pages of books long ago published in French were stuck together, exposed on their shelves to 40 years of rainstorms in this house, which had never had glass in its windows. Toothpaste, shampoo and deodorant, waiting for their owners to return, sat on the pea-green bathroom counter with its corroded faucet stuck at "On." Most of the clothes in the closet were from a time and a place I wasn't familiar with.

Outside, part of a concrete wall had been laid open, its rebar rusted to flakes. The cistern had big cracks and slimy water. When I jumped over a crumbling step, I skidded on a thrown-off shingle and landed next to a battered tin bowl that held a full can of tuna fish.

"What's this for?" Stewart asked Wesley, the caretaker of Fowl Cay who was up in years but stood clear-eyed and ramrod straight.

"Dey wild cats on dis island. I feed dem when I can. Keep de rats and such away."

Our short tour of the rundown houses was over. With an absentee owner in the States, Stewart and I felt lucky to be able to see Fowl Cay in September 1997. Only two days after we anchored off its north shore in *Crossroads* and decided to find out what we could about the ravaged houses, we had been allowed a walk-through of all three of them. As Wesley locked up, he said we were welcome to wander around if we wanted to stay. We thought we would.

"I jus' got one t'ing to say. If you t'inking 'bout buyin' dis cay, you bes' keep me on. I de caretaker here for forty-some year and you don't hire me, I gern wake up dead dat day. You guh put me in my grave dat wery minute."

After Wesley left in his tiny wooden boat, Stewart and I ducked under a four-foot spider web from where the black and orange occupant gave us a proprietary stare. In the old house known as Birdcage, we settled into the broken-down Nantucket-style chairs on its deteriorating deck. Stewart propped his feet up on the railing. With a ripping noise, the thick timber tore away from an adjoining member and crashed to the floor.

A hefty coconut thunked on the roof above us. Flaunting a blood-orange pouch below his jaw, a green lizard ran up the rotting support beam, a beautiful animal with more tail than body. He hustled into a crack in the cement porch slab to get away from a brazen gull.

Looking beyond the decay of Fowl Cay across the turquoise water, limestone boulders were turning pale pink in the sunset. To the west was a butter-cream oval sandbar with the last few inches of tide meandering in pleats across its surface. Just 15 feet from the eastern side of this neglected house ran a small sapphire inlet, probably 20 feet deep and as clear as drinking water to its deepest crevice. A sloop painted shiny black cruised with a quiet swish through the center of the 35-foot-wide passage, its reefed sails and mast striking home like a fat exclamation point on the polished teak deck.

Stewart turned to me and said, "Boy, that's pretty," in his normal tone of voice.

The captain at the wheel said, "Thank you," in the perfect acoustics of that secret spot.

Nothing looks so peaceful as a beautiful sailboat gliding to its anchorage against the backdrop of a sky whose colors run from red-orange to purple-pink. Once his vessel was secured, the captain blew a conch shell from the bow in the indigenous sound of a tropical sunset in a country where the supply of such was delightfully endless. The sweet smell of night-blooming jasmine hung in the early evening air when Stewart and I left the cay to return to *Crossroads. (Photo 3.2)*

Yes, we would do this—make a pact with chance once more. We would start the engine of our combined determination, and history predicted we would prevail.

The gas tank of our dinghy was nearly empty when we tied her up for the night, so the next morning we hooked *Roundabout* to the big hose at the Staniel Cay fuel dock. Next to us was a 100-foot yacht named *Heaven* on which a uniformed mate polished windows, and bananas hung in the sunshine to ripen. With the remains of raspberries and a croissant beside him, the owner sat in the cockpit, Gucci loafers up on the rail, reading a book, *How to Change Your Life in 7 Days.*

Change it to what? How could things be much better? From where I sat, his life seemed just about perfect.

Ironically, I would spend years in this same part of the world, living in dreamlike surroundings that looked like heaven to every person who passed by. But the only reliable thing in much of my life to come would be the problems I couldn't even dream of headed my way.

Stewart and I had acquired a habit when we ran our own business of writing down the pros and cons of important decisions. Buying an island in a land other than our own would be audacious in the most accommodating of places. But a hunk of coral rock in a country that was more ocean than land? No roads, no electricity, no septic system, no potable water. The only grocery store, pharmacy, bank, airport and hospital of note were 75 miles away, accessible only by air or water. And what about hurricanes? The pencil scratched a list partway down the page and paused. I knew my pragmatic husband was mining every conceivable downside to spending big money on so exotic an acquisition. I searched my mind for negatives to prove I wasn't being seduced by paradise either.

"Don't forget the Bahamas' history of assorted nastiness." I had just finished several books about the country's sordid past and thought perhaps that reminder might round out our perspective.

The cons side of the decision was short but fraught with reckless choices.

The pros gushed out of us until we had to rip the page off the pad and turn it over. Physical beauty alone could have filled 10 sheets. The pros of Fowl Cay bludgeoned the cons to pulp.

"It's the greatest boating area we've found in all our years on *Crossroads,*" I said after Stewart talked about the superb marina one mile away, "and by far the most gorgeous snorkeling between Florida and the Grenadines."

Stewart added to the list with his own priorities, "There's a 3,000-foot landing strip nearby, a regular supply barge that services the Exumas, bonefishing, spear-fishing, offshore fishing." I could hardly wait for him to finish writing before I added, "And the medical clinic over in Staniel Cay and the sunsets, don't forget the sunsets. We haven't even listed the most important thing—won't the kids love it here? And our families? It's much more fun than a place in Florida and not much farther away."

"Wait," said Stewart, "I can't write that fast."

I followed the outline of two sailboats moving across the aquamarine sea toward the horizon while I waited for Stewart to catch up with my fervor. He looked at me and I knew in the way you do after 30 years of marriage that we were thinking the same thing, an observation we'd voiced over and over in our numerous trips through the Bahamian out-islands. The Exuma Cays were near enough to civilization to get help in a crisis but far enough away to preserve their freedom from hordes of tourists. He flipped back to the beginning of the pros list and squeezed in that critical key to our comfort right at the top. Fowl Cay looked pretty swell on paper.

Finally, the search for a location where we could settle in the islands might have hit pay dirt. After two years of looking for a small piece of land on which to build a modest house, this perfect cay popped up like a magic trick and invited us in for a show. The wait had been worth it.

Immediately in my mind, plans for one house morphed into several, and my dream expanded to a small family compound where three generations could love and laugh for as long as Stewart and I had left. Like most people our ages, keeping our grown children close to us was at the top of our wish list. My wisecracking husband said that mature people didn't usually tie up loose strings by flinging new things against the wall to see if they'd stick. But we had been flinging out things for years and had good experience assessing what we had to gain and what we had to lose. The life we wanted on our approach to 55 and 60 years old could no longer be found in the brief encounters of transient boating. We wanted to plant ourselves in a neighborhood, a neighborhood of islands.

In our stateside neighborhood, Stewart and I had a crowd of friends we had been close to since our early-married days. Over the years, we collected new pals, our siblings married and nieces and nephews joined the fold. During the course of eight alternately delightful and deadly years' cruising aboard our first *Crossroads,* my love of family and friends took on a sharper focus. When Stewart said he wanted to put down roots now that our wanderlust was slaked, it suited me. We could build a special place for family reunions, house parties and birthday celebrations, a special place we could offer to people we cared about for making their hearts happy or soothing their hurts.

How wonderful it would be to have a life that passed like a fabulous, never-ending weekend. As people from the boating community and nearby islands stopped in for a visit, we would all sit down on the beach in wood and canvas chairs, not those cheesy plastic ones with the hollow metal arms. A broad-brimmed straw hat and sarong were all I would need in the islands, unfettered by the trappings of the life I left behind. Rum punches in hand, Stewart and I would exchange interesting stories with new friends as we feasted our eyes on endless vistas of breath-taking beauty.

But hold on. Nothing indicated Fowl Cay was for sale. And the island was not exactly modest at 50 acres. It had three dilapidated houses that took up the best building sites. Besides that, who owned it after all? Bubbling with American enthusiasm and know-how, we were undeterred by those questions as we rode back to *Crossroads* to hatch a plan and firm up our knowledge of the country we had decided to call our own.

CHAPTER 3: Why Us?

The 475-mile-long archipelago of the Bahamas is a wandering chain of approximately 700 islands. Generally divided into contiguous groups, they run in a southeasterly diagonal line with the nearest one only 47 miles from Key Biscayne, Florida. Fewer than 75 have any development to speak of. Several of the islands are large, but most of the tiny cays look like puzzle pieces flung into a dappled blue-green puddle. From the air, those specks of land are slightly perceptible outcroppings of reef, rising above one of the most crystalline seas in the world.

The coral and limestone hills ascend from white sand beaches, and their hummocky surface is scattered with sea grape bushes and low palmetto trees. High ground is a comparative concept, where the tallest place in the land stands at 204 feet above sea level. Freeport and Nassau, the "mainland" cities, are all most people know of this country. But after years of having explored the whole of it from *Crossroads*, Stewart and I knew that the real Bahamas was found in the generally small and sparsely developed cays like the Exumas.

I opened the journal I kept during our cruising years, Stewart pulled out the photographs, and we reminisced as I read aloud some of what I had written about the out-islands. "In the few places where people have settled and improved the near-barren earth, bursts of riotous color dot the green underlay of these cays. Hibiscus in flaming orange and wild magenta and spiky, purple bougainvillea have adapted to the aridity and learned to live on stingy rainfall. The blossoms look like neon signs offering a convincing message—'You're in the islands now.' Perhaps because the flora on these islands is naturally meager, the Bahamian people dress up their small cement houses in neon pink, lime green and pungent blue, much like a plain woman trying to divert attention from her plight in clothing of dazzling color." My descriptions came to life in our surroundings.

The island scene was far different from our hometown of umber-colored brick houses with gray slate roofs that snuggled into professionally nurtured foliage. That contrast was one of the many dissimilarities that drew us to the Cays like a siren song, seductive and ultimately, deceptive. We had much work to do before we could call this cay our own. Relentless work.

Our first call to the New Yorker who owned Fowl Cay in early October 1997 was a bust. Phillip Walker was in the hospital when Stewart contacted him and would be there for several weeks.

"Don't call me. I'll call you," Mr. Walker said.

With his unflagging tenacity, Stewart ignored the message and called him at the end of the month, "just checking in." He got the same result.

The third attempt right before Thanksgiving drew similar discouragement.

Spending Thanksgiving on *Crossroads* in the British Virgin Islands gave us a chance to rethink our commitment to buy Fowl Cay. Maybe it just wasn't meant to be. But with Captain Gregg retiring, we were left with three options: leave the romance of the islands and move back to the cocoon of Richmond, start the search again for a perfect island somewhere in the Caribbean, or continue living on the boat with a new captain. We weren't head-over-heels about any of those ideas, so Stewart and I doubled our determination to live on that special Exuma cay.

At home in Virginia to enjoy time with our children, we were decorating the tree when the phone rang 10 days before Christmas. Phillip Walker wanted to know if we could meet him the next evening in Washington.

During a two-hour dinner, the three of us verbally agreed to a deal. Stewart and I never discovered what changed his mind about the sale, because Phillip spent the evening charming us with the tale of how he came to buy the cay in 1974 from the original French owners.

His love of the Exumas, having been aided by excellent fortune in Nassau's casinos, turned into a desire to own a piece of that rambling chain of cays. From an airplane, Phillip chose Fowl Cay because of the magnificent water surrounding it and tried to find the details of its owner. Unable to locate the information through official Bahamian channels, he gave up, and the dream faded but never evaporated.

Several years later, the company Phillip worked for transferred him to Paris. The agent he hired to find his family a house kept promoting one in a neighborhood that he and his wife didn't like, but the saleswoman's persistence finally wore them down. They agreed to look.

The Gastons, who owned the house, were out when the Walkers met their agent for the showing. As the threesome passed through a hallway,

Phillip recalled, he jerked to a stop. On the stucco wall were six poster-size, black-and-white photographs of Fowl Cay. His Exuma dream had come full circle.

It seemed to Stewart and me that the most difficult part of buying Fowl Cay was behind us after that dinner. Although strictly verbal, we were in accord on a price range, and the agreement seemed solid and Phillip trustworthy. The stickiest remaining point was one for the Bahamian government. The Walkers did not own the cay outright. It belonged to them under a 99-year Crown grant lease that was purchased by the Gastons in 1957, well before the Bahamas won independence from England. It was now almost 1998. We would have to determine whether the present administration would give Stewart and me a free-hold, releasing us altogether from the grant, or whether they would reinstate the original agreement of 99 years in our name. We couldn't dump millions of dollars into a family compound that would revert to the Bahamas after 58 years.

Having spent so much time in the Bahamas, Stewart and I felt we were more knowledgeable about the development process than most. Other vacationers, seduced by the ubiquitous vision of palm trees and hammocks and Jimmy Buffett, rum and boats and babes in bikinis, fell to its temptations. After a couple of weeks, when paradise crooked its finger, some dreamers quit their jobs and built a place in the Cays. Or tried to.

Quite often, they never got the project started. Stewart and I had seen numerous abandoned attempts to establish homes in the out-islands. Perhaps those failures should have sent us a signal, but the two of us weren't deluded by the myth of easy island living. We were used to being outside our own country, sensitive to the differences in American and Bahamian cultures, wise to managing big projects and experienced in the logistical difficulties of the Cays. If there were ever a couple entering a project like this with their eyes open, it would be us. Wouldn't you think?

CHAPTER 4: Into the Deep End (1)

Now that our dinner with Phillip is over and we have an agreement on a price range, the hardest part of buying Fowl Cay is probably behind us. Thank goodness for Stewart's tenacity in not letting Phillip off the hook. Otherwise, we'd still be riding all over the Exumas in Roundabout looking for the perfect spot. And now that perfect spot is almost ours.

Of course, we have to find a good lawyer to handle all the usual legal mumbo-jumbo. Stewart said last night that he would call our Richmond law firm on Monday to ask for a referral in Nassau. And we've made a few Bahamian friends in the last few years who might have suggestions too. If we put all that information together, it shouldn't be hard to determine who the best lawyer is. Once that's done, we'll leave the hashing out of the contract details to him.

The Bahamas only became independent from England in 1973, and I'm told their laws are still much like the English ones of today. That's comforting, because you sure do hear nightmare stories about buying land in foreign countries. Hopefully, by week's end we'll have made contact with the lawyer who'll put this together for us. We want to get the process rolling before Phillip has a change of heart.

In one way, I wish we were right in Nassau so we don't have to put this project together by phone. The Batelco system is not very reliable. For a country with such a highly developed tourism industry, and one that promotes foreign investment, it's odd that they have so much trouble with their phones. I'm sure they're working on it.

"You've been trying to get back to us for two days with your recommendation?... I'm sorry. The phones down here are really a pain... The law firm's name is what?... Walter?... Walter?"

CHAPTER 5: Strangers in Paradise

Our search for the best lawyer in Nassau covered wide ground. By the middle of January 1998, we settled on a firm, but after repeated tries, Stewart was unable to make contact with Mr. Morley. I had a bad feeling. Stewart, who rarely made such judgments on gut feel, bided his time and left a patient message at every attempt. The attorney never returned his calls. We were doubly frustrated one day when someone on the switchboard at Hall, Kidd and Alexander told us, "Mr. Morley just say to tell you he out of de office."

"Stewart, did the lawyer call back?"

"No, Batelco was down yesterday and today."

"Stewart, did the lawyer call back?"

"No, he's gone until next Wednesday for a funeral."

"Stewart, did the lawyer call back?"

"No, he's out of the office for a four-day weekend."

"Stewart, did the lawyer call back?"

"No, he has been out of the office all day in a meeting."

By February, Stewart had made one voice contact with the lawyer. We were in serious need of advice regarding details of U.S. tax laws, Bahamian real estate laws and how a Crown grant affected them. Our attorney generally refused to take our phone calls. The assistant said time after time that Mr. Morley was in conference and would call us back at a certain time. No matter what plans we had, Stewart and I adjusted them to be available for his schedule. We didn't dare miss a chance at contact with the elusive Mr. Morley.

Hours in the Bahamas were like a drop of water in a hot frying pan; they generally evaporated with no trace. I can't remember any instance that our lawyer called when he said he would. That disregard for customers' time was the first of many experiences that made us realize the incompatibility of Americans' precise, and Bahamians' relaxed, attitudes toward schedules.

Just one full-moon night of watching starfish on the white sand bottom, turning my face to the warm breeze and listening to the rhythmic fall of waves on the beach put me back in the middle of my dream. The unpleasantness with our lawyer would pass. Fowl Cay would belong to us, and Stewart and I could close the annoying legal chapter of buying an island and move forward into the role of benevolent parents, grandparents and friends inside the utopia we had decided to create.

"Well, could you please find out a time that would suit Mr. Morley?" begged Stewart for the third time in three days.

"Certainly, Mr. Brown. Dat would be my great pleasure. I call you back before de end of de day, as you have requested. Have a wery lovely afternoon."

Stewart and I pushed our food around at supper that night. We had knots in our stomachs from waiting inside the boat for five hours for the secretary to call us back. Anger flashed inside me like lightning during a summer storm, and I couldn't resist reminding Stewart how many times we had been treated the same way. He smiled and nodded his head. The deeper his feelings, the quieter Stewart became.

"Hall, Kidd and Alexander, and a wery pleasant good morning to you. How may I direc' your call today?"

"Mr. Morley's office, please."

"It would be my deep pleasure to connec' you. May I say who is calling, please?"

"Stewart Brown."

"Oh, Mr. Brown. Mr. Morley is gone on waycation. May I get someone else for you?"

"His assistant, Alistair Smith, would be fine, thank you."

"He will also be away for two veek, Mr. Brown. Is dere someone else who could help perhaps?"

"No, thank you, Mrs. Lowe. I appreciate you trying."

"It is entirely my pleasure to do dat for you, Mr. Brown. And by de way, Mr. Morley axe dat I recheck de address to vich you vant our statement sent. T'ank you, Mr. Brown, and have a mos' pleasant time until we speak again."

This week's conversation had no reference to Stewart's three previous phone calls to her in which she said it would be her pleasure to help. It seemed a total disconnect from reality. But a very gracious disconnect.

After weeks, Mr. Morley's assistant Alistair called, and on the appointed day we flew in to meet our lawyer in person. He kept us waiting for half an hour. Although we found him reserved by our standards,

Mr. Morley seemed politely interested in what Stewart had to say. He ignored me once introductions were completed. I restrained painting myself worthy by telling him Stewart and I were equal financial partners in this venture. I had learned from observation that many Bahamian men would look at my personal business success as a threat. Narrow attitudes in the U.S. toward women paled in comparison to this country.

Finally, the date was set to hammer out the terms of Fowl Cay's sale, so I noted it in my DayTimer with a ballpoint pen. I still had a lot to learn.

Continuing to build our team for this project, we hired a Bahamian architect who was recommended by Mr. Morley. He would fly down from Nassau to see if the island's three houses, warehouse or cisterns could be salvaged. Stewart wired $900 and Jerome Young said he would report back in a couple of days. Now we were moving along.

"When do you expect him back?" asked Stewart of Mr. Young's assistant on day 11.

"I have him call terreckly, Mr. Brown."

Three days later, Jerome phoned to say he would send the report to Fowl Cay on Monday. Stewart told him we had heard mail from Nassau to the out-islands could take several weeks. "No problem, mon," said Jerome.

"OK, Jerome. While I have you on the phone, did you find something on Fowl Cay that caused your study to take longer than you thought it would?"

"No, but once we dere it turn vindy, so it a few day before I feel like flyin' out. I hate dose little plane. Since it near to my birthday and I stuck in de area, I ride to Farmer's Cay for a celebration. I have family over to Farmer's. I might charge you more 'cause I trap down dere. I send de bill for our expense."

"Who the hell is 'our'?" Stewart mumbled when he hung up.

Start and stop. Start and stop. Information bucked along in a manner recalling my first attempt at driving a straight-stick. After several tries, a firm price and conditions were agreed to between Phillip Walker and us. Stewart and I celebrated on *Crossroads,* surrounded by a flaming pink sunset with low, black storm clouds encircling the horizon. The show was a prophetic message from Mother Nature, had we only known to interpret it. Instead, we dreamed of a small resort.

After two appointment changes, Stewart and I flew to Nassau to meet Phillip and his lawyer in the offices of Hall, Kidd and Alexander. Once Mr. Morley expressed his conviction that the lease would be renewed for 99 years and that approval for the transfer of the lease from seller to buyer was "just a formality," we decided we should move forward. Those small housekeeping issues were no reason to hold up the final signatures on the contract or the transfer of money, our lawyer told Stewart. Obtaining a freehold for Fowl Cay might take a bit longer but could almost assuredly be done. We said fine, but forgot to ask in what century.

We were told it would take half an hour to finalize the wording of the contract and fill in the enormous number on the line that said "Price." Because we had all been sitting for hours at the conference table in the law offices, I needed a break and asked Mr. Morley where the bathroom was.

"The baaathroom is down the hall and on your left," he said in his English accent, except for the notable mocking of my American pronunciation of the word "bathroom."

I looked at Stewart to see if I had misread that slur and could see on his face I had not.

When I returned, Stewart was explaining to Mr. Morley and Phillip's lawyer that the two of us would own Fowl Cay jointly and that our monies would be written in two equal checks. I sat back in my chair next to our lawyer, who was at the head of the table. Mr. Morley's assistant returned with copies of the completed contract, and everyone but I received one to look over. I shared Stewart's since he sat to my right. It looked in order.

"Well, jolly. Are we all in agreement then?" asked Mr. Morley. "Shall we begin the signing with the buyers?"

He lifted the original contract over my space and placed it pointedly in front of Stewart, where he indicated the line for his signature. I didn't blink or breathe.

"Contrary to your country, Mrs. Brown, in our country, the male always signs first."

After the signatures were in place, Stewart and I left the office of our lawyer who treated me like dirt, in a country that was not our own, leaving a daunting amount of money on the table, with a contract that was meaningless until it was "approved by the Crown." No lease transfer, no 99-year extension, no freehold. We had chosen an undertaking whose enormous risk was so twisted out of recognition by our desire for a final spectacular project in our lives that we were blinded to its lopsided chance for success.

CHAPTER 6: Yes, Re-a-lly

On our next trip to Richmond, Stewart and I started telling people we had bought a remote little island in the Bahamas where we planned to build a family compound. Every time I said it though, I felt a twinge of doubt, because Phillip Walker had long had our money and we still had no tangible evidence we owned Fowl Cay. Some of the hometown reactions were similar to those we heard when we were going to start selling furniture made of crates, and when we'd said we were going to live full-time on a boat.

"You're going to live on an island? What if that doesn't work out?"

"What if it does?" Stewart and I thought.

Back on *Crossroads* in the Exumas, Stewart called our attorney first thing.

"Could you please buzz Mr. Morley and just ask him if he has received our four letters of character reference yet?"

"I am terribly sorry, Mr. Brown, but Mr. Morley is on a conference call just now. May I have him ring you back?"

"That's all right, Mrs. Lowe. I'll call him back."

Lining up the reference letters from our banker and a longtime friend had been easy, but the endorsement the Bahamian government required from a U.S. politician took some thought. Stewart and I usually tried to stay away from that crowd. Our minister seemed delighted to write of our upstanding character, although our acquaintance was intermittent. A trip to the state of Virginia and city of Richmond offices produced our clean police records within a couple of days. When a disagreement developed about turning our complete financial records over to the Bahamian government, we finally gave in because we realized noncompliance would give them reason to stonewall forever.

The demand that we present our plans and drawings for the development of Fowl Cay to Mrs. Somers in the Prime Minister's office took us by surprise, same as most things during the legal process. Stewart and I guessed the request was probably tied to the lease transfer that was still not approved. Since Jerome Young had proved himself not to be a candidate, we moved our search for a decent architect to the top of our expanding list of things to get done.

Finding one who seemed compatible with the way things didn't work in the Bahamas was more difficult than we expected. Since Jerome had reported that the three old houses on Fowl Cay needed to be torn down, all new houses would need to be designed. Several candidates we interviewed over the phone were sure they could manage in the tropics, but we knew differently by the time the call was over. Our criteria included several things: he must have designed at least one house on an outisland, not a big island like Jamaica, St. Thomas or Bermuda; he must be able to contend with a shifting start date since we didn't know when the lease transfer would be approved; and he must have had experience living on saltwater, either in a house or a boat. And Stewart and I had to like him as a person.

I lined up six architects for us to meet: one in North Carolina, three in Virginia and two in the Bahamas. In April, we decided on Ned Pinkerton who had a one-man office near Richmond. With a house and boat on the Chesapeake Bay, he had cruised much of his life, sometimes in the Bahamas. He specialized in designing waterfront homes and had done two that were built in the Cays. Smart, direct and experienced, we knew he would be capable. Stewart and I shook hands with Ned, and we left to spend Easter 1998 with Ellie and her husband Matt on *Crossroads*. The holiday was too brief.

Because lack of communication from the Bahamian government was causing permanent wrinkles in my forehead, Stewart thought he might assuage my worry by reminding me over and over that this was not our country. We had to do it their way. I tried to believe that early in the game, but the dearth of results was incomprehensible, especially since we were using the same techniques that had gotten speedy resolution to problems at This End Up. I hoped once this red tape was over, things would smooth out.

We tried not to talk about our concerns in front of the friends who arrived in late spring to join us on *Crossroads*. With a roll of our eyes, we told them the stories of mañana, making it sound amusing in a Third World sort of way. They laughed and thought we were clever and plucky.

Busting our buttons, we toured them around Fowl Cay. They were our first friends to see it. Excited for us but perhaps a bit shocked by its poor condition and scantily developed surroundings, their intelligent questions increased in depth and intensity, however overlaid with jokes about us moving slower now that we were turning Bahamian. Little did they know how our energy was being sapped.

"My hat's off to you," one of them said, hanging Stewart and me on fresh tenterhooks about the enormous scope of the development. "There's no way in hell I could do this."

While cruising around in the dinghy, our group stopped at a nearby island owned by friends from Illinois who kept their boat at the dock just outside their house. Most people who lived in the out-islands spent some part of every day trying to keep their boat engines running. Like cars in the States, boats were our mode of transportation. Without them we would all be marooned on our individual cays, so upkeep was vital. No boat mechanics down here.

I glanced at Stewart as we pulled up to Hummingbird Cay. This would be our first attempt to merge conservative Virginia with the loosey-goosey Bahamas. When Mamie from Richmond's snooty West End met Mark from the crazy expatriate population that lived in the Exumas, we weren't sure how things would go.

After introductions, I asked Mark, whose hands were covered with engine grease, "What have you been doing today?"

"Working on my lower unit."

"Your lower unit?" said Mamie. "What's wrong with it?"

"It doesn't work."

Mamie's husband, Abby, had wandered off down Hummingbird's rocky beach, but she couldn't think of joining him. This conversation was way too much fun to miss.

"What did you do about it?" Mamie egged Mark on.

"I sent it to Nassau on the mail boat to be fixed."

"You can get your lower unit fixed in Nassau? When will you get it back?"

"Next week on the mail boat."

Mamie yelled over to her long wedded husband, "Hey, Abby. Come over here and talk to Mark. He's got some great news for you."

I decided that Mamie's tongue-in-cheek humor fit right into the Bahamas, and Mark occasionally asked when "that funny girl from Richmond" was coming back for a visit.

On the last night together, we told our hometown buddies that we'd gone from having "a modest house in the islands" to planning a family compound to building a small resort. We explained that the first leap came with the decision to buy enough land to build each of our children a house near ours "so our family can have a place to be together," I said.

"OK, OK. We're bribing them," joked Stewart. The attendant group of grandparents understood completely.

"But a resort?" one of them asked, obviously shocked.

"Well, that jump was more complicated. Once we started to picture the family compound idea, a lot of questions arose, and the solutions we came up with all pointed in the same direction."

What would we do with two extra houses when our kids could come only a couple times a year? Having seen buildings deteriorate all over the Bahamas, we knew closing them up wasn't the answer... How would we keep hard-to-find staff when we needed them only part of the year? Surely their loyalty would be won faster if we could guarantee them a full-time job... With each child and spouse in a separate house, where could we congregate with those grandkids we expected to be popping out? What about our extended families that would spend occasional holidays and vacations with us? Where would they stay? A group that big would need a central place to celebrate and dine... How would two outgoing people entertain themselves with two-thirds of the island unoccupied the majority of the year? Perhaps a small restaurant would draw the lively boating community that flocked to the area.

And the biggest question: What would Stewart and I do if we didn't step out onto the entrepreneurial dance floor together one more time? A chance to prove the old team wasn't a one-hit-wonder from yester-year's contest. Entrepreneurship had been our life's work, the bond and admiration between us. A resort that felt like home was our answer. Not rustic, not glitzy, not big. Just home.

On a beautiful day in May 1998, we put our friends on a plane at the Staniel Cay airstrip and drove *Roundabout* to the village for a visit.

CHAPTER 7: Into the Deep End (2)

I keep waking up at night, my mind swirling with a mix of excitement and fear over our decision to build a little resort on Fowl Cay.
It just sort of came over Stewart and me as a solution to the problem of keeping the houses in good condition and keeping ourselves busy
and entertained. It won't be easy but we like projects and problem-solving.

The logistics of running a resort are going to take some organizing.
Since we won't have our own airstrip, getting 14 guests in and out of
Staniel Cay might be our most complicated trick. After all, Fowl Cay is
an island 75 miles away from any decent-sized town—and that accessed
only by water or air. We'll have to buy a number of small boats, hire
managers and staff and build a place to house the food and drink for the
resort guests.

The word in the boating community is there's a delivery boat that
usually comes down from Nassau to Staniel every week or two. I suppose
we'll have to line up food and liquor vendors in New Providence who
can ship goods to us on that vessel. No other way to do it. Flying all the
food in would be really expensive. We wouldn't want to do that except
in a real emergency. Bringing in the supplies by boat to Staniel is only
part of the story. We'll have to pick them up at the dock over there in
some sort of flat-bottom skiff to get them the mile back to our dock—
and that in terrible weather or the middle of the night sometimes. The
managers better be really hardy.

Stewart and I are lucky that we've lived in the islands aboard
Crossroads for so long. We won't get blindsided by "tropical" problems
of logistics like a lot of people who move down here on a whim to live.
We wouldn't dare try running a resort on a deserted cay without those
eight years of experience cruising through the islands.

"Operator, can you connect me to this number for a law firm in
Nassau? I can't get through and I'm late for a conference call…"

CHAPTER 8: Pay Up

Excitement crackled in the village, mostly among the foreigners who lived there. Electricity was coming to Staniel Cay! Electrical power was just arriving in the out-islands, and piped water was still some years off. Old-fashioned ways were never a problem for the easy-going natives. Outside influence had been unable to disturb the "What is, is" philosophy over the years. In many ways the two societies were polar opposites. Stewart and I hung around to join the festivities and introduce ourselves to the community, but everyone already knew we were the new people at Fowl Cay. The news had traveled by coconut telegraph.

"You need a good cook? Look me up to de pink house near by de airport."

"I be your tour guide for de guestis. How much you guh pay?"

"I already got a job to de Bar 'n Bites, but if you need hair braiding, I be de one."

That was a good sign. Maybe finding staff for our resort wouldn't be hard after all.

We talked to Genesta, who owned the one-room Island Market. The bright green building was in the heart of Staniel Cay, just behind the village's only church. Now that we'd be living in Big Major harbor aboard *Crossroads,* we needed to be wired in better to the schedule of the government supply and mail boat. Delivery via water would be our only source of food unless we chartered a plane for a 75-mile trip to the grocery store in Nassau.

"Oh, dat boat come mos' erry week on Wednesday," said Genesta. "'Cep' for if dey go out to Ragged Island firs'. De captain girlfrien' live dere."

"Great. We'll be over tomorrow to stock up. Do you get fresh veggies and ice cream on the boat?"

"Sometime ice cream, usually wedgeatables."

"How about fruit and meat?"

"Yep."

"What time do you open up?" said Stewart.

"'Roun' nine-turdy on mailboat day," said Genesta.

"We'll be there right when you open tomorrow then. Thanks for the information."

"Tomorrow dere won't be no food."

"Really? Why's that?" I asked.

"Cause de boat broke. It ain' been here in two mont'."

Stewart and I had homework to do on how to get food, no doubt about it, but our next few days were slated for an even bigger test.

With the selection of an architect complete, we focused on finding a contractor. We hardly knew where to start. The government, which issued all the permits we would need, recommended that the job go to a Bahamian company. By now, we could guess what would happen if we didn't follow their suggestion. But hiring locally sounded fair to us anyway. After all, Stewart and I had bought a piece of their country. Hadn't we?

A firm in Freeport named Windsor Construction had built one of the houses our architect had designed previously. After one meeting with the charming founder of the firm, we were sold. Windsor's experience with building in the Bahamas stretched the length of the archipelago and included hotels, government buildings, restaurants, casinos, condominiums and individual homes. Windsor's senior partner, John Heath, said that his firm would take on the Fowl Cay challenge.

"I swore I would never oversee another job in the out-islands," said John. "They are frightfully difficult because of the transportation, labor and supervisory issues. This one looks to be quite interesting, however, so I'll make it my swan song in the Exumas."

Stewart and I breathed a sigh of relief.

"Let me say to you both that in my years owning Windsor Construction, I have lost count of the number of people who have sat just where you are now and said they wanted to develop an out-island. Not one of them has been able to do it in all my years. It takes a certain personality to take this on. You must appreciate—no, love—dealing with problems. Resilience will be the name of the game. Think about it carefully."

Although John Heath's warning gave us pause, we were grateful for his honesty and pleased about his concern on our behalf. With a signed contract between Windsor and us, we had now hired one Bahamian architect, one American architect, and a construction company to work on a project for which we didn't own the land. I felt like a fish in a net as we signed check after check for these professionals. A bigger worry was the memory of how many dollars had been left in the impenetrable offices of Hall, Kidd and Alexander three months before, as down-payment for Fowl Cay.

In June, Phillip called to say his lawyer reported that the lease transfer had gone through. Stewart and I were ecstatic, and our first call was to the children. Even the phones being out for seven hours before we could make contact hardly put a dent in our mood. By the next day, we wanted to hear the news from our own lawyer. No luck. After several days of unreturned calls from Mr. Morley, Stewart asked for his assistant, who called back after the weekend.

"Mr. Morley has just left for two weeks on a sailing cruise, Mr. Brown. Might I be able to help?"

After Stewart explained the message we'd received from Phillip Walker, he asked Alistair about the government's approval of us as Fowl Cay's new owners.

"I'm afraid that certific' hasn't reached us yet. You and Mrs. Brown are now to be checked troo Interpol and dat process will take some time I believe."

"Interpol? That's the first I've heard of that," said Stewart.

"The guvament offices will be shut down for the holidays, but we will be in contact when we have information. Have a wery nice day."

I called Ellie and Stew to report that the good news was premature.

Through our lawyer, Stewart received a demand from the government of a substantial payment for a vague reason. When he inquired repeatedly about its purpose, he received shuttered faces and a mushy explanation about "a fee for the consent of the assignment of the lease." The bill remained unpaid. We asked to see the law that required such a fee. No results. Stewart indicated that we'd be happy to pay if anyone could show us a precedent for such a thing. Weeks passed.

In a rare piece of good news, Interpol signed off on us, but requests for the mysterious fee kept rolling in. Ten months had passed since we decided we wanted to buy Fowl Cay.

When we asked again what the delay was on the transfer of the lease, Mr. Morley said a second Interpol check was required. By this time, Stewart's jaw muscle was jumping almost non-stop, and I was back to my habit of living on Advil, Rolaids and M&Ms.

One day a Bahamian friend, whom we had known from our early years of cruising the Exuma Cays, called and said he had heard in his influential Nassau circles that the government was jerking our chain.

With acquaintances high up in the administration, he had taken it upon himself to see what he could do.

"I have a bit of news for you, but don't ask where it came from," Edmond said. "When I asked what was going on with Fowl Cay, my contact said, 'Tell Mr. Brown to stop asking questions and pay up.'"

Stewart white-knuckled his pen as he wrote a check the next morning. Our presumptions about fundamental decency in high places crumbled on the table.

Mr. Morley initiated a rare call soon after that to say we had passed our second inspection by Interpol and the Prime Minister had OK'd the lease transfer the same day. Wasn't that good news?

"So we're all set for final settlement then?" asked Stewart.

"Oh, not quite yet. The request goes to the Lands and Surveys Department now. Not too much longer I expect. Cheerio."

Later, sitting with two Bahamian buddies and some American friends who had lived on Staniel Cay for years, the comforting embrace of friendship warmed us as we watched a magnificent green flash. Reactions of the seasoned pros, as they sat in childlike wonder of the spectacle, let us know we would never become inured to the beauty of the Bahamas. "Maybe tomorrow will be better," I thought. But Stewart was unusually quiet, even in their bantering company, and I knew his silence covered inner turmoil. I wished I knew how to cure it.

Final settlement was quick and worrisome when it finally occurred. We dared not postpone it. But we were informed for the first time that the land lease could not be extended to the desired 99 years until we could get an appointment with Mrs. Somers in the Prime Minister's office. She would need to sign off on our development plans to make sure that Fowl Cay would be properly preserved. Preserved from what, I wondered— falling-down houses, crumbling cisterns and untended land?

"Please provide a book of information on why you want to do this, how much money you plan to spend and where the funds would come from, who the customer will be, how much income the resort will generate and how the business will be incorporated. Full plans showing the building sites, path layout, infrastructure needs, landscaping require-ments and recreational facilities should be included. Kindly provide four full copies as soon as they are available."

The lawyer agreed it would be better from this point forward if Stewart and I worked directly with the office of the Prime Minister, the "P.M." they called him. Perhaps it would help move things along to omit the middlemen of Hall, Kidd and Alexander now that we knew Mrs. Somers was eager to meet with us. Once everything had been sent in, she would review the plan and let us know when it would be convenient to make the oral presentation.

After that dog-and-pony show was over, we were told we would hear when the plans had been stamped and passed on to the Prime Minister. We never heard back from Mrs. Somers, so Stewart started his usual follow-up phone calls. Over many months, she never took one call from him and never returned one. Once, her assistant told Stewart that Mrs. Somers' OK for the lease extension was "on the top of the P.M.'s desk" with no problems expected. Some weeks later, the clerk said it was "at the bottom of the P.M.'s stack, very low priority, and it might not happen at all." No one ever told us it would be necessary to have a governmental visit to Fowl Cay to ensure that we had done what we said we would do before the Prime Minister would act on the extension. With assurances all around, we had been led into a contractual limbo, bound and beholden to an inscrutable bureaucracy.

The lease would stay in the hands of the law firm for registration with the proper authorities once Lands and Surveys finalized its transfer to us. We held no legal document showing the cay was ours, but another huge chunk of our net worth found a home in Phillip's bank account on closing day.

After leaving the law office, our next step that day was to obtain applications for Fowl Cay's acceptance under the Hotel and Resort Encouragement Act and The Out-Island Development Act. This would permit us to import much of our building materials and furnishings into the Bahamas without paying the 30 to 40 percent duty. If the OK for that request moved at the pace of the ones for a lease transfer and extension, who knew how many of the remaining years on Fowl Cay's lease would be available to us to enjoy?

The entire infuriating experience, which we mistakenly thought was near its end in August 1998, was just the dawning of the complexity, cost and aggravation of life while we built our resort in paradise. Eleven months after we approached Phillip Walker, we believed, but had no way to prove, that we now owned Fowl Cay. Fragile joy bloomed in the midst of spiking fear.

CHAPTER 9: Potty-Foyer

"Mr. Grayson, we don't need the dock permit yet. We won't even build a new one for at least two years."

"You NEED a dock permit, Mrs. Brown."

"But you said it would expire in 12 months. That means we would have to reapply and repay at least two more times before we actually use it. That doesn't make sense to me."

"A vord of visdom, Mrs. Brown, you NEED a dock permit."

"But I don't think we need it now."

"Mrs. Brown, you need it NOW."

When I left the payment window in the administrator's office, the clerk said, "Dere you go. I see you right here nex' year."

Stewart and I decided to open a Bahamian bank account. On the advice of Hall, Kidd and Alexander, we went to one of Nassau's largest international banks, which was run by local personnel. Our lawyer said he would call ahead to smooth the way.

For two hours, we were shuffled from office to office. Then, "Please sit in our lobby for a few moments," said one of the bankers. We left after another hour and a half as the bank was closing for the day. We had Fowl Cay's account number but that's all we had. No temporary checks, no date for the printed ones to arrive and no thanks for the business. When we mentioned the shabby treatment to Mr. Morley, he said, "You must have patience."

Ned Pinkerton, the Virginia architect, came to Nassau a day later. Along with Ned and Paul Harper from Windsor Construction, Stewart and I flew down to Fowl Cay for two days of planning. On a perfect day, we watched the undulations of white sand below a litany of turquoise shades that comprise the colors of the Exumas' water. The pilot made a lazy circle in the arch of brilliant sky above our property, craning his neck to look. *(Photo 3.3)*

"Dat you island, mon? Dat one wonnerful t'ing I see in my born day."

Ned and Paul asked for two more flyovers. Their "omigods" spilled over each other as Stewart and I gorged on the sight of Fowl Cay and basked in their reaction.

Paul agreed that the rickety dock would need to be torn down to bring in the 175-foot Windsor barge. She would be the main transportation for the tons of materials necessary to develop the cay. He thought a bit of dredging at the entrance to a new cement bulkhead should allow for the big boat to get in at high tide, a critical consideration in scheduling all our supply barges. If the boat had to wait to dock because of poor tide timing or bad weather, Windsor might add eight or ten idle hours to the $200-per-hour tab. The environmental people, however, wanted a minimum of disturbance to the natural contours of the sandy floor in Big Major. *(Photo 3.4)*

Paul left, saying, "I'm a sixth-generation Bahamian. I've been coming to the Exumas all my life. I've never seen a cay surrounded by such incredible beauty."

As he hopped on the tiny plane we chartered to take him back to Freeport that afternoon, he stuck his head out the door with a reminder. "Don't forget to have a surveyor and an environmental engineer sign off on the dock plans. We won't get the permits without that." We would need to locate a marine architect who could draw a schematic for the three piers we planned to build for our workboats, guest boats and personal boats, and then a qualified person to review the drawings who could certify that we weren't damaging the marine habitat.

Crossroads was in the boatyard in Fort Lauderdale for its annual checkup, so Ned, Stewart and I stayed at the little cottages near the marina at Staniel Cay. Each was a different color and sat beside the path that led to the restaurant next to the big dock. Having stayed there ourselves, we were used to their quirky design: you entered right into the bathroom. If a person was on the john or stepping out of the shower and his roomie opened the door with no warning, the one doing his business was exposed to the world. But we were fond of them in a funny way, and our small cottage had a dock where we could leave *Roundabout*. We took the pink house and Ned had the blue one.

When the three of us met for drinks at the bar that evening, I asked our architect if his accommodations were OK. He said they were and that his cottage had actually given him a first thought for the design of the rental houses at Fowl Cay. Stewart and I were excited to hear a concrete idea for our project.

"What is it?"

"I've really never thought of anything quite like this until now, but it might be interesting to have your resort guests enter their houses through a lovely Potty-Foyer. It seems like an islandy sort of design. What do you think?" We all laughed and raised Kaliks, the local beer. "To Potty-Foyers," we said.

The next day we finalized the agreement to build six houses: three rentals, one owner's, one manager's and one clubhouse with a small restaurant. All the existing houses on Fowl Cay would be torn down despite our wish to salvage them. I wondered fleetingly how we would dispose of that monstrous pile of rubbish.

In addition to the new houses and docks, we would need a power plant, desalination facility, rainwater catchment system, septic tanks, garbage disposal method, storage and laundry facilities, repair workshop, golf cart paths, landscaping, an office and unnamed recreational amenities. Those were the requirements that surfaced in our first meeting. Stewart and I sensed a growing gulf between our needs and our allotted funds.

During the next two days with Ned, we talked about things that would be important to the development's layout. Our experience living on a boat often brought practical consideration to bear. Some of the houses at Fowl Cay would be only 30 feet from the sea, and even the gentlest breeze would be full of salt, clogging screens and corroding metal. When squalls blew in, saltwater could course down the building exteriors and over the decks and patios and outdoor furniture. Having spent years on *Crossroads* in just such conditions we understood strong wind, blinding light, searing heat, prevailing breezes, corrosion, logistical difficulties and infrastructure odors and noise. The availability, cost and logistics of getting the particular materials required would become a daily concern.

We chartered a plane to Nassau, from where Ned flew out to the States while Stewart and I stayed to hire a surveyor to do the elevations. We needed the plans for the houses before our request for a freehold or at least a 99-year lease extension could move forward. Later that afternoon, we took a taxi to Hall, Kidd and Alexander to meet with Mr. Morley about our application for the Hotel and Resort Encouragement Act. The appointment had been arranged three weeks prior and confirmed two days before our arrival, but the lawyer wasn't there. We received no explanation, only, "Come tomorrow morning and maybe he can fit you in."

Once Ned got to the States, he provided specific instructions by telephone to George Monroe, the surveyor. When Ned called us to report on the conversation, he said, "How the hell do you get anything done on that telephone system down there? The static was so bad I could only hear half of what George was saying."

The survey would be two days' work, Ned thought, so Stewart needed to make a reservation for a Potty-Foyer cottage on Staniel Cay. George needed a boat to be rented so he could get back and forth to Fowl Cay. Oh, yes, and two $350 round-trip charter flights to Nassau, plus all of his expenses. And of course, his fee. Doing business in the Cays was always more than we had budgeted.

George said he could start the survey job straightaway. Twenty-seven days later, we paid for three men for four days at well over the original estimate and had no information in hand. Stewart joked, "Well, he did say he could start the job straightaway."

Over the phone Stewart asked, "Well, George, when do you think the information can be sent to the architect?"

"Dis de way we work down here," he said.

George grumbled about working in the out-islands, as most Nassau-born workers did. Too slow, no flashy women, no nightlife. His attitude was the opposite of those born in the Family Islands.

Bahamians referred to the Exumas as the Family Islands. Over the years, many men moved away from these little cays to look for work on Grand Bahama or New Providence, but a large percentage of them still had relatives living in the out-islands, and they spoke fondly of home when they learned Stewart and I lived there. "All my fomlee live to Barreterre... to Farmer's... to Staniel... to Black Point," they would say as we passed through Nassau or Freeport. It was an instant bond between us.

The scowling Immigration officer grunted as we came through Nassau Passport Control one day on our way from Virginia to Fowl Cay. "What are you doing in the Bahamas for seven weeks?" he asked disapprovingly as he read our entry form. A visit of that duration was an extended stay compared with the weeklong trips of most tourists.

"We own Fowl Cay down in the Exumas," I said.

"Oh! Fowl Cay over by Staniel? I got a sister, my aunt and uncle and two cousin what live to Black Point. You in God's vorl' down dere. You go on and have a wonnerful stay in de Fomlee Islands." Stewart and I were rewarded with flashing eyes and a beautiful smile before our new friend resumed his sullen demeanor and shouted, "Next!"

On the way to catch our charter flight, our taxi driver asked where we were from. "From the States," I said, "but we live down in the Exumas now."

Despite the oncoming traffic, he twisted his head around almost 180 degrees. Stewart and I could see a grin span the width of his face. "I come from down dere. All my fomlee live to Rolletown in Great Exuma. You been to Rolletown?"

"No, we haven't. We own one of your beautiful cays near Staniel and we live there now."

"Oh my. You be in 'bout de prettiest part of de Bahamas dere is. De nex' time you by Staniel, tell James Davis you rode wid Luter Rolle. He know. He my aunt sister boy."

Our particular little Family Island had developed the bad habit of swallowing up money at a stunning pace, and the clock on Fowl Cay's land lease would be ticking down to 57 years in a couple more months. I lost track of whether that lease had been registered in our name, and Stewart was so deep in thought much of the time, I didn't want to add to his burden by asking. Ned Pinkerton's clock was ticking; Windsor Construction's clock was ticking; Hall, Kidd and Alexander's clock was ticking. As for Stewart and me, the stress was about to cause our hearts to stop ticking.

CHAPTER 10: Paper Jam

Paying Bahamian vendors through our U.S. bank was difficult. Stewart called our bank in Nassau to see why we hadn't received our checks or any statements three months after opening two accounts there, one for American dollar transactions and one for Bahamian dollar transactions. We had made our choices of check style, and put in the exact amount of funds the manager requested to open the account. When Stewart had questioned the small deposit they asked for, he was told that after we received our checks and first statement, it would be proper to transfer the money needed to pay bills for Fowl Cay's development.

"I'm calling, Mr. Harding, to inquire about why we've received no statement from the bank showing the deposit we made three months ago."

"De bank doesn't send a statement until you've written at leas' one check, and dere's been no actiwity in your account," Mr. Harding said.

"That's because you haven't sent the checks to us," Stewart said.

"You not receive your checks yet, Mr. Brown, due to de fact dat you overdrew your account by choosing de expensive cover and checks. We been holdin' erryt'ing here at de bank until you take care of de overdraft. Den we can mail your checks to you."

When we asked around about changing to another bank, the opinion was unanimous. "Oh, no, don't change. You're with the best one there is."

I thought of a line I read somewhere: "A folly is a dream whose virtues have not yet been discovered." I was trying hard to keep my mind on the intended outcome of our folly, to move forward with energy and optimism, but its virtues were playing hide and seek. It had never occurred to me that I might not be adequate for this responsibility.

While we were in Richmond in November 1998, we met with Ned several times and he had rough drawings to show us, completed without the still-missing survey information. One of Ned's greatest strengths was his ability to move forward without details other architects would demand. Brimming with creative suggestions, Ned ran our meetings in his charming old office in a manner that helped us focus on the excitement of our project instead of its stumbling blocks. His can-do attitude quelled growing problems for a while.

Our *Crossroads* captain Gregg had made his last trip for us the end of October, delivering the boat from Fort Lauderdale to Sampson Cay Marina, one mile from Fowl Cay. For the first time in eight years, she waited empty until we arrived from Virginia. Imperative that we stay near the activity at Fowl Cay, we plunked the boat's big anchor at Pig Beach and for the next three years that was our home.

We hired a dock designer and a scientist to perform the environmental impact study. The two men worked smoothly together. The only stumbling block came when scientist Chris said the little dock where Stewart and I wanted to keep our personal dinghy needed to be moved 28 inches to the left. He had calculated the angle of the sun and discovered that a rare piece of coral under our dock would not receive enough light during the winter because of the structure's shadow. Unless remedied, that issue would keep us from getting a building permit. Winston, the dock designer, rolled his eyes at such minutiae.

We were assured of a speedy return of plans.

"Guess we can shut the books on this one," I said on the way to the airstrip, thrilled at this point to cross any task off our list.

"Not so," Chris said. "You need a final sign-off for this study no earlier than three months before you start building the dock. Charter me a flight when you're at that point and I'll fly back down for a recheck."

Ellie and Matt spent Christmas and New Year's on the boat with Stewart and me, but Stew was working in São Paulo, Brazil, that year and couldn't get enough time off to join us. *Crossroads* had Big Major harbor almost to herself as we turned lobster on the grill and breathed in the aroma of cinnamon from the apple crisp warming in the oven. While we waited on supper, Ellie and I laughed when we compared her winter-white complexion to my copper-colored skin.

The four of us went snorkeling Christmas Eve morning near Soldier Cay, where there were more fish per square foot than anywhere I'd ever been. On the way back, we stopped at a natural, clear pool that was protected from Exuma Sound by a cliff. High tide and a fresh easterly breeze sent seawater pulsing through a low spot in the cliff, cascading several feet to the oasis below. Rachel's Bubble Bath, as it was known locally, was the perfect place to have our picnic lunch of peanut butter and jelly sandwiches and ice-cold Kaliks, and afterward, to snooze in the sun. We waded in the sparkling water to cool off before returning to the boat.

On the first night of 1999, sunlight melted away into a rose and cream sky. The refrain of day's end echoed from a conch shell somewhere far away. While Fowl Cay shimmered like a jewel just off the boat's stern, *Crossroads* drifted on a sheet of molten gold, as if a fairy had sprinkled glitter on the water.

Before the kids' arrival, I had worried about the difficulty of keeping from them our grand plan's problems, so I was amazed by the unusual contentment seeping into the turmoil inside my head. But really, why shouldn't I feel content? I sat in good health with my family on the back deck of a boat that had given me vivid years of zestful living in some of the most beautiful places in the world. I drank a frozen Crossroads Colada and nibbled grilled lobster. My skin felt like satin under a layer of tangerine-scented lotion my daughter had brought me for Christmas.

Later, no moon shone and the monochrome black sky was a perfect foil for the dusty sweep of the Milky Way. A rising breeze caused the swishing of Big Major's palmetto trees to sing a lullaby, sending the four of us tucking into our cradle-like bunks. Nature and family knit a healing patch over my anxiety that night, and I slept straight through until the sun announced itself in stripes across my sheets.

Ned called after New Year's to say the land survey had finally arrived and seemed only half accurate, according to his calculations. He would call George Monroe for clarification later, he said. We added that tangle to a growing list of costly and time-consuming problems. I had a dozen baseball caps printed with FOWL CAY to try to make our resort seem like more than an ever-growing paper jam of red tape.

For several months in the middle of that year, Stewart and I traveled back and forth to Richmond more than usual to research choices for the exteriors of Fowl Cay's houses, including stain and paint, roofing, doors, windows, hardware and decking. I hired a friend from my This End Up days to help me wade through the avalanche of interior surface choices as well as furnishings, light fixtures, curtains, artwork and rug selections. The rest of the decisions floated between Stewart and me, depending on whichever one of us had the most interest or time for the legwork.

Locating the items wasn't half the problem. We needed every receipt for every component, no matter how small. The Bahamas Customs Department wanted each purchase to be numbered and denoted in three places: an alphabetized system of receipts, the boxes the goods were packed in and a report that would be 31 pages long, single-spaced on legal-size paper.

Stewart deferred to my organizational strength on that task, the same strength that often drove him crazy. "Plan on everything being checked on its way into the country. It could take weeks," we were told. Another former employee from This End Up joined our team to oversee the receiving, record-keeping, packing and shipping at a Richmond warehouse. When the time came, five tractor-trailers would haul the furnishings to Jacksonville, Florida, to be loaded on a transport ship to Nassau. After passing through Customs, the containers would be put onto one enormous barge for the ride to Fowl Cay.

We would undertake this venture in our entrepreneurial way: plan well, nose to the grindstone, play fair, be nice. Our rewards had always been greater than our risks, thanks in part to that mantra. We could envision success shimmering in the distance, same as always.

Stewart located warehouses, long-distance truckers, container ships, Customs brokers, barges and Bahamian movers. I didn't know squat about pool tables and dartboards, had never equipped a commercial kitchen and clubhouse, wasn't up on the latest music and had never furnished rental houses. Choosing was a constant battle between design aesthetics, human practicality and tropical durability. Although cookie-cutter interiors would have cut the time required to decorate the six buildings, that wasn't a tradeoff I was willing to make. Fowl Cay was to be our family compound, and I wanted every item to be the perfect choice.

* * *

Often, on my neighborhood stops to the gas station or the cleaners, Richmonders I hardly knew inquired about how things were going and whether Stewart and I were having fun with our new project. I warmed to their interest if not their understanding. The difficulty of matching an appropriate answer to their mild inquisitiveness grew greater as the months and problems marched on. In a city where tradition rules, many of the people who asked about Fowl Cay had ventured only to the most venerable vacation spots, and I found explicit explanations about living on a boat and developing a rock in the middle of the sea caused their faces to go blank. I learned to lighten up on the information.

"It's a hard job, but somebody's got to do it." "It is the most beautiful place." "It's so enlightening to be in a culture other than my own." "A little slower than we'd hoped for, but everything has to come on a barge." I ran dry of half-assed answers.

Sometimes the irresistible tug of Richmond and all that it represented would overtake me. Memories of my former life would rush in, and I would ache for the very hidebound, established order that I sought to escape. The more uncertainty that developed in the Bahamas—where we were and why, where we were going and when—the more obvious it became that the anchor securing my sanity was the memory of where I'd been. I marveled at my split personality, the one that yearned for exploration and roots at the same time.

CHAPTER 11: The Race Is Not to the Swift

Stewart and I had big things on our minds in October 1999. Feeling akin to butterflies pinned to a specimen board, we stuck with the risk of building Fowl Cay Resort, since we had it on paper that the lease extension would be granted when the project was completed. We told ourselves the sophistication and quality of our development would exceed the government's expectations for out-island projects. Then, no doubt, we would receive our 99-year lease—because the government promised it in writing.

The first barge of construction materials arrived 15 months after we'd hired Windsor Construction. *Amelie* was late and would never make high tide. The captain started out on time but set sail for another island named Fowl Cay four miles north of ours.

When *Amelie* was three hours behind schedule, Stewart tried hailing the captain on the marine radio. We were encouraged when he spoke back to us loud and clear, knowing he must be close.

"Dis de *Amelie,* Fowl Cay."

"Yes, Captain," said Stewart. "I was wondering, what's your ETA here at the island?"

"I at Fowl Cay right now."

Stewart and I looked around the empty harbor as we stood on our bulkhead. "Where, exactly, at Fowl Cay?"

"At de dock. We 'bout troo unloadin' your lumber. Ver you?"

What had happened to the explicit instructions we had sent to the Windsor office a week before? The ones that said, "DO NOT go to Fowl Cay north. The job to which you are delivering is located on the Fowl Cay that is one mile northwest of Staniel Cay and one mile southeast of Sampson Cay."

Even after we dredged our little harbor until the pile of white bottom-sand stood 15 feet tall on the edge of the cay, the heavy barges sometimes had trouble getting to our bulkhead. If they missed the high water window, a long wait ensued for their next chance. Sometimes bad weather kept them in abeyance for a whole day.

Amelie was carrying some of the supplies that would make it possible for the 45-man construction crew to live on Fowl Cay for two years. Plumbing equipment, bed frames, mattresses and linens were on board for the bunkhouses. Because the men needed to regenerate their supply of energy after expending it in the heat every day, Windsor shipped air conditioners for their sleeping quarters.

Pots and pans, plates, cutlery, appliances, icemaker, food and drink for the kitchen were arriving too. We needed to hire local cooks who could tolerate raunchy behavior and ravenous men, people who could stand up to the broiling heat of the kitchen 12 hours a day, who could make enormous amounts of food out of practically nothing when the supply boat froze the oranges and dumped the chicken on the dock at Farmer's Cay, where it rotted in the sun. The cooks would be the only women allowed on the island, except for me.

Housing, feeding and entertaining that many men for two years demanded an enormous amount of gear. Toilet, shower and laundry facilities were necessary, along with some method of trash disposal. Cards, dominoes, radios, TVs, grills, coolers and dive gear came in for use during time off. The barge also carried materials for the workers' housing. And an unassuming little yellow cement mixer that would make a contribution far beyond its size.

To move materials to building sites, old golf cart paths had to be repaired and new ones built, so jackhammers joined the lineup of tools set on the bulkhead. Most vital of everything that was coming, though, was a backhoe, the only thing on the whole island that would have wheels, except for a broken boat trailer and two rusted wheelbarrows.

When she came over the horizon under a magnificent rainbow, *Amelie* looked like a giant pack animal. One-hundred-seventy-five feet of stuff rode on the open deck of a monstrous red barge, pushing a three-foot wave before it.

Stewart and I were so excited we couldn't wait for the captain to get to us. We jumped in *Roundabout* and flew over to meet him. From a quarter mile away, we could see three men on the bow pointing to Fowl Cay. We roared up and paced alongside *Amelie,* David waving madly at Goliath. Smiling and taking photos, Stewart and I must have looked like we hadn't seen humans in years.

An initial contingent of our crew, the first of many Bahamian men we would live with 10 hours a day for the next 24 months, waved back and one of them put his hand over his heart and inclined his head.

I pegged him as the one who was to supervise the job, Windsor's on-site manager. John Heath had told us the man's name was Linwood Robeson, but he went by Ace. He was big, good-looking and immaculately dressed, with a cross on a thick chain and a safari hat with its brim cocked just so.

"A pleasure, Madam," Ace said in a British-tinged Bahamian accent. He removed his hat and bowed, smooth as silk, over my hand. I thought the lines of his face might reflect a long-ago relation from the South Sea Islands, the handsome features set off by a confident gaze and strong jaw line. Two gold teeth glinted in the center of his smile. He introduced Clinton and Herbert, who ambled off in the slow style we had become accustomed to in the islands, one foot flat on the ground before its mate began a slow rise from the earth. We asked the three of them to *Crossroads* for supper and enjoyed a night in their happy-go-lucky presence, and they the obvious honor to be aboard the boat.

The next day, the captain lowered the front of the barge to create a ramp, and the men unloaded supplies for a few hours using *Amelie's* Bobcat. I asked about the backhoe that was supposed to arrive on this first trip. We couldn't begin any building foundations without that machine to ram holes through the coral rock that lay under a few inches of sand.

Ace threw his head back and laughed. "Ah, wouldn't you know dat just as we were 'bout to load her on, a small mechanical problem was discovered. Better to have dat information up front, don't you agree? I like t'ings on de table myself. No surprises, dat's my motto. Don't worry, it be here on nex' week's barge for sure."

That sounded OK, but a little muscle twitched in my eyelid at our project manager's glib bonhomie.

Ned Pinkerton flew down a week later to meet with Ace. On the way from the airstrip to our island, Ned said he'd called the survey company in Nassau to clear up the miscalculations from some months back and was told that George Monroe had died. No one in that office could find any information about the Fowl Cay project, and Ned said he thought we could cross them off our list. Stewart and I agreed, but we were counting Fowl Cay's chickens before they came home to roost. A bill for George's time came months later.

I snapped a photo for my album that showed Ned and Ace using conch shells to hold down the edges of the architectural plans, which were rolled out atop a piece of plywood sitting on two sawhorses.

Six-foot, five-inch Ace had on a bright yellow hardhat, although there was nothing to fall on him yet, and five-foot, six-inch Ned wore a white baseball hat and black sunglasses. The two men stood in front of a sea of dancing peaks as waves spumed off ocean-side rocks in the distance. A new day. Maybe these two professionals could help Stewart and me see the development's plans as fun again.

Since the closest Home Depot, West Marine and decent hardware store were 250 miles away in Miami, and the closest lumberyard, building supply company and paint store were 75 miles away in Nassau, construction couldn't proceed for long without a delivery. Because Fowl Cay Resort lived and breathed by the continuous flow of materials, we sometimes supplemented the Windsor vessel with smaller ones belonging to independent operators. Runs on these little barges depended on calm seas, working generators, sober captains and a boatload of personal considerations.

Our favorite privateer missed a crucial Fowl Cay run because he had to attend a funeral in the far out-islands. "My aunty brudda' son pass over." The body had been sent to Nassau to be prepared for burial on Green Island, and our barge captain had to accompany the deceased, who made his way home on the weekly supply boat. The trip took two days since the *Island Belle* had to make her regular stops at various cays to offload pork chops, toilet paper, lumber, rum, diapers, gravel, furniture, ice cream and mail. But friends and family hopped aboard along the way, and by the time *Belle* reached her final destination, the procession of mourners accompanying the corpse looked like a state funeral. A fitting hearse and cortege, all considered.

One barge owner forgot to renew his license, and a last-second inspection had us switching a load of road-building materials from the *Allegro* to the *Grand Rose*. Another had his barge impounded for running drugs. As soon as the authorities released his boat and we had him lined up for a trip, his mate poured transmission fluid into the fuel tank. When the captain finally made it to Fowl Cay, he drove his forklift like a Formula One racecar, tipping a Bacardi bottle under the brim of his Stetson hat. With one Windsor man helping, Romeo unloaded the barge in record time, took his money in cash, and steered that sizeable vessel with its engine wide open through the narrow Fowl Cay inlet. Next time we tried to hire him, he was in prison, convicted of stealing a generator off a building site at Great Rock Island. Those obstacles were mere speed bumps compared to the veritable blockade of the boat races.

Many Bahamians planned their lives around the sailboat regattas that were held most of the year in various cays. Competition was fierce and such trifling matters as jobs would not be tolerated. Whether he actually crewed on the heavy wood sloops or simply cheered a boat on, many a Bahamian man left home for whatever far-off place was hosting that month's regatta. He might help with assembling the rudder, mast and pries, watch several days of sailing, place a little bet under the table, bemoan or celebrate the outcome, help pack up the vessel and, finally, travel back. And then time was needed to recover from the festivities. If he participated in the whole shebang, he could be gone from work for two weeks.

Stewart was unable to book some barges until he learned to ask about the dates for the Long Island, Andros, Harbour Island and George Town regattas. On a few of those occasions, he decided to join 'em rather than fight 'em. *(Photo 3.5)*

CHAPTER 12: Into the Deep End (3)

Thank God somebody as experienced and capable as Ace has entered this surreal situation—this place where I dwell every day between a dream and disappointment.

One would think, now that we've started construction and hired a big crew of Bahamians, the government will live up to its promise to extend our land lease. Mrs. Somers' assistant told Stewart during yesterday's phone call that he would make sure she saw Stewart's message the minute she came in. Pointless probably. How can Stewart hold out such optimism?

I seem unable to rise above the crummy treatment we continue to receive. I'm furious and carry a hole where hope should be. I want out but don't know how to do that.

"Hello, John Heath! What's keeping you up there in Freeport? When are you coming for a site visit?...The backhoe is leaving Nassau when?... When did you say?... John?"

CHAPTER 13: T'ree Quarter Honest

Day by day, Stewart and I got to know the construction crew. Pablo from Colombia specialized in demolition and snorting cocaine, while Reno, a Haitian, listened to evangelists at top volume on his radio. Delbon, who captained the work skiff, was a "Fomlee Island boy." He'd do anything to be one of the guys. Lyle came from Inagua and was shy and sweet and could lift two 98-pound bags of cement at once. Coming in from Nassau, Popeye smiled a lot and always wanted his picture taken. Eugene never smiled until he picked up his guitar, when a dreamy grin brightened his dark features. He hailed from the Abacos, and slept beneath a gold-framed photo of Jesus. Flea and his buddy Demetricus from Eleuthera ran separate games of dominoes at night, taking on all comers in the raucous tile-slamming fashion of the islands.

Stewart and I learned that not all Bahamian parents taught their children to say thank you. That shortcoming rankled twice over, because some of them were not shy about telling us what kind of gift or what size contribution to give. Hops could drink more Budweiser than any fraternity boy I ever knew. He was the first Bahamian of many who told Stewart and me he didn't like the local beer and to be sure to get American beer when we were buying for the Friday night bashes we put on. *(Photo 3.6)*

A Jamaican named Gilbert was missing an ear, and the resulting scar indicated either a bad surgeon or a bad fight. When Shorty saw a ghost sitting on the backhoe one night as he wandered around with insomnia, he asked to go home to Rum Cay. He was so scared he couldn't work the next day. Or the next. Sidney heckled him with ear-shattering hoots.

On Sundays, the crew's day off, the atmosphere around the bunkhouses was heavy with the odor of fried fish topped off with the sourness of sweaty tennis shoes, and pierced with high-volume screeching from call-in radio shows. One weekend, Herbert screamed that Lincoln had stolen his Leatherman tool and Lincoln yelled back that Herbert "musse crazy" because he had "defrocked" the picture of

Lincoln's girlfriend, Rodneta. They came to blows with an ice pick and a grill fork until Ace stepped in and knocked their heads together. An hour later, Lincoln and Herbert, who grew up together on Crooked Island, were playing backgammon. Bahamians seldom hold grudges.

The 45 men of Windsor Construction were scheduled for five weeks on the job and one week off, in rotating shifts of about eight people. An additional 20 subcontractors came and went. When the extras were stuffed into the already-tight living space, tempers boiled, fights broke out and if the wind was in the right direction, Stewart and I could hear the brouhaha out on *Crossroads*. I got so sick of testosterone that sometimes I had to go sit in the kitchen with the cooks, Vanessa and Cherise, where they said things that were amusing rather than virile.

After my camera was taken one day, I asked them what they thought about the person I suspected of stealing it. "Is Flip honest, do you think?"

"'Bout t'ree quarter," Cherise answered.

Another day, speaking to Cherise, Vanessa asked, "You know Uncle Henry at deat's doorstop wid ammonia?"

"Are you ladies cooking baked beans today?" I asked once.

"You know, bake bean, dey ain' in season right now," one of them answered.

Later, I asked, "Is Debbie coming in to help you the rest of the week?"

"She not guh make it 'cause she has a headache tomorrow and de nex' day."

I decided to ask Cherise and Vanessa to clear up the terms "inside" and "outside" children for me. Ever since a fishing guide in George Town had explained his family's makeup by dividing them into those distinct groups, I wanted to make sure I understood the terminology I had heard many times since.

"Inside chirren, dey de ones ver de mama and daddy married. Outside chirren de ones come wid girlfrins," Vanessa explained.

"The mother never has outside kids then?" I asked.

"Yeah, she have dem too. But she need a boyfrin for dat."

"So the outside ones are when either the mom or the dad isn't married to anyone?" I tried to clarify with my 55-year-old, American, WASP brain in full gear.

"No. Dey married. Dey jus' not married to dat outside baby mama or daddy."

"Oh. Well how do all the brothers and sisters feel about it? Do they all get along?"

"Yeah," said Cherise. "My daddy got 14 chirren, some inside wid my mudder and den dey lots of outside chirren wid diff'ren' people. Das why dey so many people wid de same las' name 'round here. We are de Fomlee Islands, you know."

Despite Stewart's perseverance, the Bahamian government remained utterly disinterested in keeping an appointment with us. Mr. Morley had assured us that renewing Fowl Cay's land lease to the full 99 years was a sure thing. As I watched the construction expenses pile sky-high, our gullibility at the hands of our own lawyer ate away at me.

Mrs. Somers refused all phone calls as we attempted to pursue the separate option of a freehold for Fowl Cay. I could have handled such ignominious treatment better if she'd said the government would work only on one request at a time. In that case, Stewart and I could have re-evaluated our commitment. Although the loss of our dream would have been monstrous, I could have tucked tail, licked my wounds and thanked my stars I hadn't gotten in any deeper. Hearing no answer was worse. Would it happen if we were patient enough? Should we hold up or pull out? What would we do with a torn-up cay containing half-finished infrastructure and temporary plywood staff buildings but no livable houses? And what about the enormous sum already spent on charter planes, lawyers, architects, surveyors, contractors, barges and materials? And on that mystery bill we had to pay to get our plans approved?

Even though we kept hoping to change the government's position into extending the lease right away, we tried to counter our apprehension that renewal might never happen by embracing the situation as it stood. Perhaps 57 years was long enough. That would give parts of four generations of Browns a family compound. How many lifetimes ahead could one couple plan? Stewart was much better at seeing the bright side than I.

We had evidence of progress in the buildings and infrastructure, but the cost was enormous, not only in dollars, but anguish, relationships and health. The burden of wondering whether we would ever see our rightful ownership of Fowl Cay poisoned the fun, joy and peace that I had planned and worked so hard for—the kind of life I felt I had earned. Constant difficult situations led to headaches, rapid heartbeat and shortness of breath, the signals of big trouble I knew so well. The faster problems developed and the more I questioned the advisability of staying with the project, the more adamant Stewart's commitment became.

When the project was over, I came to realize that he could muster unflagging perseverance because he had the capacity to continually remold the dream.

"Right decision, wrong decision, it's imperative we keep going," he said time and again.

* * *

Having lost the ability to focus on the good, I returned to Richmond by myself in hopes of finding sanity in the familiarity of home. But camouflaging my deep anxiety over the development's problems fatigued me, and alone, I was unable to keep myself safe from my own thoughts. I retired earlier and earlier at night, wondering if I was slipping into depression. Although my choice was to stay in Richmond for two months, I felt increasingly cut off from Stewart, and he was too busy for anything but a cursory phone conversation. With warning signs all around, I promised myself one sleepless night to regain a more balanced perspective. I would return to the Exumas after Christmas more positive and supportive.

* * *

Stewart called me from the cay in mid-December. The barge carrying the backhoe we needed to dig our first foundations was now two months late.

"I have good news, bad news and good news," said Stewart.

"Give it to me."

"The good news is the barge that was carrying the backhoe arrived."

"Fabulous! What's the bad news?"

"The bad news is the backhoe that was on it rolled off into 3,000 feet of water on the trip down."

"#!@*#*! Then what in the world can the other good news be?" I asked.

"The good news is they loaded the wrong backhoe. It was for somebody else's job."

"Thank God!" I said.

And that's where we stood early in Fowl Cay's growth: thankful for another "tropical" mistake, hardly focusing on the fact that we still had bad news. This example of a move away from our formerly very

American thinking—what? who? how soon?—augured well for coping in the Bahamas, but it didn't do a thing to predict a reasonable finish date for our resort. Ace could offer nothing but smooth talk when we asked if a backhoe might be delivered soon. Smooth talk was Ace's specialty. *(Photo 3.7)*

From the first day he arrived, Ace dealt with me with the false flattery of an apple polisher. My eyes, the blue of a summer sky. My figure, ravishing. My hair, streaked beautiful by the sun. My mind, so smart and organized. Why, oh why, couldn't he find a wife like me? Sometimes he just shook his head and said, "M-m-m-m."

Ace was careful to call me "Ma'am" and spoke with little trace of Bahamian patois when Stewart or the Windsor bigwigs came around, but he preened and postured when I walked alone on the site. "You men get dat cinderblock out Miz Brown way. You want huh to trip and fall?" "Flea, git yo' lazy ass—excuse me—goin' on dat sheetrock 'fore I bus' yo' head into little piece." "I t'ink Miz Brown right 'bout dat paint job, Eugene. Git dat udder color up de wall and do it 'fore she reach by here again."

One day, Ace's girlfriend came to visit from Nassau. He moved over to Staniel Cay to stay with her in a Potty-Foyer. When I met her that night at one of the bars, I felt no surprise that Chanette was a knockout gorgeous head-snapper and so beautifully dressed and made up that her mere presence was a slap in the face to most of the local women. Perhaps she thought she had a tight rein on her stallion of a man, but the fillies at Bar 'n Bites knew better.

Soon after that meeting, Stewart and I were invited to Ace and Chanette's wedding. We took *Crossroads* 380 miles to Freeport and back and stayed until the end of the six-hour celebration. We did it out of loyalty to Ace.

CHAPTER 14: "What Is, Is"

S tewart went to the Island Market for spark plugs and toilet paper a few weeks after we returned from Ace's wedding. He burst back into *Crossroads* with ghastly news. The 260-foot telephone tower at Staniel Cay had crashed to the ground killing two Batelco service people who had been sent down from Nassau to replace its rusted struts. The structure barely missed hitting a one-room school-house full of children. The accident sent shockwaves through the little cays. *(Photo 3.8)*

Now, with no way to call their families, our crew was testier than ever. I completely understood. One morning weeks afterward, when Stewart and I were approaching the dock in *Roundabout,* I could see six men in the distance balanced on the unfinished roof of the clubhouse on top of the hill.

"Wow. Look how hard all those men are working on the Hill House roof," I said when Stewart cut the engine. "If they keep that up, the whole thing will be finished in no time. But why are they screaming like that?"

Stewart burst into laughter. "They're not working," he said. "The guys found out a couple of days ago they could occasionally make a cell call through the tower at Farmer's Cay by standing somewhere high and turning back and forth to catch the signal. But if they connect, the sound is so weak they have to yell as loud as they can at whoever is on the other end."

There went the new work ethic.

Fighting and drugs were on Ace's "incident list," and he talked often about his no-tolerance policy. One awful night, though, Ace guided a group of Windsor workmen into a near-gang war against some of the men at Staniel Cay. Wearing a Windsor T-shirt, he led the drunken charge at the Yacht Club dock by brandishing the broken-off necks of two beer bottles and shouting, "You fuckin' Staniel boys guh fight? Come on. We smear your ass all over dis island." The village policeman arrived and fired his gun in the air to calm everyone.

Ace refused to apologize the next day. Windsor's Freeport office said the fight had been a regrettable occurrence, but finding a decent replacement supervisor for an out-island job would be difficult. So the rabble-rouser stayed, for a while, and I returned to the cay every day, slightly uneasy about our safety.

Stewart, Ace and I usually addressed a half-dozen things daily that needed immediate answers, otherwise some part of the building process would come to a halt. We now had no way to communicate with John Heath at Windsor, Ned Pinkerton in Richmond, vendors, shippers, government officials, our lawyer, our children or our friends. We were cut off from the rest of the world, a quarter of the way through the most difficult project of our lives.

Replacing a phone tower in the Cays would be low on Batelco's priority list, we suspected, and we were right. A year passed before phones worked again. Only our purchase of a satellite phone allowed the job to move along. Stewart settled on a rock every day with the machine balanced in his lap, aimed in the precise direction for contact, and reeled off that day's troubles to the appropriate parties. If he moved at all, say, because a lizard ran down his shirt, he lost the signal and had to start over. The phone bills brought us to our knees.

Construction continued at a steady pace during the spring and summer of 2000, but the direction was not always forward. When I questioned the uneven baseboard molding in the dining room of our house, John Heath said, "This is not a hotel in New York, Libby. You're in the out-islands." I wished I had a dollar for every time I heard that. Eugene gave me an explanation for the crooked workmanship the next day.

"Das 'bout de bes' I do. Das a happy trick between lewel and straight."

Four drizzling days caused the satellite phone to be useless. Rain, wind or clouds could block its transmission until the tropical atmosphere settled down. When I casually asked a local friend if he thought it was going to rain the fifth day, he replied, "Why you boddering 'bout vut happen tomorrow? De vedda is vut de vedda is. Nuttin' you do 'bout dat." So true, so accepting, so delightfully Bahamian.

But he wasn't trying to build a resort on an island without a computer or a fax, where the only connection to everybody and everything we needed was a telephone that could cover the 185 miles between Windsor Construction's headquarters and our development.

One late afternoon that summer, heat held over the Exumas like a lid over embers. Steam rose from the shirt that stuck like a branding iron to my back. We had slashed an opening, step by tortuous step, through thick tangles of undergrowth, Stewart with a machete and me with VHF to call for help, a rusted rebar to pull down spider webs and a can of

Cutter to discourage insects. Dust covered our faces and flies sipped our sweat as we dodged poisonwood trees, scorpions, mosquitoes and land crabs as big as cats. The only way to get a narrow curvy cart path up to the restaurant location and save the existing trees was to do it ourselves. History had taught us that if we left placement of the roads up to Zeno, the backhoe driver, they would be as wide as a highway, arrow-straight and denuded of foliage in five-foot swaths on each side. When the two of us stumbled down from our day's work, Stewart had cut himself on the exposed roots of the trees we'd chopped and had enough blood in his shoes to make a squishing sound. I was as stinking and filthy as I'd ever been in my life.

Our workmen, who had dragged their feet all day, sat under trees and tied bandanas around their necks, arms and ankles to sop up ribbons of sweat that sluiced down their bodies. In the heat of the islands, conservation of personal energy had been perfected over centuries. Many of the builders probably wondered about the fool owners who worked like beavers in a temperature that would blow the mercury out of the thermometer. We were so tired our hip joints ached in their sockets. When we left for Bar 'n Bites, Stewart and I could hardly wait for supper and a few Kaliks.

The lively wintertime façade that the Cays presented to tourists had melted away in the late summer heat and returned to the slowed-down pace of the regulars. Friends who owned an island not far from Fowl Cay joined us for supper at Bar 'n Bites. Everyone ordered grouper fingers except me. Nothing would do but a BLT, which always came loaded with a quarter pound of bacon. While we waited, the chatter around the bar was about a robbery there the night before. Someone said it was the second incident in less than a year. When a barfly off a sailboat asked what the owner would do about it, someone else said, "Nothing. That's the way it is down here." We four expats sighed as if the passerby was spreading gossip about our family.

"*Crossroad*', your dinner ready at dat table."

As I lifted the top piece of bread on my BLT to check that it wasn't swimming in mayonnaise, I saw only lettuce and tomato, not a shred of bacon.

"Vernice, they left the bacon off my BLT. Could you take it back to the kitchen, please, and ask them to add it?"

"We ain' got no bacon."

"But I asked for a BLT."

"I know dat. We ain' got no bacon." Vernice seemed annoyed at having to clarify the obvious.

"Well, OK. I guess I'll have tuna salad then."

"You want dat wid your BLT or after it?"

While our friends dug into their fish, I waited for my tuna salad and wondered if a customer who ordered a BLT when the kitchen was out of bread would receive a plate stacked with bacon, lettuce and tomato teetering in the middle of it, maybe a large dollop of mayo quivering on the top? I chuckled to myself and hoped one day to be half as unburdened by circumstances beyond my control as Vernice.

We stayed until 8:15 and listened to advice about our growing problems at Fowl Cay from local acquaintances. Under a sky black as pitch, Stewart steered us home, running lights bouncing along in sync with building waves. A light rain began to fall and we slipped into foul-weather gear we'd tucked in the boat's seat. Life in the islands would always be determined by the elements.

The minute our dinghy touched her bow to *Crossroads'* swim platform, Stewart realized he had left our handheld VHF on a barstool at Bar 'n Bites. "You go on in. I'm going back for the radio. It'll only take a few minutes," he said.

An hour and 15 minutes later, I saw no sign of Stewart. The boat swung in a jerky arc on the jitterbugging water of Big Major's deserted harbor. I tried to raise him several times on *Crossroads'* marine radio, but got no answer. When I radioed Bar 'n Bites, they were closing and said they hadn't seen him since we left together. Stewart was faithful about calling if he was going to be late. After nine years of living on a boat, we were both aware of the life-threatening possibilities when you were on the sea. Where could he be? And how could I locate him with no dinghy? By 10:30, I was in a panic.

"*Crossroads, Crossroads.* This is St. Luke's Clinic."

I was sure Stewart had had a heart attack.

"Libby, I'm OK, but I ran over a guy in a little dinghy who didn't have any running lights. I'll be home as soon as I can."

Around midnight, Stewart dragged in and told me the story.

Brian had been sitting still in his little inflatable boat immediately around the sharp southwestern curve of Big Major Island. Stewart rounded that corner, red and green running lights on, in our 17-foot, hard-bottom dinghy powered by a 90-horsepower engine. A frequent topic of discussion among boaters was the law requiring running lights on all vessels under way at night. Their gleam obscured the driver's vision of any oncoming unlit objects, but allowed other boats to see him. A further complication arose because most of the locals ignored the rule.

"Brian, I know why I didn't see you because I had my lights on, but why didn't you see me?" Stewart had asked while the nurse's husband patched Brian up in the clinic. Ted was following his wife's instructions over the phone because she was in Florida for a few weeks.

"I was looking backwards trying to restart my motor when you came around the corner," said Brian. "Since my dinghy doesn't have any running lights, I usually shine a flashlight out the bow, but I was holding it in my teeth so I could see what was wrong with the engine. By the time I heard you, you were on top of me."

Twice that night Stewart awoke with a cry, and for months after that accident, he would jerk up in the bed, dreaming of how close he came to killing somebody on a quick trip to retrieve a radio.

We never saw our VHF again, despite the Fowl Cay label on it. Especially irritating was the close quarters in which we most likely lived with the thief. Because the nearby islands were such small communities, he would know us as a friend and regular member of the neighborhood. Perhaps that was why it hurt more than a random incident in a bigger place.

With the story of the stolen money from Bar 'n Bites and the pinching of our radio, that night flogged the uncomplicated principle I had believed since childhood. The old words, newly significant—Thou shalt not steal—seemed a discretionary concept in this place of churchgoers. Theft, graft, scanty medical help and physical dangers had me alarmed that we had now discovered the fine print in our contract with fate.

CHAPTER 15: A Jump on T'ings

Birdcage, the original house's moniker from the 1950s, was perfect, so Stewart and I decided to keep the name. Whenever I had an extra few minutes, that's where I'd be, exerting my organized self over the details of our personal home. But we did have to go back to Richmond occasionally, and the short times we were away from the building site were when irreversible mistakes were made. *(Photo 3.9)*

One day, two errors showed up that caused me to close my eyes and push in on my temples. Ned Pinkerton's architectural plans clearly stated that the gas fireplace for our living room was to be "V.F.," a term understood by U.S. builders to mean "Vent Free." But Ned forgot to explain that to our Bahamian builders.

When Stewart and I returned to Fowl Cay after three weeks in the States, the team working on our house was finishing stonework on a traditional fireplace with block chimney, flue and damper. Stewart asked Lyman, the supervisor, if he had seen the designation "V.F." on the plans. Lyman said he saw it but didn't know what it stood for, so he built the only kind of fireplace he knew anything about. Stewart wanted to know why he had continued to work on the fireplace without asking a question.

"I try to get a jump on t'ings while you gone," Lyman answered.

We couldn't tear the fireplace out and rebuild it. Ned said to have them close up the damper and move forward.

I looked at the places where the uninstalled matching sets of French doors were to fit evenly on each side of the fireplace. The opening on the left took every available inch in the wall while the one on the right showed a generous amount of wall space on both sides. Prescribed molding framed that second aperture, but the first opening was unadorned because there was no wall space to accommodate the trim.

"Oh, Lyman, how in the world did the fireplace get off-center?" I asked.

"A reg'lar fireplace bigger den de archeetec' draw, so it took up extra space."

But why wouldn't Lyman at least have centered it between the matching doors? I decided not to bring that up. "Why does one opening have molding and one doesn't?"

"De trim fit on one side so I put it up dere. De udder door can't fit none."

"Please take the trim down, Lyman, so the doorways will match," I said as I turned away, sick at my stomach.

I stepped out on the new deck to gather myself and found I could have placed a bowling ball by my foot and it would have rolled, unaided, to the edge of the 12-foot-wide floor and dropped to the ground nine feet below. Whoever calculated the slope to allow for rain runoff must have been expecting a waterfall.

Disheartened, we left Birdcage on our way to lunch. Two of Windsor's crew were stomping the ground and screaming vulgarities at each other with a crowd of another half-dozen looking on. What little patience was left in me snapped after the dual construction mistakes. Running into the middle of the combatants, I pushed the furious giants apart. "You may NOT behave this way. This is my home, and if you want to act like uncivilized savages, you can go back to wherever you live, but get off Fowl Cay." After they scuffed away from the dustup, snarling and sullen, I wasn't sure which of us had acted more like a savage, while Stewart came off looking like the good cop again.

The least of it—construction mistakes and fighting employees—and the most of it—no freehold or lease extension—sent me off the deep end. It seemed that everywhere I turned there was another example of the tricky chemistry in my working partnership with Stewart.

* * *

Throughout our serial entrepreneurship, Stewart and I had approached most decisions from different angles, and this was one reason, aggravating as it was, for our successful results. We had always worked together on projects that benefited from both our strengths. That blend allowed dissimilarities to be a point of joking acceptance, even respect, instead of serious contention.

Stewart was slow to make decisions because he could, and often did, take both sides of a point with equal conviction, generally choosing whichever side I was not on. Then, once I sided with him, he flipped his argument to oppose me again. By the time that tactic was complete, we had turned up most of the options available to solve whatever problem, but, as his sparring partner, I sometimes wondered if a 50-acre island was going to be big enough for the two of us. Ace called Stewart "a bulldog with two bones."

My game was organization, control, and too often, closure before its time. One of my greatest satisfactions was checking tasks off the agenda. Although both highly competitive, Stewart and I depended on one another to fill holes in a job-sharing sort of way. But in this most towering of all our gambles, our differences had turned more detrimental than productive.

My need to get details right was no doubt a reflection of two things: the perfection affliction I inherited from my mother, and the years I spent teaching the importance of planning and follow-through. That straight edge of precision was both a source of reliability and irritability for Stewart, a common viewpoint of visionaries who need a list-making, deadline-chasing counterpart to help complete their concepts. Having filled our respective roles with compatibility in past projects, we'd danced out the exit door sharing victory. In the Bahamas, though, Stewart's patient approach and adaptability were the only ways to move Fowl Cay forward. We were involved in exactly the wrong venture in exactly the wrong country for my traits to be anything but a frustrating formula for failure. I was crushed by my own incompetence.

* * *

"Even after their awful treatment of us, we decided to go forth with building, and still we're being hassled about some permits. How many of them does it take to issue a few licenses, for God's sake? We're trying to turn a decrepit rock into a beautiful place where we can employ local people and pay government taxes. Sure they want foreign investment."

I knew I was digging in a special place in Stewart's head where he kept things under lock and key. His eyes reflected the stone wall I had seen a time or two in our lives together, the one meant to stop a conversation because he had no answers to my disturbing questions. But there was no way to turn back my ocean of pain this night.

Stewart was a mile away thinking, I was sure, about the latest twist in our overarching concern. Instead of giving us a lease extension outright, the government issued a brief letter stating that it would extend the lease to 99 years if they were satisfied with the finished Fowl Cay

Resort, which could only be determined by an official visit. In other words, you put out all your money and then we'll let you know if we're going to change our promise again. The issue of a freehold didn't merit a mention.

"Stewart?" His silence was louder than words.

As we got into bed, anger fired another charge while Stewart opened a book in the face of my ranting. I didn't blame him.

"Sticking to something is admirable, but after it smacks you in the face as many times as this decision has, it's dumb to keep going with it. They don't want us here. We made a mistake. Let's just cut our losses and go home before we spend every dime we've got."

"It's going to be fine," Stewart said. "It's their country. We knew it would be hard, but that part will blow over. You watch." He turned out his light and rolled over, back to me. We'd been married too many years for me to believe he bought into that.

CHAPTER 16: Into the Deep End (4)

It seems like I can't do anything right. For the first time in my life, I have to admit I'm a hindrance instead of a help. Precision is not useful here, but it scares me to see the amount of money, our money, that's thrown to the wind by inattention, inaccuracy and poor communication. I hate to see Stewart carrying so much of the burden for this project when we're joint partners, just like always. I hope I can shoulder my share when the details of setting up the houses move to the forefront.

The construction crew is getting restless— 45+ men on a rock island day after day. Ace is tough on them, but that may be what keeps them out of major trouble. His persona is big in every way—size, voice, expectations. That's not to say that Ace doesn't have a mischievous side himself, though. He and the men will play a joke on Stewart in a heartbeat. His sense of humor—that's one of the things we like best about Ace—even if it is mixed with an equal amount of temper. Those two things together are most likely what make him a decent manager.

The three of us have gotten to be pretty good friends. It's nice.

"Why won't my calls go through to the Exumas, Operator?... The whole tower?"

CHAPTER 17: Out of Aces

Blood flowed across Stewart's foot where a jagged branch had stuck into his ankle. Since he had started taking an aspirin a day, Stewart had become a bit of a bleeder. This was the worst one yet. As the wound continued to gush, we decided to see if the volunteer nurse at the Staniel Cay clinic would clean the cut and bandage it. When we got there, though, the sign said the nurse was away for several weeks and St. Luke's was closed up tight. That was the story of medical help where we had chosen to live, competent when available but nonexistent sometimes.

Before we decided to develop the island, Stewart and I had a serious discussion about medical matters. We knew our physical lifestyle in a remote place was dangerous and the odds against injury were not on our side. Generally speaking, MedEvac airplanes were unable to land on Staniel Cay's small, unlit airstrip. I prayed we would never get desperately hurt or sick.

Back on *Crossroads,* Stewart self-medicated with hydrogen peroxide, Neosporin, a butterfly bandage and Kalik. We ate cereal with frozen blueberries for supper and fell into bed for a 4:30 a.m. wake-up. Another small barge, which was to arrive at 6:00, was loaded with a special delivery of building materials that we couldn't afford to wait for on the regular run. The *Bahama Flower* had a new captain bringing her down from Nassau, who requested that Stewart meet him in the harbor to guide the vessel in.

At 7:00, *Flower* was a no-show. Stewart set up the satellite phone to call. "Oh, he'll be there at 10:30," said the barge's owner.

At 11:00, Stewart set up the phone again. No answer.

Stewart called again. "Just one more hour."

The *Bahama Flower* came into view at 2:30, but the tide was too low and she had to anchor until dawn.

One more day melted away as we tried to accomplish the task of leading a small barge a half-mile to our bulkhead. An inconvenient land, the Bahamas, forcing people to spend hours, money and patience on tasks to which they would, stateside, give a few minutes of their effort. Bahamians' attitude of time as an inconsequential part of life continued to hit us in the pocketbook.

On the other hand, perhaps there was something to learn from the locals.

"Good morning, Genesta."

"Okaaay. Awright."

"The last couple of times we've come over to the Island Market you've been closed in the middle of the morning or at 4:00 in the afternoon. I thought you were open 9 to 5. What's up with the new hours?" I asked.

With a grin that could have won a Halloween pumpkin-carving contest, Genesta said, "Bidness is goood."

It took me a minute to get it. The better her business, the shorter she made her hours. The ultimate reward in the Bahamas was leisure time. Islanders had been marinating for years in a philosophy of personal pleasure. They didn't strive for materialism as a measure of goodness in life.

Americans had been marinating for years in a philosophy of success and money. If business was good, the owner would have opened on Sundays, added night hours, started a delivery service, probably franchised the company. She would have made a lot more dough but had a lot less time to enjoy it.

About halfway into the development of Fowl Cay Resort, in the fall of 2000, Stewart and I felt we had found our groove with Ace. We had him to dinner on *Crossroads* a number of times so we could discuss matters without interruption and share our beef tenderloin, new potatoes, hearts of palm salad and brownies with ice cream, precious stores for which we made special trips to Nassau. Ace asked Stewart and me to bring back things from the States for him, like size 13 New Balance sneakers or a special kind of after-shave lotion.

Once, Ace wanted to borrow money and Stewart lent it. Another time, when Ace was drunk and driving the Windsor skiff at night, he ran across *Crossroads'* anchor line, bolting us upright in our bed at 12:30. We never reported it to Windsor because he asked us not to and promised he would never do it again. An ugly story floated around from time to time that Ace blackmailed some of the workers. Unless they wanted to be assigned to the nastiest jobs, like spending three days in the smelly old cistern scrubbing the algae off the side, they had to pay him off. But it was just a rumor, so we never brought it up.

Wednesday was the day Ace walked off the job without a word. Just like that, Stewart and I had 45 men on our hands with no project manager. Our cooks, Cherise and Vanessa, were hesitant to stay without Ace to keep the rowdy bunch in hand. The second tier of supervisors did their best, but not one of them came close to having Ace's authority. The workmen slept, played dominoes and fished. Our project ground to a halt.

A few days after Ace quit, Harry Brighton arrived at Fowl Cay to take over the on-site manager's position. From his piercing green eyes to his steel-toed boots, every part of his physical makeup pulsated with energy. Heavily muscled, bald and ramrod-straight, it was apparent from the start that he would coax maximum effort from the construction crew. The tall Swede was intense and plunged into work fast and hard. The difference between his work ethic and Ace's encouraged us to take a Sunday off soon after Harry arrived.

Stewart was invited to go spear fishing with some of the workmen. Still a novice at this free-diving method of hunting for fish, he jumped at the chance to learn from the locals. Bahamian men were often brought up using Hawaiian slings to spear the fish that fed their families, and diving below the water with the sharp weapon for two or three minutes was common. Rarely did you see one of them use a pole or net. *(Photo 3.10)*

"Libby, have you seen my sling?" asked Stewart. "It's been right behind the driver's seat in our dinghy for weeks and now I can't find it."

I tried to keep my mind from jumping to the conclusion it wanted, but the number of items disappearing left a stench of dishonesty in the air. Stewart had recently made an astounding statement on the subject: "I'll accept theft up to a point, but not the big things. Not the machines, not my chipper. Tools maybe, but not my chipper."

To me, Stewart's statement about pilfering showed infection festering in his values. To him, the world had a middle ground between good and bad, and if he wanted to stay sane in the Bahamas, he'd deal with that imprecise condition.

When Stewart and I were cruising the Caribbean, the Exumas had seemed innocent and somehow untouched by the chafe of life. We were usually able to find the ingredients for days of near-perfection. We selected the flavors that suited us, like we were at the bakery choosing cupcakes that offered our favorite tropical toppings—yellow with mango icing for me and chocolate with lemon-lime glaze for Stewart.

But we were no longer licking the sugar off the Cays. Every layer deeper I bit, I found things that disturbed me, and I struggled to understand the complexity of the Bahamian culture while leaving my enchantment intact. That daily scuffle began to cloud the splendor that surrounded us, and the magnificence of the place became a mocking backdrop to my former adoration. The beauty of the Bahamas spread itself thinner and thinner in the space between hurt and distrust, and our dream seemed like a fragile fantasy to me.

CHAPTER 18: Bahamacide

Stewart's only belt was too big by the end of 2000. He walked around in his ripped shorts, holding them up with his hand all day, an alarm clock in the pocket taking the place of his broken watch. "Get off my back," he growled one morning when I asked if he wanted me to order some new shorts in a 31-inch waist instead of his normal 34. Such a mean response made me wonder if I was losing the husband who had once lived happily in his less visible bones.

In a brief conversation with Ellie the afternoon before, she said she received a call from a friend of ours who said jokingly, "My calls won't ever go through to your parents down in the islands. Are they still on the verge of Bahamacide?"

"Mom, I'm worried about you and Daddy," she said. "You sound so mad or sad or tired every time I talk to either one of you on the phone. What's going on?"

I didn't dare tell her of the problems that consumed every day. And now, because Fowl Cay Resort was a Bahamian corporation, we faced another raft of issues with lawyers and government concerning incorporation, duty, labor requirements, work papers and business licenses. The balance of our patience and happiness vacillated. But not our bank account. It drained like a plug had been pulled.

Some things were over budget, many things were late, most things had huge logistical problems and everything involved asking a governmental Pooh-Bah for permission. Stewart and I worked, ate, and slept, our entire lives devoted to those basic functions.

"Oh, El, I'm sorry we sound like that. We're perfectly fine, just working hard, that's all. Wait until you see it. Now, how is Matt?" I held a dishtowel full of melting ice on the scorpion sting in my upturned palm. Water ran down my forearm and dripped off my elbow onto the boat's deck as I forced my voice into a positive tone.

"We'll be home in a week and tell you all the wacko stories in person." I closed, "Bye. I love you."

No longer able to hold up his pants with one hand, Stewart now used a piece of twine around the waist of his shorts. For a change of scenery one day soon after Ellie's phone call, we decided to take our sandwiches to the bow of *Crossroads* so we could watch the swine at Pig Beach and sit in the southeasterly breeze. The pigs were one of the favorite tourist attractions in the area, and we had become friendly with the animals after a year and a half of being anchored just off their beach.

Isabelle, an old sow that produced piglets on a regular schedule, vanished a few months back. One of her older progeny that we'd named Spot had taken her mother's place in the production line without missing a beat. We had never seen the boar. Must have been too busy. *(Photo 3.11)*

The combined litters of Isabelle and Spot were napping when Stewart and I started our lunch, but earlier we had watched as six or seven pigs, piglet to porker, roamed the beach searching for food the boaters and locals dumped for them. Having become used to humans bearing scraps, they would swim out over their heads 10 or 15 feet if they thought the people who came in dinghies to take pictures might have an offering. A family of weird-looking beasts of suspect genealogy, this porcine community had the usual large, bullet-shaped bodies, but they sprouted the longest ears, snouts and legs we'd ever seen. We called them donkey-pig-goats. *(Photo 3.12)*

Crossroads rocked a little when a powerful dinghy roared up to Pig Beach and let off two women in bright-colored sarongs and oversized straw hats. The uniformed mate off a yacht settled the two excited tourists on a blanket with the name of the charter boat emblazoned on it, helped them spread out a feast and plunked an open wine bottle in a silver ice bucket. We could hear their conversation because the wind blew across Pig Beach into our faces.

"When do you want me to return for you?" asked the dinghy driver.

"I guess about an hour will be fine, Sam."

Just as Sam pushed down the boat's throttle to return to the mother ship, Stewart and I spotted four amiable pigs lumbering out of the brush behind the picnickers, headed straight for lunch. One woman jumped up screaming for Sam to come back, but Sam couldn't have heard a blood-curdling scream over the two boat engines if his life depended on it. Stewart and I enjoyed the show—it wasn't the first time we'd seen it—while we chomped egg salad and Pringles and talked about our upcoming trip home.

We spent two happy weeks in Richmond, and flush with renewed energy, Stewart and I rushed into Birdcage, eager to see its progress. There hung the second door screw-up. A custom-made, arched doorway, designed to match an opposing one, was shown on the architectural drawings as 3'0" wide.

Mistakenly built at 30" wide, the errant frame and door had been flown in from Nassau and installed during a previous visit to Virginia. Upon our return to the cay that time, we noted the expensive mistake and asked for it to be changed. I pointed to the correct, already in-place, first door of the arched pair to make sure the supervisor understood the importance of the matched set. I was rewarded with a beautiful Bahamian smile and, "I got it, Miz Brown."

Now, nine weeks later, the carpenter was putting the last nails in the replacement frame when Stewart and I walked in. The door was a perfect 36" wide. It was also rectangular. A third door order would have to be placed.

The amount of stamina, patience and courage Stewart usually exhibited was extraordinary, but sitting on the aft deck of *Crossroads* later, his shoulders slumped and the muscles on each side of his jaw rippled in the expression of worry I knew so well.

The normally advantageous contrasts between Stewart and me continued to fight each other as the development progressed. He was hell-bent to complete the project, no matter the personal pain and deprivation involved. His commitment made him a trustworthy husband, friend and boss. Rarely, even when that intransigence affected his partner in business and life, would he pull away from a goal. For Stewart, success was born of values, vision, compromise, tolerance and never giving up. My soul mate was a man of immeasurable integrity and stubbornness.

I folded my tent a bit quicker at times, allowing unaccustomed pain and deprivation to flatten my normal tenacity. The more I thought of approaching mortality in the midst of increasing difficulties and age, the more I issued the bromide, "Life's too short." In that tired maxim were excuses, but insight too. For me, success was born of values, preparation, hard work, follow-up and knowing when to move on. I had never counted on the emotional price I would have to pay for Fowl Cay; Stewart had never added it up.

Crew chief Harry, Stewart and I were at the partially-built clubhouse and restaurant, trying to sort out a disagreement about the width of a concrete bench that topped the curving wall around the patio. Had the bench's interior side been built according to plan, it would shelter the tiny down-lights attached underneath it, and they would have cast a warm glow at night on the face of the supporting wall and onto the floor of the Hill House terrace. Instead, the depth of the bench had been so curtailed that the rope lights would simply have to be eliminated or placed on the face of the wall where all the bulbs would glare into our guests' faces.

Harry stood firmly on the side that I had OK'd that arrangement, and I was positive I never would have done such a thing. At a stalemate for the time being, Harry called timeout to give some good news about the marble and granite that was six weeks late arriving. The delay had caused an island-wide work stoppage on all kitchens and bathrooms.

"By the way, the marble and granite are in Nassau being loaded onto a barge today. It should be here midmorning tomorrow," he said. "Great news," we agreed.

As the day drew to a close, Harry's cellphone rang. He turned away to answer, and Stewart and I heard him say, "No. No. NO. Keep me informed."

"What? What?" we asked.

"They put so much granite and marble on the barge that it sank." I was speechless, but, sadly, not particularly shocked.

Harry said, "The barge was still at the dock when it went down, so they will send in divers to retrieve the materials and try reloading tomorrow."

"Pretty lucky it's something saltwater can't hurt," said Stewart.

He was right, of course, and nothing could change the situation now, but we just seemed to lurch from crisis to crisis. The difference was that Stewart never considered them to be crises. If he ever decided to get a tattoo, instead of choosing "I Love Libby," he would have to be branded, "What is, is." Stewart was turning Bahamian as the months marched on. I was turning tail.

That night at 2 a.m., Stewart and I were awake and restless.

"What are you thinking about?" I asked him.

He answered in a voice so subdued I could barely hear. "How the hell did we get here?"

CHAPTER 19: No Thanks

The windows went into three of the new houses while we were in Florida visiting Stew in February 2001. You would think we would have learned. Despite the architect's detailed schedule of placement, a number of them were put into the wrong openings. That error caused certain casement panels to crank out into the traffic path of the decks and patios. Unsealing those windows to switch them to the right places would put the job behind, and we didn't want to think of our labor cost, so Stewart and I agreed to have Windsor change only the most egregious ones.

When the custom-made doors were installed right after the window fiasco, they were an even bigger disaster. The problems were so manifold we lost count, and tracking accountability was difficult because the product involved an American wholesaler who bought the doors from the Greek owner of a Canadian manufacturing company that shipped the product to our Bahamian contractor. We wondered if Standby had been involved somewhere in the mess.

Standby was a charity case with no skills that we could use on Fowl Cay. Worse, he disturbed the other workmen by talking nonstop except during frequent naps. Although Standby refused to do any but the easiest chores for us, he was a favorite in the surrounding islands. One of several local men who came to work for Windsor, Standby was hired onto the crew for political reasons. "You have to live in this neighborhood long after Windsor leaves," said Harry. Stewart and I grimaced but appreciated Harry's sensitivity to our reputation.

One evening at Bar 'n Bites, Stewart sat down on the stool next to Standby.

"Standby, let me buy you a beer," offered Stewart.

"I guess dat'll be awright. Not Kalik."

Slide, the bartender, popped open a Budweiser and placed it in front of Standby. Stewart said, "Put that on my tab please, Slide."

Picking up his gift, Standby pivoted on his barstool in the opposite direction from Stewart and walked away without a word of gratitude.

The Bahamian government did not encourage hard work and, enhanced by recent years of overpayment from tourists for services rendered, there seemed an expectation of charity on the part of some islanders. Sometimes expats felt a bit exploited for their generosity.

Later that same night, Jessie, who worked in Bar 'n Bites' gift shop, asked me if I would buy a book of raffle tickets to support the All Age School on Staniel Cay. I said I'd be happy to, and handed over $10. While Jessie draped herself over the bar, resting her head on crossed arms, I filled out my contact information on the stubs. The recipient of the second Brown family offering of the day was ruder than the first.

She took the ten tickets from me to drop in the raffle box, raised one eyebrow and snarled, "Yeah, and somebody jus' like you gonna win de best t'ing too."

What did that uncharitable comment mean?

Those two incidents brought to the front burner a stew of emotions that had been simmering inside me. The concept of reciprocity, inherent to my upbringing, was foreign here. My treatment of the locals—generous at a minimum—did not engender so much as a thank you. I came to realize that working hard and playing fair did not return the same thing to me, that abstaining from lying, stealing or hurting people did not make everyone treat me likewise and that being loyal to others did not win their allegiance.

The problems continued. The surface of the patios on all five houses at Fowl Cay began to flake off within a month of completion. On the few occasions when it rained, puddles stood in several places on the terrace of Hill House.

When much of each patio was resurfaced, they looked better, substantial and thicker, even though the new batches of colored cement didn't match the original shade at a single house. Harry and I had argued over so many issues in the last few weeks I decided to drop my ideals about expecting the colors I chose to be the ones the houses ended up wearing. This wasn't the States after all.

Several weeks later, we had a thunderstorm. Afterward, in the Hill House's outdoor cocktail area where I had envisioned greeting my guests, a dip in the surface contained a quarter inch of rain. I acquiesced once more as the patio of Fowl Cay's flagship building had a white plastic drain inserted rather than a third resurfacing. When the custom-made doormats arrived for the six-foot-wide French doors, we couldn't use them in several places because the second application of cement caused the mats to stick up too far for the doors to open.

The doormats fit perfectly at the Sweetwater house, however, although it turned out to make no difference. All eight were stolen one night soon after we opened for business.

After a couple of nasty weeks of wet cold fronts, a beautiful, warm day slid up from the Gulf in March 2001. Dawn was breaking when I awoke, and an orange blade of sunlight cut through the cloudbank outside my window. Stewart and I took a day off, and late in the afternoon we waded beside a sandbank that trailed off for a quarter mile with no footprints. Retreating to a seat at the water's edge, Stewart opened the cooler for Kalik and Oreos, no stranger choice than the combinations we had a lot of days.

A little distance between Fowl Cay and ourselves provided time for talk of hope.

We did, after all, have a letter from the Bahamian government saying the lease would be extended to 99 years if we improved the land per our written plans. We were certainly doing that. Most people in the know said no one was receiving a freehold for their cay now, and even 56 years would see us into great-grandchildren.

Florida seemed about to sink with the weight of its growing population. New people coming along would want to find less crowded places to rent by the water. Every travel magazine said the hottest thing in leisure property was a private island. And there sat Fowl Cay, our Fowl Cay, in about the prettiest water in all the world, only 200 miles and change from the U.S.A. How could an investment with diminishing competition and increasing demand be anything but good?

The next morning, my head was screwed on straighter. Even when I fell three feet into an open hatch in the floor of the boat, I just bandaged my wounds and got on with the day. As I hung the clothes from the washing machine on *Crossroads'* rail to dry, though, I hoped the answer to the clothes dryer's contrariness could be found.

We had been waiting on the repairman for 10 days. I no longer even blinked at the cost to fly in people from the States to fix things, but occasionally I drove my business-trained mind nuts by trying to figure their cost per minute. The time somebody brought the wrong part and had to come back again did set our teeth on edge. But we learned to live with it, as long as he had the answer. When I returned to the boat from the cay at noon to take in the clothes, a midmorning squall had left the items dripping wet—the ones that hadn't blown away.

CHAPTER 20: Into the Deep End (5)

*S*tewart is the most optimistic, resilient person I know, so now I'm really worried. His whole personality has changed and, now where there used to be practically no temper, he flies off the handle over the mildest questions. Sometimes it seems as if this project is going to take us both down.

Although even this doesn't put a smile on his face, the one place Stewart is the happiest is helping to build Fowl Cay's infrastructure. He rides around from site to site in his Bobcat to see what he can help with — septic tanks, water pumps, landscaping. He's a sight driving the little yellow machine, sometimes wearing a red hardhat, smoking a stogie and adjusting the carpenter's pencil behind his ear. The men all like him, I can tell by their greetings when he shows up where they're working. They call him "Stu-art." They call me "Miz Brown."

I think I'll get my husband back soon, though. The end of construction is not too many months off, and we do feel like the development is in good hands with the crew from Windsor.

"Hey, Frank. How're things in Richmond?... I couldn't hear you — say it again... Who died?... WHO?... Frank?"

CHAPTER 21: The Right Footings

Windsor Construction and its subcontractors installed Fowl Cay's infrastructure in stages, some of it during Ace's tenure and some during Harry's. But Stewart was the person who really honchoed that complex part of the development. Septic tanks, pressure pumps, junction boxes and tar were his favorite parts of the whole project.

With sand-filled noise abatement blocks and air circulation fans in place, the building for the power plant would be complete once the diesel fuel-feed lines went in. For a month, three generators had been scheduled to arrive any day. The big machines would produce the heart-beat of the entire island. Without their perfect performance, especially under tough conditions, such as seven hairdryers, five AC units and both watermaker machines turning on simultaneously, we would have no electricity and no water.

Once the facility was finished, Windsor laid the lines for the diesel that ran 200 yards from Fowl Cay's dock to the 10,000-gallon storage tank next to the generator house. Word had it that when the Shell barge-men arrived on a tight schedule at our bulkhead every couple of months to fill us up, they would have no patience for malfunctioning parts and would move on, leaving our island on empty. The generators had to run without a hitch.

Connected at the far end of the generator house was the workshop that would be filled with things that broke faster than we could fix them. Buying the equipment to repair 14 icemakers, 75 ceiling fans, 10 golf carts, 8 boats and engines, 16 toilets, 18 showers, 30 appliances, untold pumps and air conditioners, path lights, stereos, shingles, sprinklers, gut-ters and the occasional fishing rod, just to take a sample, would require a massive shopping spree. Usually, shopping was something my husband avoided with the cunning of a military general. But Stewart set off on the errand of outfitting Fowl Cay's workshop grinning from ear to ear.

When we met with the people who manufactured the reverse osmosis machines that would make Fowl Cay's fresh water out of seawater, we had to decide what size equipment the resort would require. The first questions were directed at me: "How many guests will the resort hold, how full do you expect to be at your peak and what percentage of the renters will be Americans?"

I could make an educated guess on the first two questions, but I had no idea how many guests would be Americans. "Why do you ask that?" I said.

"Because those three pieces of information give us our best shot at accurately sizing your watermaker machines," said the salesman. "The information on Americans helps us gauge how high to boost your capacity since they average using 70 gallons of water a day compared to 50 gallons or less for non-Americans. It's a case of bathing more and conserving less."

We decided on two separate machines and pressure pumps. Running both watermakers wide open for 24 hours would give us 8,500 gallons of fresh water, more than enough for Fowl Cay's daily drinking, bathing, flushing, cooking, laundering and irrigation needs, even if we had all American guests. And it would be purer water than in most big American cities.

For each of the six buildings, we dug a separate waste system. We couldn't let one disaster bring the whole island to a halt. The men working on this part of the infrastructure joked that they were the No. 1 team on the No. 2 job.

Trash disposal on an island is a gigantic problem, and we had no better solutions than the next guy. Incinerators were expensive, burying rubbish was not a good alternative in a place where holes were limited to a foot deep by hard rock, and we didn't want to haul it to the Staniel Cay dump that was already nearing capacity. We decided to burn it and pay to return beer bottles for recycling in Nassau. The permanent burn pit, with protective berms, would be in the middle of the island, hidden from the eyes of guests.

Because the number of people living on Fowl Cay during construction generated huge amounts of garbage, we dug a temporary burn pit in a rare sandy spot at the western end of the 15-acre development area, convenient to where all the workers ate. Since it would be covered once the men left and the regular pit would be dug far from the building sites, this large makeshift hole was placed for convenience, not aesthetics.

Keeping the garbage burned down to a pile less than five feet tall was an ongoing battle. When Ace sent one of the workmen to the pit with an extra big load, he found the last debris had been reduced to a pile of ashes. William deposited his collection of refuse into the hole but decided the breeze was too stiff to put fire to it, so he rejoined the crew at the building site on the easternmost end of the island, thinking he would return to finish off the trash when the wind died. By the time someone saw the fire, it was already out of control, gobbling small trees and moving fast in the 20 mph wind. Our handheld fire extinguishers were useless, and most of the men could only beat at the edges of the flames with pieces of insulation board.

Stewart rushed into the conflagration, pushing dirt with our little Bobcat, while Fowl Cay burned like a wildfire in a drought. As he backed out of the flames to change direction to where things were worse, he saw Elias sitting in one of the backhoes watching the action. He yelled, "Elias, get over here and help us put this out!" *(Photo 3.13)*

Elias said, "Why? I didn't start it."

Demetricus shoved Elias from the controls and drove it into the flames to join the other backhoe. The machines and the rest of the Windsor crew, on foot, battled the fire for hours at great danger to themselves to save our cay.

Later, when William was questioned, he said he had seen smoke rising from the pile of ashes but he hadn't seen any flames, so he dumped the load of scrap wood and cardboard boxes on top and weighed it down with cinder blocks so it wouldn't blow away, an ideal scenario for smoldering embers looking for action.

Quite another challenge was stoking the stomachs of dozens of laborers on a remote rock in the sea. Food was stacked to the ceiling in the canteen's kitchen. Sometimes Cherise and Vanessa fed meals to 65 people, three times a day. They were itchy for the Fowl Cay food warehouse to be built, the big one we needed for the resort. It would eventually hold four freezers, two refrigerators, liquor, wine, beer and soda storage, food for the houses, food for the restaurant, food for the staff and food for our family. Cleaning and laundry supplies, batteries, light bulbs and paper products needed space too. And for the time being, it would store food for an army of hungry workers.

The central laundry facility and bunkhouse were in the only old building worth keeping, a big warehouse hidden in the center of the development area. Washer/dryer, overflow bedrooms, staff bathroom and break room with a TV were added. The original boathouse was repaired to hold beach chairs, umbrellas, grills and outdoor games, and we built a boat ramp for pulling out the resort's kayaks, sailboats and dinghies, which would need constant maintenance.

Once the cart paths were laid out, the whole crew had to leave for five days while they were surfaced. During that downtime on the cay, dock installers sank huge "dolphins" into Fowl Cay's harbor, five pilings leaning together and held taut by circles of heavy cable. The big barges that would service us as long as we lived on the island would use these to brace against while they offloaded cargo.

Wesley, the old caretaker, built lovely stone walls and paths, collecting the rocks from "secret places" he would never disclose. He said he wouldn't charge us too much for the materials since the Lord wanted the stones to be used in a beautiful way. One day, Stewart rounded the corner at the undeveloped end of Fowl Cay on a trash pickup mission. There was Wesley, loading his dinghy with our rocks off our beach for our walls. When he presented his bill, which showed a separate charge for materials, Stewart never said a word as he wrote the check to pay for our own stones.

The cement work was never ending: six house foundations, floors for generator and watermaker buildings, steps and retaining walls, bulkheads and ramps, pads for air conditioners, pumps and tanks, fireplaces and a wishing well, swimming pools, stone work and cistern repair, and cinderblocks filled for stability. Windsor's single mixer measured 36 inches tall, wide and deep, and had an 18-inch diameter opening, where gravel, sand, water and bags of cement mix went in by the shovelful and cement came out exactly the same way—if its little generator didn't give out that day. A queue of laborers stood with buckets wherever the tiny mixer had been rolled on its trolley, and, one by one, they stepped up to the mini-machine and someone shoveled out enough cement to fill his pail. The workman carried it to the spot where the buckets were being emptied and rebar set, and by the end of the day there was one significant accomplishment of masonry. The hardest worker in two years of construction was the little yellow cement mixer that still abides with us on Fowl Cay. *(Photos 3.14 and 3.15)*

The new phone tower had been up for a while, and Bahama Telephone Company continued to supply erratic service and poor reception. After the better part of a year trying to get Batelco to agree to reconnect our local phone line, a man finally came down from Canada, of all places, with the equipment needed to replace the antiquated system. Two months after installation, the local rep arrived to do the hookup. That accomplishment was almost easy compared to setting up Fowl Cay with the account rep at the phone company's billing office in Nassau. When we explained we had bought the cay from their former customer, Mr. Phillip Walker, and wanted to change the name on the account, Mrs. Peters said Mr. Walker could do that the next time he was in the area. I responded that Mr. Walker wouldn't be coming back to the area, whereupon she said Mr. Walker was the only one who could take care of this name switch for the phone service. And only in person.

"Can you set us up a whole new record under our name then?" I asked.

"Dat is impossible because dat de number Fowl Cay has and it belong to Mr. Walker."

We gave up trying to straighten things out, and to this day, our Batelco bill arrives in the name of Phillip Walker.

The landscapers came for four weeks and stayed for nine. By the time the palm trees arrived, we were nearing the end of construction. Many people in the boating community cruised in and out of Big Major's harbor and anchored several hundred yards from our dock. Between their own activities, they watched our development's process, and after a few days, moved on. Many boaters revisited this safe anchorage several times during Fowl Cay's two years of building. The cruisers recognized our distinctive trawler with the dark green hull, which never moved from its spot at Pig Beach, and they recognized Stewart and me as the crazy people who left home at dawn and returned at dusk almost every day, rain or shine.

Lady Margaret came over the horizon at breakfast time one morning, carrying 75 full-grown palm trees, their burlap-wrapped root balls stacked high and the fat red tie-down straps dancing in the wind with the trees' waving fronds. With Stewart and me leading the way in *Roundabout,* the big barge inched its way among anchored vessels in Big Major's crowded harbor, and the little tug with the Canadian flag started a song of celebration with three high-pitched toots. Then, echo-like, sailboats, powerboats, charter boats, workboats, big boats and small boats added their individual tunes to the chorus. A man blew his conch shell and an air horn topped off the symphony as most of our neighbors came out on their decks and toasted us with coffee cups and various sound effects.

Stewart and I had been too busy during construction to pay attention to our boating neighbors, but they had taken great notice of us. A couple of years after the heartwarming welcome of the palm trees,

I introduced myself to a man who had come to dinner at our restaurant. "Hi. I'm Libby Brown."

"Oh, I know who you are," he said.

"Really? How so?"

"My wife and I cruise the Exumas regularly, and our favorite place to anchor is by Pig Beach. For over two years, as we would come and go, we watched you and Stewart drag home from your island to that beautiful trawler as the sun went down. When Stewart went to check things on the flybridge every night, you turned on the lamps and you might as well have been in a spotlight because you must have been too tired to close the blinds. Almost any night we were anchored near you, you put out a box of Cheerios, Stewart got a Kalik and you sat at opposite ends of the dining room table and both put your heads down on your arms. We were there the day you brought the palm trees in, too, the ones who rang our ship's bell when the barge went by." *(Photo 3.16)*

Several months after the *Lady Margaret* delivered the coconut palms, we were ready to build the three docks. With two years of Mr. Grayson's useless permits for that project already, our environmental man Chris came down from Nassau again, signed off on his study and delivered the report himself to the administrator's office in Nassau. Permit No. 3 came in six weeks, requiring only one rescheduling of the pile driver. Stewart put in an order for the three guest boats that would share space at the new piers with *Roundabout,* the beat-up Windsor work skiff and *Crossroads* until our house was ready for us to occupy it. Once that move was made, the trawler would be sold and our live-aboard years would be over.

CHAPTER 22: Sex Toys and Snow Jobs

Construction on Fowl Cay wound up the way most jobs do: a few disagreements, some people we were sad to see leave but most we weren't, and a punch list of things that would be completed by a couple of workmen who would stay on awhile. Considering the magnitude of the task, two years of construction from start to finish was a timeframe I wasn't sure could have been bettered in big cities anywhere. Stewart and I were proud of the final results.

As good as Windsor was, Fowl Cay Resort would not have risen to our expectations without our having been on site. No hired overseer would have tended it like the owners, and I'm sure we almost sent Harry Brighton to the funny farm with our requests. The project at Fowl Cay was irrefutable testimony to Windsor's island savvy, Ned Pinkerton's flexible approach to discrepancy, and Stewart's patience. And maybe a little bit to my over-the-edge, shut-that-woman-up perfectionism. One of the best things that came out of the risk we took to develop a resort on a rock island in a foreign country was the mutual admiration engendered between a Bahamian contractor, who understandably doubted we could pull it off, and an American couple, who realized in the end we never could have done it without him.

Stewart and I flinched when people told us construction woes were the same where they built—at the river, on a Blue Ridge mountaintop, in St. Croix, at Fisher's Island, on the Upper Peninsula of Michigan, at Vail, on an island in Maine, in Nassau. No one would ever convince us of that.

The time had come to furnish and decorate our house, the managers' house, three rental houses and the clubhouse. I wasn't too worried about that with my home furnishings background, although my recent experience in the Bahamas caused a fitting prickle of foreboding. Finally, we could set up our business. Interviewing candidates for the manager and staff positions would be a nice change of pace, and the responsibility presented no foreseeable problem since we had interviewed many people for our previous business.

We anticipated the arrival of our first guests with the excitement of brides having finally arrived at the church. The learning curve that had been so steep between the cay's purchase and completion was finished, and now Stewart and I would move into areas where we knew the ropes: team building and customer service. Thank God the hard part was over.

Dawn broke with a sliver of color where sea meets sky. From the anchorage on the north side of our island, the silhouette of coral and limestone boulders that shielded Fowl Cay from the surging ocean were limned with a faint light, which melted away as the sun spread a golden veil across the rising tide. *Crossroads* floated on a turquoise ribbon of water that augmented the panorama of sunrise changing night into day. The yellow Birdcage glowed at us, sure and solid, waiting for its furnishings and occupants. With three months left in 2001, the allure of adventure seduced me again as I turned myself toward the opening of the island for family, friends and customers.

Stewart and I were leaving for Nassau that morning to interview nine couples who had applied to manage Fowl Cay. The first couple we had hired looked perfect on the surface, including degrees in hospitality management from a stateside college and good references from three years at a hotel on Paradise Island. With seven apparently happy weeks at Fowl Cay under their belts, Lizzie and Trey came forward one day to say that the out-islands were too remote for them, that they missed tennis games, nightclubs and their German Shepherd. And that Lizzie had a skin cancer on her nose that couldn't be shaded adequately by a hat because she needed to be outside so much of the time.

"It's been a gas, you two," Trey said. "We'll miss you, but better to move on now, don't you think?"

With that, the "perfect couple" returned to Nassau, leaving us back at square one on the hunt for managers.

The second set of advertisements in the Nassau paper was more descriptive about the job and asked for two people with a combination of bookkeeping skills, mechanical ability, computer proficiency, people management and customer service experience. For the most part, no one who came to the lobby of the Marriott where we had set up our hourly meetings fit that description.

Each interview lasted 45 minutes, with 15 minutes of down time for Stewart and me to make notes and prepare for the next couple. Then appointments resumed, back-to-back, straight through nine hours. The two of us alternated the questioning.

"So, Chanardo, what are you doing right now for a job?" Stewart took his turn at interviewing the much younger male half of couple No. 3 on our schedule.

"I in sales," he answered.

"Really? Do you work in a retail store?" asked Stewart, no doubt thinking of what a common bond he would have with Chanardo in such a case.

"No, I work from home." Chanardo's face was just on the border of handsome and his collarless white linen tunic shirt set it off to advantage.

I could almost see Stewart thinking how unusual it was to find a Bahamian entrepreneur.

"What type of sales are you in?"

Chanardo fidgeted in the Marriott's burgundy suede swivel chair. "I, um, I sell sex toys."

In an effort not to show he was nonplussed, Stewart continued, "So you sell them out of your house and have them shipped to the customer?"

"Oh, no. When dey arrives to me, I deliver dem in person to de client. In case dere any questions."

When Milly, Chanardo's girlfriend, spotted the shock on our faces, she piped up in defense of his products. "Dey really nice ones, too."

It crossed my mind that Stewart and I were probably envisioning a similar scenario on Fowl Cay: Chanardo, hosting dinner in the club-house, pulling his "Superior Sex Toys" catalog out from under his tunic to sell to, say, some cruising guests from the New York Yacht Club.

Couple No. 6 was two people all right, but it was comprised of a pretty woman and her three-year-old child.

The combined age of couple No. 7 seemed about 35 years old. No computer experience, never worked on a generator, never driven a boat and lived in an overcrowded house. "We try get away from de jam up at home."

Stewart and I were discouraged. By now we realized finding a per-fect couple for such an unusual job was going to be quite difficult, so we lowered our sights several notches before meeting couple No. 9.

Jillian Canady handed over a perfectly typed résumé for each of them and our hopes ticked up. Jillian had ten years' experience in the legal department of a fast-growing liquor distributing company where she'd been in charge of the section specializing in labor issues, but her former company wanted an attorney in that job now. As a bright young Bahamian, she had been awarded a scholarship for her secondary school education in England and afterward returned for two years of secretarial school in Freeport. What she had gained in education, however, she lacked in humor. From pursed lips she discharged the perfect grammar of her precise thoughts. Once we met Ike, Jillian's husband, Stewart and I were pleasantly distracted from initial worries about her stuffy formality and glum manner.

The big American could be legally employed in the Bahamas because he was married to Jillian. His recent time working construction in Freeport was a bonus to the other experience he could bring to the Fowl Cay job. A résumé that showed little formal education didn't bother us, because he had years of work on oil rigs in Texas plus an 11-year stint working on machinery at a power plant in Alabama. He offered much of what we needed in the mechanical area. Ike's speech was energetic. His spirited eyebrows moved in perfect synchronization with the inflection of his voice. Although he was fun to talk to, underneath I detected an expression of stoically endured sorrow.

The two of them wanted to get away from the crime in Freeport, Ike said. And yes, they were knowledgeable of the computer. Yes, both of them had managed people. Yes, he had experience driving boats and backhoes. No, he didn't think being a black American would affect his relationship with our Bahamian staff. The six children of their combined families were grown and all of them lived in the States. Outside of work, she wrote poetry and he played chess, the banjo and a hot game of darts. Should they get the job, Ike and Jillian agreed they could easily get out of the contract for their Freeport rental house.

Stewart and I were eager to hire Bahamians for these managerial positions, but there had been not one prospect in our neighborhood of islands. Of nine interviews, this half-Bahamian couple looked to be the best of our choices. Although we figured we could cheer Jillian up over time, there remained a worry about their appearance, not a good concern to have for front line, customer service jobs in a resort.

Ike was stained with a dark birthmark that bounced across the left side of his constantly moving brow and drifted down his cheek to end in a salt-and-pepper beard. Big ears sat akimbo, nestled into an Afro-style mass of tight gray curls that settled inside the neck of a rumpled Hawaiian shirt. Our prospective manager had a forest of hair falling out of ears and nose, sprouting from shirt collar, and popping off his head in every direction. His yellowed fingernails were longer than mine and needed a good cleaning. Messy was the word that came to mind. Messy, but with dancing black eyes, relevant experience, a great sense of humor and strong people skills. Stewart and I were willing to try to manage messy in exchange for the best candidate we'd seen all day.

Jillian was anything but messy. Prissy and pinched-looking with her narrow shoulders held in tight, her demeanor made me wonder if she was constipated. Below wide-set, reptilian green eyes were two deep dimples that bracketed thin, vermillion-red lips. That brilliant slash was a startling contrast on her extraordinarily white skin. A thick russet braid hung almost to her ample hips. Although she was clean and her clothing tidy, Jillian lacked the warmth and conviviality Ike oozed, but charmless though she was, her background with Bahamian labor law would be helpful. We were willing to try to manage prissy and pinched in exchange for bringing Ike to us.

In our haste to hire managers, Ike's suggestion of stoically endured sorrow would be the one signal we passed over too quickly. With help in sight, though, we could almost touch our life of carefree fun now, the life we'd been dreaming of, and flummoxed by, during four years of uncertainty. Stewart and I had high hopes for Jillian and Ike.

When we checked the Canadys' references, they were satisfactory, if not glowing. After a second interview, the four of us agreed that a visit to see Fowl Cay would be worth their time. Moving to the out-islands from Grand Bahama would be a big change. They would need to close up their lives in Freeport and move their personal goods to the cay on the supply boat. The managers' house was not yet finished, so we would find Ike and Jillian temporary living quarters, introduce them to the local community, train them in Fowl Cay's mission of customer service and learn to trust and share our lives with them. Stewart and I would have the opportunity, again, to show people with whom we worked that jobs and fun were not mutually exclusive.

A two-day visit to Fowl Cay had Ike smiling and asking smart questions. Jillian wanted to know about salary, vacations and an employment contract. We decided her former training guided her in that direction. Her field was personnel, after all. And she did have an exacting sort of personality. Deep inside, though, I kept thinking she wouldn't have made it to the second interview at This End Up. As we'd heard so many times, however, we lived in the out-islands now, not America and, practically speaking, Stewart and I needed to get these jobs filled and open Fowl Cay to customers. Most likely, we could get these two intelligent people to work out just fine. We offered Jillian and Ike the jobs.

After they accepted, we agreed that Ike would come down ahead of Jillian, since she needed a month or so to take care of their Freeport arrangements. During the discussion, they smoked cigarette after cigarette, a habit carefully hidden from us until now, and asked if they could bring their two cats. One of Jillian's children would be in the Bahamas soon, and she wanted to come stay at Fowl Cay for a week. Ike's brother often dived in the Exumas. Could he leave his equipment somewhere on the island? They made no further comments about the job, only requests about personal wishes now that the deal was closed. Although I had learned to accept the local attitude of "What can you do for me now?" I would never learn to like it.

CHAPTER 23: Fowl Behavior

We hired son Stew, who was back in the States from Brazil by 2000, to create the website, and daughter Ellie to take customer reservations from her home in Richmond. The three of us coordinated efforts on a brochure to be sent when people inquired about coming to stay at Fowl Cay. One day, I asked Stewart to read over the final draft for that marketing piece to make sure the message was to his liking. *(Photo 3.17)*

"I want every person who comes to stay with us to leave feeling that he or she got more from these out-islands than our advertising could ever express. We must never overpromise, but let the customers experience it themselves. That way, they'll go home feeling as lucky as we do to have discovered them."

Stewart's innate generosity, one of the reasons I had fallen in love with him 33 years before, never failed to touch me. He always gave the benefit of the doubt to the Bahamians, who had returned the favor with corruption and broken promises, while exploiting his belief in kindness without motive. My wish for the Bahamians was that one day they would appreciate a man like Stewart as much as he did the country he had chosen to make his home.

Arriving for work from the island where they lived nine miles away one morning, the local staff we hired said it was cold. Rowena, who moved to the area from Acklins Island in the southern Bahamas, was to be head cook for the Hill House. It was 72 degrees when she climbed the ladder from the boat to the dock in a sweater and windbreaker. I had been pleasantly surprised with her skills when I asked for a trial run on a dish I hoped to serve in the restaurant, especially since she used a teacup instead of a measuring cup to follow my recipe.

"We don' use dose to measure. Bahamians know how it 'pose to be."

Evelynn must have been colder-natured than Rowena because she sat huddled on the boat's back seat in a fat ski jacket, orange with fuchsia racing stripes. She had lived on a nearby island all her life. Hired as our waitress in the dining room, she told me during the interview that she was "wery good wit' wisitors." The third Bahamian woman on the staff was pretty Cozetta, who had moved to the area when she married a local man. She was the only person on the cleaning crew five days a week. On Saturdays, which was turnover day for the rental program, she would bring friends to help clean and restock the three houses. Even with a sweater zipped up under her chin and a towel draped around her shoulders, Cozetta shivered and rubbed her hands together.

The two men were more bundled than the women. If I hadn't known Rupert for the two years he worked on the construction of Fowl Cay, I wouldn't have recognized him. Wrapped up in a scarf and ski hat with bouncing pom-pom on top, his wraparound sunglasses completed the disguise. Only his slow, shuffling gait gave away his identity as he ambled down the dock to start the day as our main all-purpose helper. Close on his heels came James, Rupert's younger brother. He was No. 2 all-purpose helper, definitely No. 2, as Rupert let him know every minute as he stood over James and gave directions. The two of them refused to be separated on tasks. One might think in that case they would finish things in half the time, but in reality we often paid two salaries for one job. James pulled off his earmuffs, stuffing them in his parka along with his gloves. Stewart and I sat on the wall by the bulkhead in shorts and T-shirts.

Chatter. Chatter. Chatter. The five Bahamians fussed and yelled as they came down the dock, conducting animated conversations, or maybe an acrimonious argument—it was hard to tell. Twenty feet from us, in unspoken unity, silence took over until we were all face-to-face. We exchanged "Good Mornings" in the polite way of the newly acquainted. Twenty feet past, rollicking conversations in the local musical dialect began again as the group moved *en masse* down the newly-surfaced golf-cart path to the staff break room. There, they would pass the first half-hour of their day at Fowl Cay eating breakfast and drinking tea. In some odd way, Stewart and I felt a diminished sense of belonging on our own island.

A few days later, after the "cold front" passed, I asked one of the workmen if he could put my washer and dryer in the Birdcage laundry room. I was looking forward to using the larger size of standard machines after years of stack-packs while living on boats.

"Hey, Rocky, did you get my washer hooked up?" Rocky was a leftover Windsor worker we'd hired for a few months longer to do carpentry during the decorating process.

"Yep. Right in de spot you show me."

A great load of our work clothes filled the big General Electric tub, and it was roundly satisfying to toss a double dip of detergent in the big tub of dirty duds. My eager finger punched the middle of the Start button. Nothing.

After a 20-minute search of the grounds to locate Rocky, who was busy adjusting shutters, we both looked down into the stinky morass of shorts, shirts, socks and underclothes.

"The water won't come in. I know I have it set right because I have the same machine in the States. And the spigot in the laundry sink works, so water's not the problem," I said.

"You wan' me connec' de vater for you?" asked Rocky.

"Didn't you do that yesterday?"

"You axe me put in your machine. You didn' say nuttin' 'bout turnin' on no vater."

Three of Windsor Construction's regular crew were also on Fowl Cay finishing off the punch list. Including them, our five staff members, Rocky, two day-workers from Staniel Cay, Ike, Jillian, Stewart and me, there would be 15 of us to join the six moving men who would arrive at our dock on Intercontinental Shipping Company's super barge. A crowd of 21 would offload and place the hundreds of boxes and pieces of furniture, each of which had been tagged by our Richmond shipping coordinator indicating to which house and which room the item should go. Stewart would direct each of the five shipping containers to their individual locations. Jillian would guide the workers at Blue Moon, Ike at Sweetwater, Stewart at Hill House, and I would oversee Birdcage. The managers' house and little Lindon cottage would have to receive their furnishings with no team leaders. *(Photo 3.18)*

Per our instructions, the five containers were to be placed in the order in which they needed to come off the barge, the one on the bow, slated to go to the house farthest away, would be offloaded first. Once the massive storage units were in place, the narrow paths would be blocked. We guessed a two-day event, at least, to unpack and return the empty containers to the mother ship.

Logistical planning for this had been monstrous. From the purchasing and record-keeping of thousands of items, from trucking it all from the Richmond warehouse to Intercontinental's piers in Jacksonville, Florida, from moving the goods onto the transport company's ships to unloading and storing the whole lot in Nassau, the effort required months of complicated work for Stewart and me.

But not as complicated as organizing the transfer of those goods 75 miles from the Bahamas' capital to one of its tiny out-islands.

"No, Mr. Brown, we have no 'pecific Customs officials in Nassau who awailable dis week to check troo your containers. Dat temperwary but I not sure how long it is."

Stewart called Intercontinental. "I'm sorry, Intercontinental. I have to release the barge I reserved because we haven't cleared Customs yet. Of course I understand that I lose my deposit."

"Dose Custom document doesn't conform to vut ve require, Mr. Brown. Ve need a rewised report before ve go forward."

"But the information is in the format you requested when I lined this up with you a year ago." Silence. "Please send the new requirements to the Batelco fax number at Staniel Cay. I'll pick them up there," said Stewart.

"We need you out de Customs Warehouse No. 9, Mr. Brown. Please arrange a vay to transfer your goods by Friday."

"It's been four days and I still haven't received the faxed copy of the new Customs form," said Stewart. "How can we make this work out between you, Intercontinental and us?"

Oh. That again.

Stewart wrote a check, again. We were too close to the end to argue. Suddenly, Fowl Cay's containers didn't need moving from one place to another, we could forget bothering with any documentation and the barge we had reserved in the first place was free.

Magically, the *Tropic Moon* appeared at the dock with our belongings, and no one ever asked to see my 31 legal-size, single-spaced pages of minutiae.

Intercontinental had brought its own truck cab to handle the job, and Murphy, the driver, sat high inside as he drove down the barge's lowered bow hauling one of the containers, bumped over the cement bulkhead, and roared down Fowl Cay's path to dump it off as fast as possible at the appropriate house. With the tide falling, he had to get all five units off the boat before low water caused an untenable degree of angle from the barge's ramp to the golf cart path. Then, out to deep water, waiting to reload the empty containers and cab for their trip home.

Exhausted after two 12-hour days of nonstop labor unloading boxes and furniture, Ike, Jillian, Stewart and I were trying to put enough nutrition back in our systems to drag ourselves to bed, us on *Crossroads* and the Canadys in their rental house on Staniel Cay. Supper from Bar 'n

Bites, a case of warm Kalik and a bag of ice sat on an unpacked carton in Birdcage. The refrigerator and stove weren't hooked up yet, so fried takeout was the best we could muster.

The four of us were draped over the tall box to get as close to the meal as possible, because none of us had the energy to raise food to our mouths. Stewart's beer sat on top of perky handwriting that said "Birdcage Dining Room," and Ike's plastic fork dripped tartar sauce onto "Dining Room Chair: 2/4." Right house, right room, right item. I fell in love again with organization.

As we dropped our new managers at the house we'd rented for them at Staniel Cay, Stewart said he would pick them up the next morning at 8:00 to start the unpacking process. Ike indicated he'd be ready. Jillian announced she was taking tomorrow off to recover from the two-day "ordeal" of directing the movers. She said she planned to spend it looking for a new place to stay.

"I won't live in that house you rented for Ike anymore. It's falling apart. It doesn't even have a bathtub. I take baths, not showers."

If I hadn't been devoid of strength, I might have popped her one. Stewart and I headed back to our boat, worried we had made a colossal mistake. Little did we know.

Once the rugs and furniture were in place, we moved off *Crossroads* and into Birdcage to continue unpacking. Stewart hung curtains while I put new sheets on our bed, and then the two of us hauled belongings from the boat to our new home until we could hardly put one foot in front of the other. Our beautiful trawler, with a delivery captain at the helm, was off to Florida in a few days to be put on the block.

A delicious November evening settled around the island that had manhandled me since 1998. Stewart and I prepared to live permanently on land in 2001 for the first time in almost 11 years. My frame of mind was far from the unfettered happiness and excitement I wanted on this first night. But, finally, here I was and for that, a little smile of delight.

On our third night as a Birdcage couple, we walked down to Blue Moon, the rental house the Canadys decided to try. Even though finishing touches remained to be done on the house, Jillian said it was better than anything at Staniel. Completion of the managers' house was just a few weeks off, and most of the Canadys' boxes were piled up there, an inconvenient but short-lived situation for them.

"Hi, Ike. Do you and Jillian want to take a drink up to the Hill House and watch the sunset?" Stewart asked.

"Well, um, I tell you, Jillian is a bit out of sorts. Just one of those lady things, you know. It really made her angry late this afternoon when one of the workman walked in the house to work on the cabinet hinges without knocking. Jillian is a very private person. Actually, I've reserved a room at the Yacht Club for us for a couple of nights, just until Windsor is finished with this house. Or until our own house is done. We're getting ready to leave now."

As the rose-colored hour of sunset took hold, I didn't even register the end-of-day fusion of turquoise waters as they turned into a pond of pink glass. I wasted that short, sweet moment by acceding to anger, one of many short, sweet moments I allowed to be stolen from me by Jillian.

"Who does she think she is? She knew what it was going to be like on this cay. We paid for them to spend two days down here just so they could see for themselves what the conditions were. And now she has to move because one workman walks through the front door without knocking, for God's sake? What kind of conditions does she think *we've* been living in for the last two years?"

My outburst was like the last fierce jump of a fighting fish just before it surrenders to oblivion from having its head clubbed.

"I don't think Jillian's the kind of person who cares much about our problems," said Stewart lying back on a chaise lounge. "Maybe she'll calm down once the dust settles and the business starts up, but I hope she doesn't make Ike miserable enough to leave in the meantime."

CHAPTER 24: Into the Deep End (6)

Even Jillian's behavior during last week's moving-in spectacle has edged its way out to the fringes of my mind. Finally, Stewart and I live in paradise. In what must be the world's most beautiful homesite, the Birdcage's flaws pale to obscurity.

It's payback time. The risk to build a resort on a remote island in a foreign country is offering its reward at last as I look at the view from three sides of my living room. The house seems to float in the clear turquoise water, so close is it to the sea's edge. I am ashamed of myself for all the times I wanted to give up, and proud of myself that I never did.

Thanksgiving will be here in three weeks. It will be our first Fowl Cay family holiday, one I many times doubted would ever arrive. And before we can blink, the resort's first guests will be here to celebrate New Year's with us.

I expect the new year, 2002, will begin to reverse the toll that choosing this risk has claimed from us both. I'm breathing easier already.

"Windsor Construction?... Can you speak up please?... I need to talk to Harry Brighton right away if you can put me through... Yes, very important... Hello?... Hello?"

CHAPTER 25: Taken by Storm

I was more pleased with the outcome of Birdcage every hour I lived under its roof. My drive for accuracy, usually a heat-seeking missile, had struck a truce with perfection. I stood beside my husband on the deck of our new home, overwhelmed by living in a land of such beauty.

Earlier in the day, at the Bar 'n Bites, there was mutter around the bar about a late season hurricane somewhere out in the Atlantic. Without TV at Fowl Cay yet, Stewart and I were out of the news loop and hearing for the first time about a potential storm. November hurricanes were so rare, though, that no one paid much heed.

The many violent gales that had hit our beach house on the coast of North Carolina over the years had made Stewart and me veteran storm worrywarts, and I noticed a wrinkle between his eyes identical to my own. But we were too tired and too busy to spend time thinking about the small chance our resort might get blown down. Our first six customers were coming right after New Year's. We had their money in the bank.

Five days after we moved onto Fowl Cay, on November 5, 2001, Hurricane Michelle hit. The announcer on the Bahamian radio station made it sound as if the storm would give us only a mild brush. The eye was predicted to pass at least 30 miles north of Nassau, 100 miles north of us, and most likely the central Exumas would sustain winds of only 35 or 40 mph. But just before the edge of the enormous eye passed over our area, local instruments measured Michelle's power at 115.

The electrical junction box for our house lay beneath an isthmus that connected Birdcage to the rest of Fowl Cay. Once the torrent of seawater filled it, our power went out. Ike, Jillian, Stewart and I tried to play cards in the semi-darkness, but we gave up and recoiled in our seats from the scream of a Category 3 hurricane.

In the beginning, the wind hit in gusts, slamming into the front wall of the house. Running over a 100-mile fetch when the wind switched to southeast, the waves grew from two to six feet. Overriding our dock, they exploded onto the cement wall immediately below Birdcage, where they took flight and crashed against the French doors of the living room in which we sat. Eighteen feet above sea level and sounding like buckshot, wall after wall of wind-driven water pounded our unprotected front doors whose glass moved in and out like the stomachs of cartoon people on TV who have eaten too much.

Wind wailed like a person being tortured. Shingles flew off the roof, a pack of cards thrown into the air. Shutters and fan blades sailed away, banging and cutting the exterior walls. And the roof creaked as if it were about to fly off and leave the rest of the house to fend for itself. When a heavy palm tree outside the house uprooted and ripped through the screened porch, coming to rest inches from the master bedroom's glass doors, Birdcage keened in protest as if the house were speaking its mind against such abuse.

The wind stopped shrieking, like a screaming baby given a pacifier. During that troublesome calm, the four of us went outside to look for golf carts, rocking chairs, potted plants and hoses we hadn't put away in the face of the mild forecast. With the water rushing furiously from one side of the island to the other across the low bulkhead at the bottom of Birdcage's ramp, we were trapped on the knob of land. We could only guess at damage to the other buildings on the cay. The knowledge that Michelle was only half-finished with her assault made me feel like I was stuck in the crosshairs of a howitzer.

After the eye passed, the angle of attack swung around 90 degrees and staggered us with its might. This second part of the storm was longer and meaner than the first, and the wind ripped up already weakened pieces of our resort. Birdcage, not even settled into its new life, shuddered under the weight of its fate while fear and I huddled together, curled up on the brand-new couch.

From a window facing the interior of Fowl Cay, the sky looked like it was raining palm fronds and shingles. Trees partially standing after the first punch were now going down by inches, and the ones already on the ground were mud-covered and awash in debris-strewn water, their canopies shredded. When Michelle moved on, our five days in paradise were over. *(Photo 3.19)*

A week later, I sat on the horizontal trunk of a dying palmetto holding the satellite phone from our early construction days. It looked as if a New England autumn had come to the Exumas, a country that doesn't have seasons. Still coated with salt, everything that had been green two weeks before was now rust-colored as far as I could see. The normally turquoise sea around me was gray-brown, foamy and still washed up an amazing assortment of trash onto our eroded beaches.

We were halfway to getting 35 palms back up, but the delicate smaller trees and new ground plantings were 90 percent ruined. Shingles and screening were already on order from Florida since Windsor Construction had called to ask what they could do to help. Windows, shutters and radio antennae had to be replaced, as did fans, path lights, terrace furniture and gutters. The project list was long and the complexity of the tasks dismaying: docks to rebuild, electrical repairs to complete, beaches to resculpt and a watermaker intake pump to dig out of an undersea sandbank. Massive amounts of cleanup and burning awaited us in our crawl back to normalcy. The terraces of the rental houses had disappeared under a layer of mud while some of the new furnishings and rugs were marked by saltwater driven beneath doors.

The last thing Stewart and Ike had done before coming inside on November 5 was to partially bury *Roundabout* in the sand for protection against the hurricane. As the storm surpassed the forecast, we feared Michelle would sweep away our big inflatable in its surge, but in that regard, we had been fortunate.

On this day, the wind was 20 mph. Neighbors from other cays were beginning to surface like groundhogs do in spring. We touched base by VHF, but few moved about in their dinghies. We were all too busy with the immense task of setting our properties right. Silence abounded in the normally bustling island neighborhood.

I looked down at a little patch of ground, listening to the tinny ring through the Sat phone. Several tiny pink flowers, portulaca I thought, bounced around in the light breeze. Their quick recovery time reminded me of watching flowers come to life in time-lapse photographs. How long would it take us to bloom again? I knew that parts of the tangible ingredients of our dream were ruined. It would be months before Fowl Cay could be restored to her newborn beauty. After four years and millions of dollars, risk had almost devoured us.

I watched as Stewart lined up the palm tree expert to fly down from Nassau to advise on the cost of the damage, heard him talk to the man with the pile driver about coming over from Long Island to check the security of our docks, followed a conversation about getting two of the Windsor Construction crew back from Eleuthera. Right after lunch, he transferred money from our U.S. bank to our Bahamian bank for the second time since the storm struck.

Michelle's cameo appearance brought to mind a joke that floated around among people who ran businesses in the Cays: "You know how to make a small fortune in the Bahamas? Start with a big one." We were on our way to that being a self-fulfilling prophecy. And we hadn't even opened our doors yet. Not for our children, not for our friends, not for our business.

"Hello," said the person on the line.

"Hi," I said. "This is Libby Brown calling from Fowl Cay Resort."

I cancelled the first of our initial families in that phone call. There were two more groups just like it. My message was two-fold: "Where would you like your refund sent?" and "I have no idea how long before you could rebook."

When those conversations were over, fading daylight backlit a tall anvil-shaped cloud on the western skyline. It was six o'clock. I closed the curtains in our bedroom anyway and went to bed in search of obliterating sleep.

CHAPTER 26: Fowl Play and Fair Maiden

Once we set the major problems from the hurricane on their way to recovery, Rupert asked one day if he could bring his two youngest children to swim in our pool on Sunday afternoon, "jus' for a few minutes before de guestis start being here all de time." We said it would be fine.

I looked north three days later, watching four winding boat wakes obviously traveling together. Each one was loaded with bouncing little bodies in bright bathing suits. As they closed in on Fowl Cay, I realized this was Rupert and his "two chirren."

Five adults, twelve children, two pounds of jellybeans and a case of Coke later, they left. Neither Stewart nor I had yet been in our swimming pool.

During the second week in December, Evelynn was appointed spokeswoman by the staff. Their demand was made crystal clear, as is often the way with dictates in the Bahamas. That's the opposite of when you seek general information from island folk. Then the answers are clear as mud.

"De res' of de staff and me want our Christmas bonus today. We goin' to Nassau and do our shoppin' nex' week."

The subject was launched as if the word "bonus" didn't mean an unsought or unexpected extra benefit. Evelynn's approach left no question that they expected it, and on their terms. Stewart wrote checks for each member of our new staff, and we handed them out at the end of the same day, thinking they would be pleased with our prompt attention to their bidding.

"We like cash, not checks," said Evelynn.

When Stewart explained that we took in little cash on the cay, the crew frowned, folded their checks, picked up their belongings and boarded the skiff home to enjoy their bonus, as well as a surprise paid week of vacation.

The next afternoon, Jillian offered to snap some photos for possible use on the website. When I saw her by the pool later with her camera, I walked up to the Hill House to see what view she was considering.

"Hi, Jillian. See anything good?"

"Hello." She faced away from me and made no eye contact.

"Don't you want both the Bahamian and the American flags up if you're going to photograph the harbor with the flagpole in the foreground?" I asked.

"I don't think the American flag should be seen in publicity shots. Most of the world hates America, and personally, I don't care for people in Freeport or Nassau to know that I work for Americans."

I must have misunderstood her meaning, I thought to myself. With anyone else I would have asked for clarification on such a statement, but Jillian was so distasteful to talk to I took the chicken's way out and left without saying a word. How in the world did Ike handle living with her? On the way back to Birdcage, all I could think of was how difficult it had been to find anyone marginally acceptable to take the managers' job. The thought of starting over made me cringe.

A few days later, Jillian's daughter arrived to stay at Fowl Cay for a week. Diane had been raised in the mold of her mother. Once I heard her pontificate about how awful everything was in America, I knew I hadn't misunderstood Jillian's statement about the flags that afternoon at the Hill House. Jillian stayed in the house with Diane much of the time while Ike worked harder than usual trying to cover his job and Jillian's. The distribution of their workload was often imbalanced in that way.

While Diane was still visiting, I noticed the cushion of the new porch swing at the house where Jillian and Ike were living flung over the railing as if to dry. Gaping from the middle of it was a large burn hole. None of the family had mentioned it to me, and I wondered what other damage they had done to the house. We hadn't had even our first customer stay there yet.

When Ike came back from picking up our Christmas tree off the freight boat, he brought an envelope addressed to Stewart. The letter read, "Mr. Rolfe has served 16 years as the Head of Police on Hooper Island. There will be a party at the Reef Nightclub to celebrate his retirement December 30. We suggest a contribution from you of $300 in food, drink, T-shirts and hats or cash. We need to know what you are giving to this worthy cause right away." Contact information was included.

Solicitations were starting to come in on a regular basis. The one before this had asked for a contribution to the Miss Bahamas Budweiser contest. The one before that had invited me to a baby shower on a nearby island. I had no idea who the mother-to-be was, but she wanted infant clothes, size 0-6 months.

Unsurprisingly, Stewart and I disagreed over how to handle such requests. Actually, not since the day we vowed "I do," had we two hard-headed people agreed easily on much of anything, but until Fowl Cay came along, we knew how to manage that conundrum.

Although we had never met the police chief who was being feted, nor did we know the people who were collecting the money, and although we had lived on Fowl Cay for only five weeks, Stewart discounted my ideas that Mr. Rolfe's retirement party might be a scam or that it might open Pandora's box. He gave the money, saying, "We're part of this neighborhood now." I added "stingy wretch" to the list of how I felt about myself, and "gullible pushover" to the list of how I felt about Stewart.

A couple of weeks after the freight boat brought the Christmas tree, the thermometer stood at 80 degrees. We picked up Ellie, Matt and daughter Gracie, who had flown in from Richmond, at the Staniel Cay airstrip. Wearing a blue checked dress with a scalloped collar, baby Gracie clutched a stocking as her mom carried her off the plane. Matt looked like Santa, loaded down with presents wrapped in Ellie's signature glossy red paper with white satin bows. I couldn't stop touching that little family as if their skin and hair carried an antidote for the rancor that was eating my insides.

Later that day, six more of our family arrived, coughing and pale from hard work in snowy cities. Next came four of Ike and Jillian's children on the freight boat from Nassau. And on Christmas Eve morning, Stew flew in from Miami with his girlfriend, Johannah, and her brother. We numbered 20 for the dual-purpose visit—celebration of the Christmas holiday and the opening of Fowl Cay. Our toasts that evening were full of good wishes for the success of our business and for the happiness of our families.

On Christmas night, we sat at a long table surrounded by place cards, poppers, candles and tiny reindeer that found their place among island decorations of miniature shells and bougainvillea blossoms. The tree glistened with ornaments that every family had brought. Empty stockings drooped, tired but satisfied they had done their duty for another year, and Santa's largesse lay scattered about the Hill House.

Dinner was Bahamian style—conch salad, lobster, steak, peas and rice and guava duff. We could return to turkey and dressing, green beans and sweet potatoes another year, in another land. The laughter rose and fell and rose again as the different families merged in the cheer of the season. I looked at Stewart and he at me, and the 18 other people in that room disappeared during our brief, unuttered message, "This is why we built Fowl Cay." For family and friends, for celebrating and rejoicing, for gratitude and for love.

"Ding, Ding!" Unwrapped table favors sat in front of every person except for Amazing Gracie, who slept in the nearby Porta-Crib in her angel pajamas. Stew walked the table and refreshed wine glasses.

"Ding, Ding!" The laughing group was hard to settle.

"I'd like to give a toast," said Stew, standing at one end of the long Christmas table where dessert had just been served. He raised his glass. "To old friends," a nod to Stu, Johannah's brother, "to new friends," a nod to the Canady clan, "to family," a nod to his aunt, uncle and cousins. "To Ellie and Matt and my new niece." He put his hand on his father's shoulders. "And to my parents who have made this beautiful place for all of us to enjoy. Merry Christmas."

"Hear, Hear!" Clink, clink.

"But I want to focus mostly on family tonight, because ours will be increasing." I could hear the rhythm of the waves through the open doors. "Today, Johannah agreed to marry me."

Johannah's brother and I teared up while the younger cousins whooped in celebration and yelled, "I knew it!" Ellie ran around the table to scoop up Stew and Johannah in a happy embrace. Ike brought out the new champagne glasses and popped the corks on two bottles of bubbly while his children high-fived. Stewart planted a kiss, first on Johannah and then on Stew, and said over and over, "That's great, just GREAT." Uncle Bob toasted a new member of the in-law club.

Jillian offered up a joyless glance and sour silence, and a few minutes later Ike followed her out the Hill House with a look of sad apology over his shoulder. I could see the headlights of the Canadys' golf cart swinging through the darkness on their way back to Sweetwater.

I turned back to the goodness of the moment.

CHAPTER 27: Here and There

One of our generators had a problem soon after the holidays, so Stewart chartered a plane for Ham, the repairman, to come down from Nassau with new parts. What the problem might be was only a guess from phone conversations between Stewart and Ham. "What does the machine sound like? Look like? Smell like?" That kind of reading, correct only about 50 percent of the time, was the best we could do without a costly round-trip flight just for diagnostics. But half a guess was better than none.

If all went swimmingly, we would get four hours of Ham's work and pay for eight hours of Ham's time: two hours for the loading and round trip from Nassau to Fowl Cay, an hour offloading equipment from dock to power plant, setup and finding tools from our workshop that he forgot to bring, and an hour for lunch. The tab rose if Ham brought a helper, and, of course there would be the bill for parts. Add in the cost of a charter flight with the pilot's wait time, as well as the hours spent by our staff on Ham's behalf, and we'd closed in on a figure that would be equal to a bill for 30 guests to eat dinner at the Hill House. The combination of salt air's abuse and our remote location made for sky-high upkeep. Fowl Cay averaged a couple of repair calls a month from Nassau or the States.

At the airstrip, James picked up Ham, they loaded the box of generator parts onto the section of the work skiff behind the driver's seat, and headed the mile across water to our dock. Because the two men failed to secure the top of the container, some of the items flew over the stern of the boat and left a bobbing trail in the water, as if Hansel had decided to drop generator seals instead of crumbs. But the only people who noticed the runaway goods were other boaters, some who picked up the pieces and some who just ran over them.

Once James and Ham got to Fowl Cay, a long conversation ensued about how to handle the fiasco. By the time they left to search for the missing parts, and showed up again empty-handed, there remained only two-and-a-half hours before we needed to have Ham back to the airport for his return trip to Nassau—actually less, once he'd eaten his lunch.

At 3:15, on his way to take Ham to the airstrip, Stewart called Preston, the local Batelco representative, to see what time he was closing the office. Work hours varied with his whim. "Oh, I here 'til at least 4:30 today," Preston said.

Unable for several years to get Batelco's system to accept our U.S. address, the Bahamian phone company continued to send the telephone bill to Phillip Walker's home in New York. He forwarded it to us when he got a chance. Without fail, the envelope arrived in Richmond well after the payment date was due, even if we had our bookkeeper check for it every day. Despite our repeated recitation of the problem, Batelco cut off our phone every month.

"You jus' keep a balance wid us," said Preston. "Das de onliest t'ing dat work."

Stewart planned to stop by the office after his trip to the airstrip and leave a check with Preston to cover our next several months of phone service, such as it was, and he didn't want to dock the boat and walk over the ridge to Batelco if it was going to be closed. Three quarters of his workday had already been wasted.

Uncommon frustration showed in Stewart's eyes when he arrived back at Fowl Cay at 4:00 with our phone bill unpaid. "The man painting the Batelco building said Preston left for the day around 3:30. I guess I'll try again tomorrow."

Now that Fowl Cay Resort was completed, our lawyer arranged for Mrs. Somers to come down from the Prime Minister's office for the official tour. Afterward, we would finally receive our lease extension. The afternoon before she was to arrive, she cancelled.

Stew took off a week from work in January and appeared on the island one day to help speed up the repairs from Hurricane Michelle, so we'd be ready for the rental guests Ellie had booked for late March 2002. He confided to Stewart and me much later that he and his sister had been concerned enough about our exhausted voices on the phone that they had hatched a plan to see for themselves how the 'rents were really faring.

Young and healthy and part of a family with a king-size work ethic, Stew labored 12- to 14-hour days without breathing hard. From the first task, he was a natural with everything mechanical. Although he'd had no such training, his abundant gift of common sense and his willingness to delve into repair manuals solved a wide variety of problems. Banking and auditing jobs in South America had provided him experience only with financial work, and he was as surprised as we were at how often he could fix things. Boat motors, watermakers, generators, icemakers, golf carts, water heaters, swimming pool pumps, electrical wiring—it was an uncommon thing that Stew couldn't repair. The Guardian Angel of Breaking Points must have seen how close Stewart and I were to her *raison d'être* and sent salvation in the form of our son.

After Stew went back to Florida at the end of January, time raced past us. Stewart and I wanted to reconnect with the world beyond our Bahamian borders before we made the final preparations for the first guests who would arrive the end of March. We had been away from Richmond so long that, for me, it had become blurry with distance. When I had to look up the phone number for a close friend, I knew we needed to head north.

Nearing the Nassau airport in our small charter plane, we could see a solid gray curtain of rain approaching fast from the east side. Cephus, our experienced local pilot, said, "No way," after the control tower put three commercial airliners in a holding pattern. "We gat to land at Norman's Cay," he said and made a gentle U-turn away from the squall that would slam into Nassau in a matter of minutes. Heading back 20 miles to an abandoned runway, we touched down like a feather on the airstrip that had rampaging railroad vine and a couple of dogs wrestling at its edge. It became the first of several times I was glad to be flying the Cays in a small, single-engine plane. While we waited for the weather to clear, the three of us walked across to McDuff's for an early lunch. After a quick up and down flight, Stewart and I boarded a jet to the States, arriving home in February for a week's visit.

Ellie picked us up and I listened to the charged city sounds on the way from the airport: car wheels thumping over the asphalt, quarters clanking into the toll basket, siren screaming from an ambulance. The noises rang foreign because my ear was tuned to the putt-putting of dinghy engines, the snapping of flags, the chattering of a VHF.

When we got to our house, the telephone rang and a friend asked us to go out for dinner to a new restaurant in the neighborhood. I heard every word he said without static or interruption.

"A little dressier than usual," he warned, and Stewart went to put away his salt-caked deck shoes and look at the condition of his loafers.

The sky was drizzling when our buddies picked us up, and we popped open a golf umbrella instead of climbing into foul-weather gear. We rode dry and warm in the back of a Lexus, and I rubbed its leather seats while I thought of windy, rainy rides to dinner in an open rubber boat.

Pat and Gene walked with clarity of purpose and brisk steps, so Stewart and I ramped up our Bahamian pace.

The climate control at Harvest Moon eliminated humidity and the aroma was of tabletop roses instead of oft-used grease. I patted my hair to smooth it down but found it in the same condition as when I left home. I smiled because my city clothes smelled of Tide instead of salt.

The women chose salmon and the men had roast beef. Both were slightly pink in the middle and accompanied by scrumptious sauces rather than Tabasco in a bottle. The waiter called me Mrs. Brown instead of *Crossroads*. For a second, I wondered who Mrs. Brown was.

The four of us talked of grandchildren and travel and politics, of books and health and home, of missing one another and of where our lives were headed, the soft conversation of longtime friends who know they are growing old together.

When I said the construction at Fowl Cay continued to be difficult and Pat said she sort of understood because they were renovating an old farmhouse, I empathized and resisted comparisons.

When Gene questioned if things were settling down in paradise, Stewart gave a wan smile and I looked down at the table.

On the way home, I spread my hand flat on the inside of the car window. Cold. Sleet came down in a steady curtain, and trees were bare with spiky branches poking skyward. I thought of the warm breeze we'd left that morning and missed the gentle swaying of the floppy palm fronds as I looked outside. In the staid, old Richmond neighborhoods, elegant Georgian houses shone with a patina of age and good taste but offered no wintertime color to delight my eye. No raspberry bougainvillea or coral hibiscus or blue plumbago.

Before I got under the heavy blanket in my socks and flannel pajamas, we sat for a moment in front of the embers from an early evening fire and listened to a train in the distance. In bed, the comfortable clatter of a heat register filled the room, a cozy accompaniment to sleep, opposite and delightfully equal to the tickling flutter of my cotton nightgown under the whir of a ceiling fan.

The alarm clock went off when it was still gray outside to get me up for an early appointment with the dentist to fix a nagging toothache. The insistent buzz was a far cry from the lazy rise out of sleep I was used to when the sun turned the color of a ripe pumpkin and snuck in my warm room to ask if there was any reason to get up yet.

I jumped into my cords and heavy peacoat and then into the frigid car. I forgot all about gloves and my hands were stinging with cold. I turned a sharp right and then a sharp left. I yielded and stopped and put on my blinker. My seat belt treated me rudely and so did the blast of a horn at the stoplight. Cars had tall chassis and rear windshield wipers on the dark windows. The drivers, all blonde and thin, looked straight ahead as they talked on their cellphones.

While I sat in the waiting room, I daydreamed of a morning ride in *Roundabout* where there was a curvaceous cay around every turn, a coral reef under every colorful fish and turquoise water that covered the ostensible earth. Everyone I passed waved hello, and open boats were filled with fishing rods, coolers, snorkel gear and beach towels. If it sprinkled, I didn't care. I had no watch to protect, no windows to roll up, no upholstery to ruin.

Afterward, I bought a decaf latte at Starbucks and Sally Lunn bread at the bakery and had them for breakfast while garbage men whisked away the neighborhood trash to I didn't know where or care. When my trash compactor wouldn't start, the repairman came and fixed it, handed me a bill for $61, thanked me for the business, didn't ask for lunch and left without expecting me to get him home. My friends arranged a bridge game for me because they kept track of my comings and goings and knew I would want to be included. Ellie and Gracie and baby Anna arrived, trailing scribbly drawings and Pie Pie the Bunny and love in so many fragile forms it all but healed my heart.

* * *

As if someone had turned an hourglass on its side, the sand that had run in one direction for so long settled in the middle. My experiences in the Bahamas, cruising on *Crossroads* and developing This End Up — 27 years — had forced me through a portal of change, marked by a return to peace with my Richmond lifestyle. Because the world around me had become crazier and crazier, I took another look at the value of tradition, and every day I was home I found myself happier in the town of people who had continued to touch my mind, my heart and my soul over the years.

Out of desire for a more diverse lifestyle, I had pushed back from steadfast Richmond and cast aside its essence. Perhaps because many of the days where I lived now were spent fighting to hold on to staunch values, I yearned to be in a place where I could be enveloped in their core belief, a place where I could find serenity in their virtue.

Although disparaging words were never meant as a rejection, in the past I had occasionally diminished the place I came from, so focused was I on a life of exploration. Now, bruised and battered and in need of some balance to my life, I longed for the comfort of familiarity. I marveled at the grip of good memories, at how precisely I could recall them while I was home. On this trip, I began to regain patience with my hometown and to stop weighing its bad points against its good. Perusing pages in the mental ledger I had kept on Richmond for years, I recognized myself as a fickle admirer who now circled back to my jilted friend, a friend who had waited with forbearance for my return.

CHAPTER 28: Human and Inhuman Resources

No soft opening for us. On the fourth Saturday we had all the rental houses booked coming and going—14 guests leaving and 15 guests arriving. Most of them had found our website, but pictures on a computer screen were static and e-mail reservations were just words. Reality was a crapshoot in both directions. Would they love it or want a glitzier atmosphere? Would they be disappointed in the Raisin Bran and oranges we put in their houses for breakfast? Thank God the supply boat had come in this week. But perhaps they were expecting granola and raspberries. Maybe the ones flying out would whisper to the newcomers that the kayaks weren't arriving for three more weeks or that the female manager had an attitude. Our dream of showing people the Exumas on our terms was upon us. The question was whether our terms would be the same as theirs. Calm weather was key, but the 18 mph wind this morning had the boats bouncing around at the dock like jumping beans. So was my heart.

Every person on our day staff knew that coming in on changeover day was imperative. Flipping the cay, as we called it, took three of them plus Stewart, Ike, Jillian and me working at a clip to clean the cottages inside and out, change the linens and, assuming we could procure them, put in the selections each group had ordered from the food and beverage list that Ellie sent out a month ahead. The golf carts needed to be cleaned and charged, the boats washed and gassed, the pool scrubbed, the grounds picked up, the snorkel gear rinsed. Laundry had to be washed and the garbage emptied. All between checkout at 10:00 and check-in at 3:00.

We confirmed everyone's outgoing or incoming flight. Reconfirmed. And reconfirmed. Planes almost never ran on schedule, and attaining correct information on arrival times was beyond difficult. Our bye-bye company and bags had to get to the airstrip, each group at a different time and, although we were drowning in preparations for our hello company, Ike stayed with departing passengers until a tardy wheels up, smiling like he had nothing else to do.

Same as the night staff, one of our guys drove the three day staff members nine miles home in our work skiff to the island where they lived, an arrangement that kept Ike and Stewart from making four hour-long round trips every 24 hours to transport them. By 8:30 a.m. on this first full Saturday though, Cozetta, James and Rupert were an hour late. Because Batelco was out of service, we couldn't call and Rupert had dropped the VHF we supplied him a month earlier into the water. It looked like the island changeover would be up to Stewart, Ike, Jillian and me.

The bye-byes had started moving about, wondering when their luggage would be picked up and if their flight was on time, the question to which there was never a good answer. Could they get another pack of bacon, had we seen a pair of sunglasses around anywhere and was it possible to get into the gift shop to buy one more Fowl Cay T-shirt? "Absolutely," I said, swallowing stress like it was part of my breakfast.

All I could think of was the 15 new guests who were boarding planes in Atlanta, Chicago, Baltimore and Boston, all of them expecting clean houses, stocked kitchens and fueled boats when they arrived in a few hours. Jillian didn't last long because she had a headache, so that left Ike, Stewart and me to make several round trip airport runs and convert the cay from pawed-over to pristine. No way could any of us take the time to hunt down our workers.

Ike was at the airstrip, I was swishing toilet bowls, and Stewart— his retirement looking a touch different from what he'd dreamed—was loading outgoing baggage into a boat when the bow of our skiff bumped the dock at 10:15. Our staff ambled off at their regular tempo. Bahamians never felt pressure, as far as I could tell, and worked in the same relaxed manner no matter how important the issue, how close the deadline, how many promises had been made or how much money was on the line. Stress had no life in the Bahamas. Almost always, if it had to be done in a pinch, it had to be done by us.

"Hey, Rupert," called Stewart. "Why are you so late?"

"Dey borrow de prop offen de skiff."

"Who has the prop? What do you mean 'borrowed'?"

"I don' know who it was. De prop guh offen de motor dis mornin' ven ve start vork," said Rupert.

"What do you mean by 'they borrowed the prop'? Did you get it back?" asked Stewart.

This was way too much pressure for Rupert, who looked off to the side in silence.

"Rupert?"

"Prob'ly won' get it back," mumbled Rupert.

"Stolen" didn't seem to be in the Bahamian vocabulary, but it was clear that stolen was the present condition of our propeller. After Rupert walked on, it occurred to us that we didn't know how he got our skiff's engine to work without one. Most likely he "borrowed" a prop off some other boat.

I couldn't tell if the locals didn't have much of a conscience or whether they simply found it an easy thing to compromise. Although most of our possessions could sit unbothered, we regularly discovered small items missing from the cay—tools, cleaning supplies, liquor. A couple of times, the culprits were caught red-handed, but generally the thefts went unsolved. Stewart and I were told by others to chalk it up to "toting rights," an attitude of the locals that as long as the purloined goods were necessary for everyday living, they were entitled to take them. When subcontract carpenters came to add new rental houses as Fowl Cay grew, our workshop was all but stripped. The connection between the devout heed they paid religious services and their actions seemed tenuous to me, because many of the locals ignored moral codes that burdened them, a riddle that was hard for me to understand.

Thursday before Easter, Duncan, the bartender we had added to our staff, said he wouldn't work on Good Friday. We had a signed employment contract with him stating that he knew the job entailed working on national holidays because Fowl Cay was part of the tourist industry.

"I ain' doin' it."

"Duncan, I'll have to let you go if you don't come in tomorrow," said Ike. "Do you understand? This is fair warning."

Duncan didn't show on Friday. Stewart tended bar for a packed Hill House dinner crowd, paging through *The Bartender's Bible* to find how to mix a Bahama Mama and a Goombay Smash and praying the next customer wanted just a beer. As I went from guest to guest introducing myself, one of the people who came in off a boat for dinner asked me, "Where'd you find an older white guy to be your bartender?"

The "older white guy" scared me to death that moonless night when he and Ike were long overdue from taking the staff home. The boat's prop hit a reef and he had to limp back to Fowl Cay at idle speed. Normally, Duncan drove everyone back at top speed with no lights.

Duncan returned on Saturday with a note that said he'd had the flu Friday. Signed by the government nurse on the island where he lived, there was nothing we could do about the absence. When Ike asked him how he felt, he waggled his eyebrows and said, "Oh, much better today. Mussa be one of dose 24-hour t'ings."

Stewart and I got in *Roundabout* on Easter Sunday and headed toward the church at Staniel Cay where the coral-colored stucco building with a red steeple sat out on the edge of the water. I could see the women's irrepressible hats through the open windows, and as soon as we were floating abreast of that heady display, we doused the engine, threw the anchor over and listened to the exuberant songs of the day from the congregation of Mt. Olivet Baptist Church. No stuffy, half-swallowed Episcopal hymns for us.

At the end of April, Stew and Johannah came to visit so we could work on their wedding plans, a happy event to look forward to in the face of continued silence from the Bahamian government, ornery behavior from some of our staff and unrelenting truculence from Jillian. The four of us breezed through plans for a week-long celebration to be held in November at Fowl Cay. The logistics of housing, feeding and entertaining 65 guests for that long had me trembling in anticipation of all the delicious details that would need my attention.

Over dinner the second night, Stew and Johannah threw an astonishing question at us.

"What would you think about the two of us moving down here to run Fowl Cay for you?"

Such an idea was so far from anything we had ever thought that Stewart and I sloughed it off. But two weeks after Stew and Johannah returned to Miami, their résumés arrived in our forwarded mail. The cover letter began, "Dear Mr. and Mrs. Brown," and detailed exactly why they wanted the job, what expertise they would bring and how that might affect the bottom line.

"Not a good idea," Stewart said to me. "Who could know the pitfalls of working with family any better than you and me? Let's not put that pressure on a new marriage."

The next time Stew and Johannah came down, they asked for another meeting. What did we think about the idea?

I was sold on the suggestion, and not just as a release from the Canadys. Ignoring Stew's excellent aptitude for the tasks of Fowl Cay during the hurricane crisis and his lack of comment on 14-hour workdays was impossible. And now our grown son and his future wife wanted to live and work with his parents. How could we turn our backs on that kind of gift?

"Stew, if you come here to work, your career path could be diverted forever. Have you considered that? You would be setting aside an MBA and years of financial training. And Johannah would, too. Do you really want a job where you are serving the public?" Never one to sweep away reality, Stewart spewed out negatives until the table was piled high with unpleasant possibilities. Nothing his dad said seemed to change Stew's mind.

"Go home and work the pros and cons list. I think you'll both find it would be a risky thing to do," said Stewart.

Hearing him warn Stew against taking a chance early in his career was amusing and sad at the same time—amusing in its "do as I say and not as I do" message, and sad because I knew our difficult experience with Fowl Cay was the ingredient that had made Stewart gun-shy about risk for our son.

After numerous talks with Stewart, Jillian told him she would think about resigning: the job wasn't what she thought it would be, she was worried about the sublease on their Freeport house, her cats didn't like the wind, our American management style was abrasive and unproductive. In answer, Stewart used his masterful statesmanship.

"Jillian, we know this position isn't using your experience, and that makes you unhappy. I can understand that. As you know, we weren't sure exactly what the job would be since we'd only had managers for seven weeks before the two of you came, so I can empathize with your feelings. I'm not sure what Libby and I can do to change how we manage—it's the way our background is—but we're willing to try. Every person deserves to be happy where she lives and where she works. Think about it for a week, and if you decide that can happen for you at Fowl Cay and you want to stay, we'll be with you 100 percent. We want it to work out for all of us."

I had seen Stewart work this diplomatic magic time and time again at This End Up. "If you want something from someone, always give that person a way to hand it to you," he had taught our senior management team for years. We had never had a complaint from any employee when we parted ways. I couldn't wait for next Tuesday.

CHAPTER 29: The Charm School Option

Only one of the original families whose week with us was cancelled because of the hurricane eventually came to stay. The daughter tilted a lampshade and burned a hole through it. Eager for her child to learn a lesson about other people's property, the mother wanted Katy to pay for the damage.

"How much would it be to replace the shade?"

"Don't worry about it," I said. "We count on an occasional thing like that happening."

"But I want Katy to learn about responsibility."

"You're nice to offer, but it's OK. Just an accident."

"No, I insist we pay for a new one. How much do you think it will cost?"

I told Martha I would let her know, but I had no intention of doing so. The expense and time it took to replace one small thing in one house on an out-island in the Bahamas defied belief.

Several $2-per-minute phone calls would be the first task toward restoring this hard-to-find item, the kind of item that made the rental houses on Fowl Cay special. The decorator in Richmond who hunted down an appropriate shade charged $100 an hour. She bought two shades since it involved a matching pair of lamps. The originals, made in Morocco of embroidered cowhide, cost around $75 each, plus the decorator's ten percent commission.

Continuing my phone calls, I asked Ellie to pick up the shades from the decorator's office and take them to the mailing store where each one was boxed separately due to their fragile nature. The cost of shipping, handling and insurance was charged to my MasterCard, and off they went to Fort Lauderdale by UPS. Once the boxes reached Florida, they were transported, along with the airfreight bill, to the hangar where the little airplane was kept that flew goods in to Staniel Cay.

On the way over to the Bahamas, the plane stopped on Andros Island to clear Customs, and we were charged 42 percent duty and stamp tax on the invoiced lampshades. After the plane landed at Staniel

Cay, a truck took the boxes to the partially covered holding area, and today was a good day so someone radioed us to say we had "pockages" before rain blew in on them.

Then we dispatched one of our men by boat to ride over and pick up the boxes—gasoline in the Cays at that time being $4.50 a gallon—and hoped the goods could weather the wet, bumpy trip in the bottom of the dirty work skiff. Upon his return, after Rupert pitched the fragile items from the boat up onto the dock, I unpacked them and had James take the packaging to the burn pit where Wesley added it to the day's pile. I took the new shades to Blue Moon, but not until Saturday when I could get in, and was able to restore the lamps to their former condition. That miracle happened only because there were no screw-ups in the eight-week, nine-step, three-country, $565 process. No charge for my time.

During that undertaking, I found the expensive new sheets I had bought for the master bedroom at Birdcage neatly folded on our bathroom counter where somebody on the staff had left them after washing and folding. When I shook the set out to make the bed, both sheets and pillowcases were riddled with holes. It must have taken a long time to fold those items so they looked perfect from the top, because there wasn't much intact material to work with. The next day, I took the bottle of bleach out of my laundry room and called the decorator in Richmond to add replacement linens to the box when she shipped the new lampshades.

Day after day, Jillian walked in the little office we all shared with her face squeezed tight as a fist, hardly a "Good Morning" straining out of her mouth. Our staff complained on a regular basis about her high-handed ways, and I knew what they meant because she treated me that way too. One morning when I looked out the window from Birdcage, I watched Ike running after her, waving his arms as she ripped a furious turn out of the parking spot in her golf cart. He slowed after a few futile steps, squatted on the cart path and held his head in his hands.

One customer asked, "Why don't you send Jillian to charm school?" and one said, "She really brings the place down." Friends in Staniel Cay asked if we knew how she complained about her job and told how angry it made them on our behalf while they watched us work to build up Fowl Cay's reputation. A normally non-judgmental Bahamian, one of our sub-contractors from Nassau, said, "Vut in de vorl' de madder wid her?"

Stewart and I had used every management skill we knew to uncover the source of Jillian's bitterness. She refused to talk. Although we knew

Ike was doing much of her job as well as his own, we didn't think it proper to speak about one person's performance to another person, even if they were married. We wondered what she was telling Ike at home.

Often she complained about how direct I was in my verbal communication, so I offered to start writing down my requests and comments. Jillian penned angry responses all over my writing, circling certain phrases and calling them nasty and unprofessional. She left those on top of my desk.

We had a mix-up about the dates a couple from Germany was coming to stay. When I asked Jillian in writing for help, she responded with the original set of dates we all had on our calendars. It felt ridiculous to be sitting eight feet from each other passing notes when a 30-second conversation would clear things up, so I floated an inquiry aloud to see if we could settle such a simple matter.

"I have that same week down, but Ellie says she sent an e-mail with the change. Can you check back to see what the new date is please?" I always said "please" to Jillian.

"Ellie's lying. She never sent me any e-mail."

It took powerful coaxing on Stewart's part to persuade me to keep managing Jillian. I only could leave my written comments and requests on her desk when she wasn't in the office. I simply could not be in the same room with her. Never in my working days could I have imagined agreeing to manage someone by avoiding contact with her.

How could we stop this? Stewart and I alone couldn't manage the resort. It was too big. What would we tell a government that was notoriously touchy when you fired one of its citizens? That we let her go because she was hateful? Where could we find someone decent to take the job? And Ike was good, so was it better to endure his wife than to flush him out along with her? Discouraged, but feeling we needed a backup plan, I pulled out the want ad we had placed in the Nassau newspaper less than a year ago for a couple to manage Fowl Cay and faxed it to the appropriate section.

Our This End Up philosophy was to manage people to their own conclusion about resignation. This idea was hard for me to swallow in Jillian's case, but Stewart wanted to try it. I wanted to kick her butt back to Freeport. Like so many times in the last few years, I didn't like the problem and I didn't like the solution. The Bahamas were on thin ice with me.

CHAPTER 30: Into the Deep End (7)

I don't know if I can keep going, as wrung out as I am trying to make things look good on the surface for the customer's sake. My stomach hurts almost every day while I go behind the staff straightening and wiping and fluffing and coaching uninterested students. I know things can't be perfect in this environment, but good should be attainable, shouldn't it? In my entire life as an entrepreneur, I've never had anything with my name on it that wasn't at least good. I don't want to start now.

Jillian continues to be the most difficult person I've ever managed. Maybe if Stewart can get her to resign, though, I won't have to listen to any more comments about my child "lying." What an incredible thing to say to your boss. Let alone Ellie's mother.

"Hi, Ellie. Daddy and I can't wait to see you and Matt... In the EMERGENCY ROOM? For what?... You're fading out... Ellie?... Hello?"

CHAPTER 31: Culture Clash

When dinner was put on the buffet counter at the Hill House, the sign that read "Hot and Spicy" was next to the apple-sauce that went with the pork tenderloin we weren't serving. On an old English chest sat the coffee machine, holding two 12-cup pots. One pot was the color of weak tea and one was black enough to hold a dipstick straight up; there was no way to tell which was regular and which was decaf and, for 24 diners, there were six cups of coffee in one carafe and three in the other. For the third night in a row the coffee was all wrong, despite my daily efforts to cure it. I would try again tomorrow.

"Evelynn, can I get you to do two things for me? Would you use this measuring spoon when you make the coffee, please? A heaping one of these per cup will make it the perfect strength every time. And let's make enough coffee to fill each pot every night."

There. Clear directions like that should make it simple. I put the spoon on the kitchen counter beside her.

Looking me straight in the eyes, Evelynn told me what she thought. "I don' do it dat vay, we never done it dat vay, and you can't make me."

My desire to run a proper business in the Bahamas fell flat as a bad joke. As with others on our staff, Evelynn acted like a child at times, and I found I had little patience with adults who threw their tempers around, demanding to be coddled. In the face of such behavior, I was less and less disposed to understand that often it wasn't a matter of me being right and them being wrong. Rather, it was one more example of the thousands of small ways our cultures battled, and mine lost.

On Tuesday, Evelynn called to say she wanted us to come pick her up and bring her to Fowl Cay so she could resign in person. How thoughtful. Stewart said no, because it was her day off and she would probably charge us double time to quit. When Rowena came in the next day and discovered she had to fix dinner without Evelynn, she refused to cook, even though Jillian said she would help. We had to pay for our guests to dine at Bar 'n Bites.

One day, Ike asked Rupert, "Can you please clean the ceiling fan blades in the master bedroom of Birdcage?"

"Men don't do no work inside de house. Das a woman job."

"Cozetta," said Ike, "can you please clean the fans in the Browns' bedroom and bath?"

"Women don't nevah do no work what need a ladder. Das a man job."

When I went in the house that afternoon, Ike was on a ladder cleaning the fan blades.

A few weeks later, Administrator Broome called and said to come pick him up at Staniel Cay. He had come to the area from the office of local government, which was located 15 miles away on Green Island. No matter if Fowl Cay was grinding to a halt with mechanical attacks, guest requests and staff no-shows, the administrator with no appointment took precedence.

"How many golf carts you got on Fowl Cay?" asked Mr. Broome.

"Eight," said Stewart.

"Ver dere license plate?"

"They don't have license plates. They're private carts on a private cay on roads that we built and maintain."

"Dey need license plate."

"Really? Why is that when they don't run on government roads?" asked Stewart.

"Just do. It's $70 a cart."

Having been through similar no-win drills with government officials during the buying and building of Fowl Cay, Stewart paid up once again. As he walked The Man down the dock for Ike to take him back, Stewart said, "Well, I guess I'll see you this time next year."

"Nope," said Mr. Broome. "I'll be back in t'ree mont'. Das ven dese plate expire."

Later we heard when other private island owners stood up to the administrator about the unfair levy, they were the recipients of typical arbitrary Bahamian law. "OK, if you t'ink das too much, den jus' pay half." "Still too much? Den forget it." And off Mr. Broome would go to his next victim.

In the years when we lived aboard our Hatteras, May mornings were full of warm water and gold-dust sun and hours to fill with idle time. Stewart and I went out early in *Roundabout* to stickybeak around in whatever neighborhood we happened to be. That wonderful sort of purposeless meandering had been off our agenda for years, but as sunrise stole into day, we decided not to put off recapturing lost pleasure.

As we lay in the shallow water at the edge of Osprey Cay, the easy, joking conversation I had hoped to revive was not to be. We talked about how to handle the problem with Jillian when we met with her and Ike on the appointed day. Once again, the subject of the Canadys sapped our capacity for fun.

"Do you think she'll resign?" I asked.

"Don't know," said Stewart.

Walking the low-tide sandbar, I tried to focus on the loveliness of the Cays and to keep at bay the almost certain unpleasantness to come. A broken sand dollar lay along our way, its five perfect dove-shaped prizes spilled out of the center of it at the edge of the water. A good omen maybe.

On Tuesday, Jillian resigned in writing, giving us two months' notice. Ike said little and shuffled out behind his wife after the brief meeting was over. The good news was she was leaving. The bad news was he was leaving. Where would we find replacements? How long would it take?

James came to us that same afternoon and said we were supposed to give each person on the staff one paid banking day per quarter to go to Nassau to cash his paychecks because no banks did business in the small Exuma Cays. When Stewart asked James if "banking days" were a Bahamian law, he said yes, but we were unable to find it in our outdated copy of the labor laws. This year's booklet was well overdue. So was last year's.

Stewart called the administrator in George Town for information about banking days.

"So this paid banking day is not a law in the Bahamas?"

"You need to pay dat, Mr. Brown."

"Is it the law that I have to?"

"You need to do it to keep your staff happy."

"But it's not a Bahamian law, right?"

"I adwise you to keep your staff happy, no matter what. You vant dem to be happy, don't you, Mr. Brown?"

If we didn't pay, we could envision our request for the extension of Fowl Cay's land lease falling into a governmental black hole. We included the extra money for a banking day in that week's payroll, even though we felt sure it wasn't the law.

Stew and Johannah flew down from Miami for Memorial Day. They said they'd tried to think of every angle, pro and con, and they still wanted the job.

"Have you considered that you'll have practically no free time for 14 hours a day, six days a week?" They had.

"What about no people your age down here? No social life?" They knew it.

"How are you going to feel when some drunk jerk yells at you in the restaurant?" They could handle it.

"What about children?" Children could live on the cay too.

"I still disagree, Stew, even though Mom thinks it would be fine."

For such a positive person, Stewart could really go off on negativity.

"OK, Dad. I'll have to give in to your decision. But I guess unless I really screw up, Fowl Cay will belong to Ellie and me one day, and I can't think of a better way to be a good steward of your and Mom's investment than to run it. Can you?"

I watched as Stewart's eyes slid off to the side. The sight of our child silhouetted in front of Fowl Cay's diamond-studded water spoke of the power of the dream, a vision that had made us leap when we could so easily have sat back. Acceptance flickered at the corner of Stewart's mouth, a twitch so tender only I knew it was there.

Before Johannah and Stew left, they decided to be married right away at the courthouse in Miami, because their Bahamian work papers would be easier to obtain as a husband and wife entering the country. They would tuck away that legal certificate in their files, and in November, the real ceremony would take place as planned at Fowl Cay. As they left the Bahamas to dismantle their lives in Florida, we hoped they would be on the job by the first of August.

Jillian, with her legal background, spearheaded the complicated Bahamian work paper issue. Who was more perfect to make sure the required attachments for Stew and Johannah were in order: birth, marriage, police and citizenship records. And the proper payment. One of the main reasons Stewart and I had employed her was so she could use her experience to keep us straight and in compliance with all things having to do with Bahamian labor laws.

That hiring rationale would take a turn so ironic as to be unimaginable.

CHAPTER 32: Laughter, Lies and Larceny

Once in a while, Ellie regaled us with a few of the questions that came in over the website or toll-free number. She said they sometimes made her feel like she was the caretaker at a zoo. Whenever I had a day that lasted a month, she flabbergasted me with some of the choice inquiries she had to field.

"I must be able to bring my dog. She's smaller than a stick of butter, she doesn't shed a single hair and never goes to the bathroom—ever."

"I'm a corporate planner in New York City, and I mean a big corporate planner. If you can please me this first time around, I can keep your island rented 100 percent of the time. My clients are big Wall Street tycoons with so many rich, important friends that you'll be able to close your doors to all those nasty little people that must come there now."

"I see on your website that you specialize in fowl. Can you please tell me what parts of a bird are most edible and how do you carve it up?"

"This e-mail has nothing to do with coming to stay at your resort, but I know you must have a lot of clouds down there and I am a cloud artist. Please tell me, in your opinion, when are the good times of the day to paint clouds? You know, when the light and colors are the best?"

Whenever my daughter shared wacky people stories with me, I felt a renewal of my sense of humor, a lightening of my insides. Kooky material was abundant, and still is.

I was not amused, however, when our lawyer called to say Mrs. Somers from the Prime Minister's office was canceling another appointment to tour Fowl Cay, her third rejection.

Even less amusing was Jillian's attitude, which had only deteriorated. She handled my outgoing e-mails for me on our lone computer. After years living on a boat, I was woefully behind the world when it came to that machine. I wrote e-mails out longhand, about one a week, and she typed and sent them. At the end of June, I left her an e-mail to take care of with "please" and "thank you" and "no rush" written on it, as always. The message was to a friend with the good news of Stew's impending island wedding to Johannah and their decision to move to the

Exumas and work. The second paragraph began, "Young Stewart will be married on the beach at Fowl Cay on November 14th." It was a message full of happiness from me, and I put the text on Jillian's desk in the same place I always left my requests. *(Photo 3.20)*

On Sunday, when Jillian never went into the office, I slipped in and sat at my desk to write in the journal I kept about Fowl Cay's development. Squarely in the middle was a copy of the e-mail Jillian had typed and sent to my friend. With a red pen, she had circled the statement about Stew and Johannah being married on Fowl Cay. In an attached note she said, "I do not appreciate being put in the position of having to support your lies. An e-mail, which you requested that I send today, stated 'Young Stewart will be married... on Nov. 14th.' That is not true. He has already been married. In future, word differently." Jillian was quick to accuse the Brown family of lying.

And I had to pay to live with this woman.

Stew and Johannah moved in and were trying to learn how to manage the highest priority jobs from Ike and Jillian before their departure, but the lame ducks were not cooperative in the training. Even Ike told Johannah to "just figure how to order the proper amount of food from the records." The Canadys were focused on packing their possessions so there would be no holdup on Friday when they were scheduled to leave Fowl Cay. Maybe Stewart's determined optimism would somehow see us through to the end of this relationship on a civil note.

When Stewart met Ike the morning he and Jillian were to leave, Ike presented a list of overtime pay he said the two of them were due—$29,500—for work on behalf of the cay during holidays, on Sundays and in Freeport when they went there for R&R. Not in the entire year of their employment had either of them mentioned one word about such an issue, and Jillian had been hired for her expertise in the field of labor laws, which stated that out-island managers were exempt from having specific days off. Additionally, the Canadys had signed an employment agreement stating, "This job encompasses all responsibilities entailed in running Fowl Cay as a resort." When Stewart turned down Ike's claims, he felt in the right and covered by Bahamian law in doing so. He was a bit miffed at the couple's attempt at highway robbery, but true to his kind soul, never reacted in an adversarial way and, in fact, wrote their final paychecks with gift bonuses and relocation funds included.

The four Browns gathered at the dock to say goodbye to Ike and Jillian, wish them good luck and thank them for their contribution.

Jillian refused to speak or make eye contact with any of us, but Ike returned our waves and smiles, saying, "Call anytime I can help."

I reflected most of the night upon why this experience had gone so sour, looking deep inside myself. Any single explanation ultimately came up short. I tossed and turned, wondering whether Jillian had an answer.

The relief Stewart and I felt over the Canadys' departure had us giddy the next night at the Hill House. We had a full complement of dinner customers—resident guests, Staniel Cay people and customers off charter yachts. When one of them asked Duncan for a scotch and soda on the rocks, he looked a little puzzled, so she asked if she could help him.

"Das OK. I know dat one. You want Coke or Sprite wid your scotch?"

Stewart and I were sitting with the two people staying in Lindon because the dining room was full. At dessert, a conservative-looking, but very drunk, woman stood up to tell a joke and all 25 other guests politely stopped to listen. The punch line was so vulgar it left even the rowdy crowd of boaters dumbstruck, and in the uncomfortable silence the man at our table said to the room, "Well. I haven't heard that word since I was in the boy's bathroom in high school." The moment was saved as the diners erupted into laughter.

At closing time, a young couple approached me with a bottle of port as a gift to Stewart and me.

"Melanie and I wanted to thank you for squeezing us in tonight," said the man. "We're on our honeymoon and my best man told us if we didn't go anywhere else, we had to come to Fowl Cay for dinner. This is our last night in the area, and if you hadn't taken us, we would have missed out on an incredible night."

Three examples of generous people in one evening in the Hill House made me realize how blind I had been to small kindnesses for the year Ike and Jillian had ruled my roost.

But the next morning my happiness was brought up short.

"Stew, where's dinghy 'A'?" asked Stewart.

"I thought you must have put it on the north dock."

"No, I haven't seen it since last night."

Stew went to examine the security of the cleat, knowing that, as always, the last thing he'd done before retiring was to check the holding of all our boats' lines and back anchors. The cleat sat secure on the dock and Stew located the missing boat's anchor and cut line on the bottom of the harbor. Dinghy "A" and its new 70-horsepower Yamaha engine had vanished on a calm night, 100 feet from where Stewart and I slept. Twenty thousand dollars of goods stolen, most likely for a single engine part, by a thief who knew he would get away with it.

"You prob'ly find it to Staniel," said the police at Black Point. "Check for it over to Black Point," said the policeman at Staniel Cay. The two islands sat six miles apart.

Our staff looked at their feet and shook their heads when we asked what they knew. Local acquaintances said, "We ain' hear nuttin' 'bout nobody teefin' a boat." From a tight-knit community of several hundred mostly-related people, all of whom knew our boats and us, an impenetrable wall. We could sense the information hiding in the bars, houses and workplaces of the neighborhood.

Never will I forget the silence. I wondered again what sort of place we had chosen to give our loyalty, our assets and ourselves to. The sight of that empty space at the dock was a reminder of the gulf that lay between us.

CHAPTER 33: Into the Deep End (8)

I n all our years of hiring people, this is the first time Stewart and I have ever had someone leave our employment on such a bad note. I'm not sure how we'll work this nightmare out, but Stewart is incredibly fair in trying to keep employees happy—always has been. I guess we'll end by coughing up a few undeserved dollars to get them off our backs. Anything to close the file on these Canady characters!

"Counselor Treadwell, please... Hello?... Hello?... Damn. Batelco's down again."

CHAPTER 34: You've Got to be Kidding

Stew called Ike with questions numerous times over the next several weeks, but Ike never answered his cellphone so Stew gave up. Mid-August, Stewart received an e-mail from Jillian restating her opinion that Fowl Cay owed $29,500 in back pay. "Unless we shall receive said sum within 14 days of this e-mail, we shall take immediate steps to enforce our rights." It was signed, "Yours faithfully." Stewart e-mailed back a rejection of the claim and, since they would never answer their phones, he asked the Canadys to please call him to discuss the issue. A week went by before Jillian wrote that she and Ike would not communicate further on the matter. We knew where Jillian and Ike were headed.

Our law firm assigned William Treadwell to defend Fowl Cay before the Industrial Tribunal. Labor disputes were his specialty, we were told. Fourteen months later, the trial was set for the end of April 2004. Two days before our appearance in court, our lawyer still had not called to discuss the pages of documentation Stewart had sent in November 2002, updated, and re-sent directly to Mr. Treadwell several weeks prior. When Stewart reached him, the lawyer said he hadn't had time to read the information yet and to call back at 5:15.

"Oh, Mr. Brown. Mr. Treadwell has left for the day," said the receptionist at 5:05.

"Any message?" asked Stewart, although he knew better.

Two of our former employees who had worked on Sundays agreed to testify that Jillian and Ike almost never worked on that day. They were waiting outside the courtroom when the trial began. In that room were the Canadys and their lawyer, Treadwell, Stewart and the judge.

The trial went poorly from the start. Our lawyer put up almost no fight. When the time came for him to present our case, he never brought up the fact that the Canadys resigned of their own will. Nor did he say that Jillian had a background in labor law and was in charge of all legal matters, that she was responsible for bringing questions of non-compliance to our attention and had never once questioned not being paid for holidays or extra time worked, although she was the person who wrote the monthly paychecks. Mr. Treadwell never deemed it suitable to show where Jillian and Ike had both signed a contract that stated, "The job encompasses all responsibilities in running Fowl Cay as a resort," nor where they had agreed to a stated salary.

Our lawyer's failure to advocate in our behalf, however, was nothing compared to the judge's behavior. Stewart decided that if the lawyer wasn't going to present the facts, he would, so he stood and asked to speak. Flatly rejected by the bench, Stewart tried a second time, when the judge told him to "Shut up and sit down." Mr. Treadwell requested that the judge have the employees testify, to which he responded that no underling could ever testify against a manager in his courtroom. No point of law or legal reasoning was discussed on either side. Before we even had a chance to present our case, the judge blurted out, "It is unconscionable the way you treated these people—UNCONSCIONABLE."

The whole procedure was over in an hour, and Stewart wrote a check to Ike and Jillian for a negotiated, but significant amount, on the spot. When Ike stuck out his hand to shake Stewart's, the most forgiving man I have ever known said, "You've got to be kidding," and walked out the door. By those five uncharacteristic words, I knew the rage he felt at being muzzled and unable to defend himself. Such as it was in the Bahamas, the law of the land had spoken.

CHAPTER 35: Traces of God

After our legal battle was lost in 2004, the resort settled into a smooth course, as if it had been waiting for closure on that unpleasant matter. Not a well-oiled machine, exactly, but disruptions became the exception. Our staff came to work reliably, traveling over an hour in an open boat each day, sometimes in dicey weather. With little turnover among them, familiarity paid off in more compatible day-to-day communication. Relationships among everyone who worked on the cay grew warmer, lubricated by Stewart's joking, happy demeanor that was so like the out-island Bahamians themselves. A Fowl Cay family budded that spring.

In September, we closed the business for the month, as always. Hot weather, mosquitoes and the height of hurricane season made it the right time to shut down for repair of houses and equipment. Fowl Cay turned upside down then, with newly painted signs left to dry in the sun, hardware off doors so hinges could be oiled, paths blocked off to allow resurfacing, boats pulled out to have their bottoms painted. We were in no shape for polite company during maintenance month.

Things were slow everywhere—the Potty-Foyers, Bar 'n Bites, the yacht club. Even the pigs could hardly be bothered to amble out of the brush for food scraps. Except for an occasional game of backgammon with a friend, most of our expat buddies left the Bahamas for cooler climes, and our weekly card game and dinners on surrounding islands came to a halt. *(Photo 3.21)*

It was during this quiet month that I stepped out of Birdcage with a great book tucked under my arm and pulled one of those old-fashioned collapsible lounge chairs into the shallow water. Late morning sun warmed the top of me and water from the ocean cooled the bottom of me. The contrast in temperature felt wonderful, and the rhythmic sound of the lapping waves was soothing. Their melody spoke to me about the sweetness and freedom of solitary moments in Paradise made possible by our staff.

Wesley, the old caretaker, cruised up to the dock to start his job of burning the trash we'd generated the last three days. On his way to the burn pit, he stopped by my chair. "'Scuse me, ma'am, if I not bodderin' you could I show you de stone I found for dat special place you vant in de wall? If you don' like it, I hunt down anodder one, no pro'lem." My feet curled and flexed in the baby powder sand as he returned to his dinghy to retrieve the homegrown prize.

No doubt about it, with age, Fowl Cay and I were growing compatible. But the out-islands being the out-islands, service glitches continued to nag us whether they happened on, or to, our island.

Johannah paid the bills for Fowl Cay out of the Bahamian bank account we had opened several years back in Nassau. With the balance too low to cover the upcoming withdrawals, she e-mailed a request for a transfer of $50,000 from the American dollar account to the Bahamian dollar account. Her computer showed the electronic transmission was opened, so Johannah wrote the monthly checks and sent them by freight boat to be mailed by a woman who worked for us in Nassau.

The checks started bouncing the next week, and Johannah called our account rep at the bank to straighten things out.

"I transfer dat money when you call," said Mr. Harnett. "I have to check on it for you."

Knowing that checking on something in the Bahamas was a lengthy process, and knowing that creditors to out-island customers were quick to close charge accounts, Johannah asked Mr. Harnett to locate the missing money as soon as possible but, meanwhile, to transfer another $50,000 immediately so we could keep the resort supplied with goods from our now-perturbed vendors. Then she rewrote the checks to cover the late bills and sent them off by charter pilot to Nassau.

The next week, most of the checks bounced again. Johannah called the bank.

"Did you transfer the second $50,000 when I called you last week, Mr. Harnett?"

"To be honest wit' you, I forgot for a couple of days. And den I remember, but I couldn't recall de amount so I jus' switch $25,000."

"Did you ever find the original $50,000?" asked Johannah.

"Not yet, but it jus' jam up in de papervork," said the banker.

"Mr. Harnett, please get that straight and e-mail me a statement of our balance today."

"Dat might take a little while, because I gat to figure how much overdraw to charge your account for all dese checks you bounce," said Mr. Harnett.

Needing a little breather after that conversation, Johannah walked down from the office to where I sat in my favorite place on the Birdcage beach. She patted her cheeks with a little cool water. You couldn't blame her.

Duncan called over the wall above my spot after Johannah returned to work, "Miz Brown. Dey didn't have yo' Diet Coke at de place JoJo order from, but I got some Diet Pepsi offen de mailboat. If dat OK, you vant me take yo' case up de house?" Seawater gurgled under my back, singing its eternal song.

Rupert walked off the dock at Birdcage where he was pounding nails that had worked their way partially out of the decking. I had told Stew the day before that I got a mean scrape on my foot from a raised one near the ladder. "Mornin', Mornin'," said Rupert as he walked up the steps from the beach to his work cart. "You doin' good?" The sky was bright blue and the clouds looked like islands sitting in it.

October flung itself, exultant, over the Exuma Cays in 2004, and Fowl Cay cast her spell week after week on our customers. Stewart and I were sweeping the sand off the bocce court on the south beach one day when his cellphone rang. It was a representative from Batelco.

"How you enjoy de call waitin' we install on your phone for free las' mont'?" she asked.

"I didn't know I had it," Stewart said. "No one notified me it was on there."

"OK, but was it good enough for you to sign up for de regular service?"

After Stewart hung up, someone we didn't recognize drove by in his boat and hailed Stewart to the water. The man handed him an envelope, nodded and drove off. The delivery was from the officials at Green Island that hosted the Kids' Regatta. Stew had sent a check several days prior for $200 in response to a solicitation for the upcoming event.

The envelope contained three things: the original contribution request letter, Fowl Cay's uncashed check and a note from one of the organizers. The man called our donation unacceptable for a business such as Fowl Cay. If we were going to be part of the neighborhood, he wrote, we needed to show that we valued its traditions with more than $200.

Later, when we sought advice from a long-time resident, she said if we were ever going to need permits from any central Exuma representative who lived on that island, we'd better pay.

Cozetta walked into Birdcage to clean the salt spray off the door and window glass. She put away the towels from the dryer and placed a bowl of Rowena's conch salad in the refrigerator. Cozetta's beautiful smile was like a spotlight on a dark sky. With no need to worry about cooking our midday meal, doing the laundry or cleaning my house, I could devote the rest of my day to being angry over the returned donation if I wanted to. If I wanted to.

When I returned to Birdcage to eat lunch, James was putting the screen back in the door that opened out onto the covered deck. Zeke and Lulu, the yellow Labs, had pushed their noses through it, lured by the smell of warm banana bread that had been delivered from the Hill House kitchen, as usual, on Thursdays. I held the door for James while he carried out a ladder. I was trying to keep him from backing into a thorny riot of bougainvillea that spilled over the pool's retaining wall outside. "Miz Brown, " James called back. "I clean off de blade of all de ceiling fan earlier." A hummingbird flew between us, in search of its lunch. *(Photo 3.22)*

Almost every day, resident guests brought interesting stories, vacation laughter and, when their time with us was over, promises to return and to tell others about our little cay. People off boats that were anchored at nearby Big Major came to dinner at the Hill House, bursting with cheer through the front door, glad to have secured a reservation in the 28-seat restaurant. Seldom was there a night that wasn't filled with happy laughter. Seldom.

By now the father of one young son, with another on the way, Stew had been a tireless manager. From tending cranky generators to teaching guests to water-ski, he handled it all without complaint. It was past time for him and Johannah to take a stateside break, especially after one night's experience. Every seat in the Hill House dining room had been full, as usual in the winter months. Coordinating kitchen, bar, boat transfers and customer service by himself pressed even easy-going Stew to his limit.

"You won't believe the scene at dinner last night," he said. "What an uproar."

After cocktails and about 10 minutes into the meal, a couple that Stew had ferried over from Staniel, along with a babe-in-arms, started arguing at their table. Then shouting. Other customers were cutting eyes in the direction of the increasing volume, and, along with our staff, becoming worried about the baby who was jostling around in the mom's lap as the disagreement picked up heat. When the woman stormed from the dining room to go out on the terrace with her child, everyone breathed easier.

"When I asked the husband if I could do something, he lurched out of his chair and went outside, leaving a full plate but taking the wine bottle," said Stew. "In two minutes, Rowena came in the dining room where I was trying to make things cool with the other diners and said she needed to see me. The kitchen staff had watched out the window and saw the man belt his wife in the face while she was holding the baby."

The woman ran into the kitchen crying and begging for protection from her husband. Incensed by the injustice of such treatment, the female staff wanted Stew to call the policeman on Staniel, and making an unusual offer, they agreed to stay until the cop arrived in order to be witnesses for the abused customer.

"Let me hold dat baby for you. I calm her down," said Rowena, who like most Bahamians, was a soft touch when it came to children.

Most of the other customers in the dining room cleared out before the coffee was served, and the man said he wanted to be taken back to Staniel without mom and baby. Stew asked what the customer wanted him to do with the rest of his family.

"I don't care. Keep them here for the night. I never want to see them again."

Stew called the manager of the Potty-Foyer complex and reserved one for the night under an alias. Rowena tended to the woman's bloody mouth, and one of our rental guests rocked the screaming baby while Duncan took the husband back to his boat at the yacht club dock. After the terrified woman calmed down, Stew drove her and the baby to their Potty-Foyer by a circuitous route, looking over his shoulder the whole way, and waited to leave until he heard the door lock.

"This morning about eleven o'clock, I was picking up a workman at Bar 'n Bites and there was the family—the baby playing on the bar and mom and dad holding hands and sipping Bloody Marys. I don't think they even recognized me," Stew said. "It was kind of a long night."

Even that experience, however, couldn't dampen our spirits as we anticipated a family holiday. On Wednesday before Thanksgiving, Ellie, Matt and their daughters Gracie and Anna had come in from Richmond to join Johannah, Stew, our two grandsons and us for the holiday. A Bahamian pal from Great Exuma, who happened to be in the Cays on business, dropped in for a visit late in the afternoon. He sat under the umbrella at the Hill House swimming pool where baby Henry slept in his portable seat. Usually full of jokes and teasing, our friend was quiet as he sipped a glass of wine and watched Simon and his cousins jump in the water, only to be pulled up laughing by their parents time and again. I saw our visitor's eyes drift beyond the pool as the moon came up behind Big Major. He stared over the harbor with an expression of open wonder and turned his face slightly upward, as if he were connecting to something bigger than us all.

"You're a lucky mon, Stewart Brown," he said. "T'ree generation of fomlee in a beautiful place like dis. Dere's traces of God at Fowl Cay."
(Photo 3.23)

CHAPTER 36: Hill House

More and more often, Fowl Cay provided a venue for fun and laughter. The sunset-colored focal point of our dream, Hill House, became a place where people who were unconnected discovered improbable links, people who were hurting experienced a moment of respite, people who were aging regained a taste of carefree youth, and I found happiness. Inside the pink stucco house with white gingerbread molding and two yellow Labs wagging at its door, joy kindled and spread and blessed my beleaguered heart. *(Photo 3.24)*

Connecting. "You're from Oakboro? I grew up there." "You were at Camp Happy Hills in '68? No kidding. I was a counselor there that same year." "She's your sister? We played in the state finals together." "Today's your birthday? It's mine too." "You work for Merrill Lynch? So do I."

Reviving. Stew talked computers and music the entire cocktail hour with a young man about his age whose useless legs hung limp. At dinner with his tired-looking parents, Blair was rosy-cheeked and animated in conversation, a different person than the one we'd brought up the back service entrance in a golf cart and lifted into his wheelchair to roll inside. "I have no adequate words to thank Stew for his kindness," said Blair's father to me as he left. "Our son hasn't been alive like that in years."

Healing. My childhood friend stayed in one of our houses for a week. On the last perfect evening, we sat after dinner in the rocking chairs overlooking heaven's nighttime gifts and reminisced about the old days when we were attached at the hip. "Libby, today was the first time since I was diagnosed that I didn't think about having cancer. Thank you for that."

Mending. I'd never met my dinner partner, but people we knew asked us to sit at their table with friends who were visiting. Tony was charming and warm but sad around the eyes in a way that brings me to my nurturing best. When he left for the evening, he hugged me, as many guests do in our home. "This is my first night out since my wife died, the first night I haven't wished I'd gone with her. Thank you."

Rejoicing. All four children had planned the 50th-anniversary trip for their parents as a surprise. We worried that it might not be a surprise the Wyricks wanted because Fowl Cay was mostly about physical activity—sailing, kayaking, snorkeling, tennis, boating, fishing—and earlier questions had arisen about allergies, steps and medical help. But Theresa and Fredrick wanted only to be surrounded by children and grandchildren, and to have that happen on a tropical island was almost beyond the ken of this midwestern couple. For the anniversary party, we decorated the dining room, signed a card, brought out a giant cake called Chocolate Thunder, and Stewart made a funny toast, saying their children, their grandchildren and their Fowl Cay friends were glad that, in 50 years, they had never chickened out. With that, he put our signature felt hat with a chicken on top on Theresa's head and tied its yellow legs under her chin. Every guest in the dining room stood, lifted glasses and snapped pictures. Theresa grinned and Fredrick cried. *(Photo 3.25)*

Celebrating. A gutsy woman we'd met when we first opened Fowl Cay was back for her fifth or sixth dinner with us. She came to the Exumas on the boat she and her husband had shared for years before he died. Dinghied in by Captain Kyle, Louise and her three friends clambered up the dock ladder like they were 40. Kyle had arranged for a birthday cake to be brought out after dinner for Louise's celebration, and it was big enough to share with the entire dining room. She grinned and sliced and passed plates around while everyone sang the good old song. After dinner, Louise sat on the leather couch in the game room to receive congratulations from the crowd. Her infectious enthusiasm let anyone know she was happy, she was vital and she was game. She was also 80. After cranking the music all the way up, one of the guests off a charter boat reached over the back of the couch, lifted Louise like a baby and deposited her flat on her back on the cleared bar. As Stewart, Kyle and I watched horrified, Mr. Inebriated lifted Louise's shirt a few inches, lowered her elastic-waist pants a few inches and poured tequila in her belly button. Before he imbibed from the human shot glass, he planted a sloppy kiss right on her smacker and screamed, "Happy Birthday!" With a loud slur-r-r-p, he sucked up the liquid while his seven drunken friends shouted, "BODY SHOT!" I rushed over to our guest who had been stood upright by then and said, "Oh my God, Louise. I'm so sorry. Are you all right?" The gutsy lady said, "I'm perfect. Haven't had such a divine time in years."

Giving. Before dinner, a little girl's voice sang out clear and high, a child unfazed in the room full of adults. The other tables fell quiet, captivated by her blessing and by her gumption. After she said "Amen," she picked up her spoon as if it were nothing special. But it was to me.

Toasting. One happy evening, a man I'd barely met stood up in the dining room to make a toast during dessert. He spoke of what a special atmosphere the Hill House had, how fortunate he felt to have found it, what a jewel it was tucked into the out-islands. "I'm a Bahamian," he said, "and unless you've lived in these islands all your life, you have no idea what the Browns have accomplished here." I thanked him for his kind words as he was leaving, and he said, "You're welcome. It was really nothing." But it was to me.

Loving. My two-year-old grandson came to the Hill House for hors d'oeuvre and cocktail hour every evening in his pajamas, and he was as big a hit with the guests as the conch fritters. Simon frequently picked hibiscus blossoms from the prolific bushes and handed them out to every woman, saying, "Here's a fower for you." After his parents hauled him off to bed, people would tell me what a loving child he was, and I smiled as if it were nothing. But it was wonderful to me.

Reconnecting. When a man and his teenage son arrived for a week, the boy seemed angry and uncommunicative the first night at the Hill House. The father told us they had been estranged for several years, and this vacation was his attempt to close the distance between them. By the end of their time with us, two different people stood on the dock to leave, jostling and teasing each other. The son boarded the boat for the airstrip first and was arranging luggage and fishing gear in the bow. Seizing that moment out of earshot, the father said he couldn't have chosen a more perfect spot for the two of them to reconnect and heal, that it had been seven days in paradise. "I'm sure you hear that all the time, so it probably sounds trite." Not at all.

Believing. The child beside me at the dining room table said she'd been studying angels in school, and that sounded right for five years old. Angels apparently lived in a beautiful place and were surrounded by people who loved them and could fix their wings in case they broke. Of course, angels were always girls. "You know where I think angels live, Mem?" asked my first-born grandchild Gracie. "I think they live at Fowl Cay." And off she ran with her sister to pass the bowl of jellybeans to all the guests as if suddenly angels weren't important. But they surely were to me.

Happiness arrived at Hill House on angel wings and wheelchairs, in songs and prayers and funny toasts, and fortune smiled once more on me.

CHAPTER 37: Into the Deep End (9)

The worry the government causes by its failure to extend our land lease never goes away, it only fades while Stewart works with our lawyer to try to set up another appointment for an official review of the Fowl Cay project. When the date is agreed upon for the visit, I still harbor a tiny glimmer of hope for the end of my suffering while the Bahamian bureaucracy continues to ignore our plight. We busy ourselves at their whim, hustling around, cleaning and primping to show off our baby at her very best. We're scared not to.

When the inevitable cancellation comes—sometimes after a plane has been chartered at our expense, after the staff has planned a special lunch, and after Stewart and I have arranged our schedule to be on the cay—we're backhanded again by the disregard of the powers-that-be.

Most people we talk to say this government is the hardest one to work with in years. But a promise is a promise in my book. Could they be trying to get us to leave the Bahamas? For what reason? To let Fowl Cay fall back to ruin?

Stewart and I are not short on tenacity, so for now, we'll keep trying to get what is due us. But I guess I won't hold my breath.

"The screen on my cellphone reads 'No Service' again today. I understand the message in its entirety."

POSTSCRIPT

In my daily effort to appreciate the good things at Fowl Cay, the hours are too brief to collect them all. I start early in my sea-scented bedroom, where the orange-gold dawn sneaks through gossamer curtains that flutter in a fine breeze. The family compound we dreamed of is at its best today. My 21st-century grandchildren come up to visit me at Birdcage to play with my grandmother's 19th-century doll Tommy, which sits in a child's chair by the fireplace. The girls show me their shell collection with a miser's joy, and the boys, led by Simon, ask to swim with the nurse sharks at Sand Dollar Cay. Lulu and Zeke bark at an airplane, as if someone might parachute in and kidnap the children, but give it up when they spot a lizard they can snuffle. *(Photo 3.26)*

The sandbar across the way is the color of shimmering opal in the shallow water, but time is too short this morning to hunt for its bounty. No matter. Mother Nature's gems wait patient and happy, and I am learning to do the same. Looking for Stewart to remind him of our date for lunch and cards, I find him pruning the firecracker plant that sprawls around the edge of the pool. Sitting in *Roundabout* is a magic carpet ride, because the boat barely touches the velvet, turquoise water, so smooth is its surface. Halfway to Bar 'n Bites, little ripples rise with the first harbinger of a cooling breeze.

Friends await us for a meal of grouper fingers and the finest French fries this side of heaven. Bahamian believe-it-or-not stories abound in our laughing conversation of can-you-top-this. Ben, who owns a large island eight miles from Fowl Cay, huffs in.

"I'm so furious," he says. "You all know my caretaker, Juan, and what a great worker he is. Well, Paulie from Cross Cay was over to do some landscaping for me on Thursday and spotted Juan straining to drag our broken flagpole over some bushes. He came over and told Juan to stop working so hard, that it made it tough for the local fellows with people like him around."

In solid understanding, the lunch bunch gives its usual nod. "What is, is." Ben, a bit more of a newcomer than the rest of us, isn't ready to accede so easily, and I smile knowingly. "It seems like around here, the more someone accomplishes, the less of a person he's considered to be," says Ben.

A letter sits on the kitchen counter when we return. It comes from a guest who rented last month. I'm eager to read its contents, because you have to really want to say something to figure out how to get mail to people who live in the out-islands. It's a thank you for their week with us, a quick read with the requisite list of favorite activities. I flip it over. "But, most of all, we appreciate reaping the benefits of your adventuresome spirits, hard work and positive and persevering can-do mentality. You are an inspirational couple with a loving and working relationship that encompasses your family and guests, a model for us all. Thank you for sharing your island and yourselves." I walk outside with that letter, warm as if it were alive in my pocket.

Rupert lowers the flags of our sweet resort in paradise against a backdrop of early evening sky that is dressed in cooled-down tints of lavender and lemon. The Hill House glows in the sunset, waiting for love and laughter to fill it up again.

* * *

Fowl Cay Resort remains a family business. Stew and Johannah, Simon and Henry continue to make the island their home. From Virginia, where she lives with Matt, Gracie and Anna, Ellie takes customer reservations for the five rental cottages. *(Photo 3.27)*

* * *

Despite the joy our investment in the Bahamas brought me, it has burdened me with an implausible amount of woe. It will take outrageous guts to go back for a rematch with risk now that it has shown me its stuff.

I realize with the futile clarity of the unexplainable that I will never understand this country in the way most people do their homeland, but faith grows inside me that serenity is all around, and I am learning to harvest it despite my hurt. Because I have been among the world's luckiest risk-takers, I am inept at fighting off fortune's backside, which had never truly shown itself to me before. It is difficult to be loyal to one's code of conduct, yet walk with others in understanding and compassion, and the struggle to make attitude more important than success or failure is a hard battle. Disappointment seems easier to find than determination.

That said, I have discovered my footing once more and a certain dignity in staying as long as I have. After all, it is my choice to be here. Yet I retain the open wound of unrequited love of the Bahamas. The ongoing skirmish with this country shadows me, although finally I understand that no arms can put me on a level battlefield. The scars from that inequity have transformed me from happy anticipation to agitation to fragile acceptance.

Stewart and I spend 80 percent of our time on Fowl Cay and do as we please every single day. On July 19, 2006, Mrs. Somers canceled her sixth appointment to visit our island since 2002, so we still wait for the Bahamian government to keep its promise to us.

* * *

As this book goes to press, Stewart and I have signed a contract for the sale of Fowl Cay.

Photo 3.1 ~ This 53-foot trawler, also named Crossroads, the Browns' home for two years while building Fowl Cay.

Photo 3.2 ~ Mother Nature's daily show, sunset at Fowl Cay.

Photo 3.3 ~ Fowl Cay, seen from the air, is sheltered from the Atlantic Ocean by a string of large boulders.

Photo 3.4 ~ This barge arrives at high tide to deliver five tractor-trailer loads of household goods.

Photo 3.5 ~ Bahamians compete in sailing regattas with handmade wooden boats.

Photo 3.6 ~ Libby and Stewart throw a Christmas party for the construction crew and neighbors from Staniel Cay.

Photo 3.7 ~ Excavating foundations from coral rock for buildings on Fowl Cay.

Photo 3.8 ~ The demise of the 280-foot Batelco telephone tower ended communications with the rest of the world.

Photo 3.9 ~ An aerial shot of Birdcage, the Browns' home on Fowl Cay.

Photo 3.10 ~ Stewart and his friends back from spear-fishing with the day's catch.

Photo 3.11 ~ Denizens of Pig Beach.

Photo 3.12 ~ This little piggy went swimming.

Photo 3.13 ~ Stewart, here in his Bobcat, always happiest at work on Fowl Cay.

Photo 3.14 ~ Layers of concrete can't repress big smiles from Randy and the tireless little yellow cement mixer.

Photo 3.15 ~ Foundations for each building are cut from coral rock and reinforced with iron and concrete.

Photo 3.16 ~ The "Captain."

Photo 3.17 ~ Ellie fields the questions of guests
worldwide from Fowl Cay's reservation desk.

Photo 3.18 ~ *Unpacking one of the five tractor-trailer loads of furniture and household goods at Fowl Cay.*

Photo 3.19 ~ *Surveying the damage from Hurricane Michelle, five days after the move into Birdcage.*

Photo 3.20 ~ Johannah and Stew at Fowl Cay on their wedding day.

Photo 3.21 ~ A friendly game of backgammon, Fowl Cay-style.

Photo 3.22 ~ The Fowl Cay public relations department, LuLu and Zeke.

*Photo 3.23 ~ Fowl Cay's swimming pool under
a harvest moon.*

Photo 3.24 ~ Hill House offers hospitality to resident guests and yachters.

Photo 3.25 ~ Our bartender eggs Stewart on as he models the Fowl Cay chicken hat.

Photo 3.26 ~ Granddaughters Anna and Gracie explain to friends how to swim with the sharks.

Photo 3.27 ~ Stew and Johannah with sons Simon and Henry in the family vehicle.

AFTERWORD

Life is a risk. It attends our delivery into this world and abides with us from that point forward. Avoiding risk can preserve life — don't play with matches, don't take candy from strangers, don't drink and drive. But seeking risk is vital. It's a paradox, but if you avoid life's risks, you'll never really live.

Risks are relative. One woman's small risk is another woman's bold dare. My soft swell on a lazy sea might be your tidal wave — or vice versa.

Risks are fickle. You might gamble your life's savings in a hedge fund and make a killing — I might take the same chance and go bankrupt.

And risks are scary. It's frightening to step into the unknown. But if you never risk it, you'll never know what might have been. And simply by taking that step, win or lose, you succeed.

Risk has been good to me and risk has chastened me. I have been humbled by my blessings and made larger by my losses. I have put my friendships, my money and my life on the line and, in this case, the gambles have yielded handsome returns. Despite knowing through experience the disquietude of placing my destiny up for grabs, my heart races at the thought of another shot at challenge.

As a child of the conservative South, where tradition is the soul of society and women the guardians of the faith, the choice to imperil a privileged lifestyle, not only for myself but also for my family, might have been selfish if not reckless, and I would have been the first to find myself guilty. The hardest struggle for me has been to indemnify my deepest, most traditional values against the compulsions of my risk-seeking spirit.

Pursuing my own individuality was the path to liberation, and I thank good fortune for the heavy weather I had to endure to gain it. I do not wish to die untouched, untried, unspent. I want life to use me up and, when it's over for me, I want to race through that finish line without looking back. Although my love of taking chances didn't always love me, I will rest in my final moments void of regret — I would never risk regretting.

Real triumph sometimes requires us to yield and to trust and so, to rise above. My soul is at peace, but it sleeps with one eye open.

"Life is either a daring adventure
or nothing at all."

— Helen Keller